Elizabeth Barret Browning

Aurora Leigh

Elizabeth Barret Browning

Aurora Leigh

ISBN/EAN: 9783741163296

Manufactured in Europe, USA, Canada, Australia, Japa

Cover: Foto ©Andreas Hilbeck / pixelio.de

Manufactured and distributed by brebook publishing software (www.brebook.com)

Elizabeth Barret Browning

Aurora Leigh

EACH VOLUME SOLD SEPARATELY.

COLLECTION
OF
BRITISH AUTHORS

TAUCHNITZ EDITION.

VOL. 124
AURORA LEIGH BY ELIZABETH BROWNING
IN ONE VOLUME.

LEIPZIG: BERNHARD TAUCHNITZ.
PARIS: C. REINWALD & C°, 15, RUE DES SAINTS PÈRES.

This Collection is published with copyright for Continental circulation, but all purchasers are earnestly requested not to introduce the volumes

COLLECTION
OF
BRITISH AUTHORS

TAUCHNITZ EDITION.

VOL. 1248.

AURORA LEIGH BY ELIZ. BARRETT BROWNING.

IN ONE VOLUME

TAUCHNITZ EDITION.
By the same Author,
POETRY . . . . 1 vol.

AURORA LEIGH.

BY

Elizabeth Barrett Browning.

COPYRIGHT EDITION.

LEIPZIG
BERNHARD TAUCHNITZ
1872.

The Right of Translation is reserved.

DEDICATION

TO

JOHN KENYON, ESQ.

———

THE words "cousin" and "friend" are constantly recurring in this poem, the last pages of which have been finished under the hospitality of your roof, my own dearest cousin and friend;— cousin and friend, in a sense of less equality and greater disinterestedness than "Romney"'s.

Ending, therefore, and preparing once more to quit England, I venture to leave in your hands this book, the most mature of my works, and the one into which my highest convictions upon Life and Art have entered; that as, through my various efforts in Literature and steps in life, you have believed in me, borne with me, and been generous to me, far beyond the common uses of mere relationship or sympathy of mind, so you may kindly accept, in sight of the public, this poor sign of esteem, gratitude, and affection from

Your unforgetting

E. B. B.

39, DEVONSHIRE PLACE,
October 17, 1856.

CONTENTS.

	PAGE
FIRST BOOK	9
SECOND BOOK	43
THIRD BOOK	80
FOURTH BOOK	117
FIFTH BOOK	154
SIXTH BOOK	192
SEVENTH BOOK	230
EIGHTH BOOK	268
NINTH BOOK	306

AURORA LEIGH.

FIRST BOOK.

Of writing many books there is no end;
And I who have written much in prose and verse
For others' uses, will write now for mine,—
Will write my story for my better self
As when you paint your portrait for a friend
Who keeps it in a drawer and looks at it
Long after he has ceased to love you, just
To hold together what he was and is.

I, writing thus, am still what men call young;
I have not so far left the coasts of life
To travel inland, that I cannot hear
That murmur of the outer Infinite
Which unweaned babies smile at in their sleep
When wondered at for smiling; not so far,
But still I catch my mother at her post
Beside the nursery-door, with finger up,
"Hush, hush—here's too much noise!" while her sweet eyes
Leap forward, taking part against her word
In the child's riot. Still I sit and feel
My father's slow hand, when she had left us both,
Stroke out my childish curls across his knee,
And hear Assunta's daily jest (she knew
He liked it better than a better jest)
Inquire how many golden scudi went
To make such ringlets. O my father's hand,

Stroke heavily, heavily the poor hair down,
Draw, press the child's head closer to thy knee!
I'm still too young, too young, to sit alone.

I write. My mother was a Florentine,
Whose rare blue eyes were shut from seeing me
When scarcely I was four years old, my life
A poor spark snatched up from a failing lamp
Which went out therefore. She was weak and frail;
She could not bear the joy of giving life,
The mother's rapture slew her. If her kiss
Had left a longer weight upon my lips
It might have steadied the uneasy breath,
And reconciled and fraternised my soul
With the new order. As it was, indeed,
I felt a mother-want about the world,
And still went seeking, like a bleating lamb
Left out at night in shutting up the fold,—
As restless as a nest-deserted bird
Grown chill through something being away, though what
It knows not. I, Aurora Leigh, was born
To make my father sadder, and myself
Not overjoyous, truly. Women know
The way to rear up children, (to be just)
They know a simple, merry, tender knack
Of tying sashes, fitting baby-shoes,
And stringing pretty words that make no sense,
And kissing full sense into empty words,
Which things are corals to cut life upon,
Although such trifles: children learn by such,
Love's holy earnest in a pretty play
And get not over-early solemnised,
But seeing, as in a rose-bush, Love's Divine
Which burns and hurts not,—not a single bloom,—
Become aware and unafraid of Love.
Such good do mothers. Fathers love as well
—Mine did, I know,—but still with heavier brains,

And wills more consciously responsible,
And not as wisely, since less foolishly;
So mothers have God's licence to be missed.

My father was an austere Englishman,
Who, after a dry life-time spent at home
In college-learning, law, and parish talk,
Was flooded with a passion unaware,
His whole provisioned and complacent past
Drowned out from him that moment. As he stood
In Florence, where he had come to spend a month
And note the secret of Da Vinci's drains,
He musing somewhat absently perhaps
Some English question . . whether men should pay
The unpopular but necessary tax
With left or right hand—in the alien sun
In that great square of the Santissima
There drifted past him (scarcely marked enough
To move his comfortable island scorn)
A train of priestly banners, cross and psalm,
The white-veiled rose-crowned maidens holding up
Tall tapers, weighty for such wrists, aslant
To the blue luminous tremor of the air,
And letting drop the white wax as they went
To eat the bishop's wafer at the church;
From which long trail of chanting priests and girls,
A face flashed like a cymbal on his face
And shook with silent clangour brain and heart,
Transfiguring him to music. Thus, even thus,
He too received his sacramental gift
With eucharistic meanings; for he loved.

And thus beloved, she died. I've heard it said
That but to see him in the first surprise
Of widower and father, nursing me,
Unmothered little child of four years old,
His large man's hands afraid to touch my curls,

As if the gold would tarnish,—his grave lips
Contriving such a miserable smile
As if he knew needs must, or I should die,
And yet 'twas hard,—would almost make the stones
Cry out for pity. There's a verse he set
In Santa Croce to her memory,—
"Weep for an infant too young to weep much
When death removed this mother"—stops the mirth
To-day on women's faces when they walk
With rosy children hanging on their gowns,
Under the cloister to escape the sun
That scorches in the piazza. After which
He left our Florence and made haste to hide
Himself, his prattling child, and silent grief,
Among the mountains above Pelago;
Because unmothered babes, he thought, had need
Of mother nature more than others use,
And Pan's white goats', with udders warm and full
Of mystic contemplations, come to feed
Poor milkless lips of orphans like his own —
Such scholar-scraps he talked, I've heard from friends,
For even prosaic men who wear grief long
Will get to wear it as a hat aside
With a flower stuck in 't. Father, then, and child,
We lived among the mountains many years,
God's silence on the outside of the house,
And we who did not speak too loud within,
And old Assunta to make up the fire,
Crossing herself whene'er a sudden flame
Which lightened from the firewood, made alive
That picture of my mother on the wall.

The painter drew it after she was dead,
And when the face was finished, throat and hands,
Her cameriera carried him, in hate
Of the English-fashioned shroud, the last brocade
She dressed in at the Pitti; "he should paint

No sadder thing than that," she swore, "to wrong
Her poor signora." Therefore very strange
The effect was. I, a little child, would crouch
For hours upon the floor with knees drawn up,
And gaze across them, half in terror, half
In adoration; at the picture there,—
That swan-like supernatural white life
Just sailing upward from the red stiff silk
Which seemed to have no part in it nor power
To keep it from quite breaking out of bounds.
For hours I sate and stared. Assunta's awe
And my poor father's melancholy eyes
Still pointed that way. That way went my thoughts
When wandering beyond sight. And as I grew
In years, I mixed, confused, unconsciously,
Whatever I last read or heard or dreamed,
Abhorrent, admirable, beautiful,
Pathetical, or ghastly, or grotesque,
With still that face ... which did not therefore change,
But kept the mystic level of all forms,
Hates, fears, and admirations, was by turns
Ghost, fiend, and angel, fairy, witch, and sprite,
A dauntless Muse who eyes a dreadful Fate,
A loving Psyche who loses sight of Love,
A still Medusa with mild milky brows
All curdled and all clothed upon with snakes
Whose slime falls fast as sweat will; or anon
Our Lady of the Passion, stabbed with swords
Where the Babe sucked; or Lamia in her first
Moonlighted pallor, ere she shrunk and blinked
And shuddering wriggled down to the unclean;
Or my own mother, leaving her last smile
In her last kiss upon the baby-mouth
My father pushed down on the bed for that,—
Or my dead mother, without smile or kiss,
Buried at Florence. All which images,
Concentred on the picture, glassed themselves

Before my meditative childhood, as
The incoherencies of change and death
Are represented fully, mixed and merged,
In the smooth fair mystery of perpetual Life.

And while I stared away my childish wits
Upon my mother's picture, (ah, poor child!)
My father, who through love had suddenly
Thrown off the old conventions, broken loose
From chin-bands of the soul, like Lazarus,
Yet had no time to learn to talk and walk
Or grow anew familiar with the sun,—
Who had reached to freedom, not to action, lived,
But lived as one entranced, with thoughts, not aims,—
Whom love had unmade from a common man
But not completed to an uncommon man,—
My father taught me what he had learnt the best
Before he died and left me,—grief and love.
And, seeing we had books among the hills,
Strong words of counselling souls confederate
With vocal pines and waters,—out of books
He taught me all the ignorance of men,
And how God laughs in heaven when any man
Says "Here I'm learned; this, I understand;
In that, I am never caught at fault or doubt."
He sent the schools to school, demonstrating
A fool will pass for such through one mistake,
While a philosopher will pass for such,
Through said mistakes being ventured in the gross
And heaped up to a system.   .
                           I am like,
They tell me, my dear father. Broader brows
Howbeit, upon a slenderer undergrowth
Of delicate features,—paler, near as grave;
But then my mother's smile breaks up the whole,
And makes it better sometimes than itself.

So, nine full years, our days were hid with God
Among his mountains: I was just thirteen,
Still growing like the plants from unseen roots
In tongue-tied Springs,—and suddenly awoke
To full life and life's needs and agonies
With an intense, strong, struggling heart beside
A stone-dead father. Life, struck sharp on death,
Makes awful lightning. His last word was, "Love—"
"Love, my child, love, love!"—(then he had done with
    grief)
"Love, my child." Ere I answered he was gone,
And none was left to love in all the world.

There ended childhood. What succeeded next
I recollect as, after fevers, men
Thread back the passage of delirium,
Missing the turn still, baffled by the door;
Smooth endless days, notched here and there with knives,
A weary, wormy darkness, spurred i' the flank
With flame, that it should eat and end itself
Like some tormented scorpion. Then at last
I do remember clearly, how there came
A stranger with authority, not right,
(I thought not) who commanded, caught me up
From old Assunta's neck; how, with a shriek,
She let me go,—while I, with ears too full
Of my father's silence, to shriek back a word,
In all a child's astonishment at grief
Stared at the wharf-edge where she stood and moaned,
My poor Assunta, where she stood and moaned!
The white walls, the blue hills, my Italy,
Drawn backward from the shuddering steamer-deck,
Like one in anger drawing back her skirts
Which suppliants catch at. Then the bitter sea
Inexorably pushed between us both,
And sweeping up the ship with my despair
Threw us out as a pasture to the stars.

Ten nights and days we voyaged on the deep;
Ten nights and days without the common face
Of any day or night; the moon and sun
Cut off from the green reconciling earth,
To starve into a blind ferocity
And glare unnatural; the very sky
(Dropping its bell-net down upon the sea
As if no human heart should 'scape alive,)
Bedraggled with the desolating salt,
Until it seemed no more that holy heaven
To which my father went. All new and strange;
The universe turned stranger, for a child.

Then, land!—then, England! oh, the frosty cliffs
Looked cold upon me. Could I find a home
Among those mean red houses through the fog?
And when I heard my father's language first
From alien lips which had no kiss for mine
I wept aloud, then laughed, then wept, then wept,
And some one near me said the child was mad
Through much sea-sickness. The train swept us on:
Was this my father's England? the great isle?
The ground seemed cut up from the fellowship
Of verdure, field from field, as man from man;
The skies themselves looked low and positive,
As almost you could touch them with a hand,
And dared to do it they were so far off
From God's celestial crystals; all things blurred
And dull and vague. Did Shakspeare and his mates
Absorb the light here?—not a hill or stone
With heart to strike a radiant colour up
Or active outline on the indifferent air.

I think I see my father's sister stand
Upon the hall-step of her country-house
To give me welcome. She stood straight and calm,
Her somewhat narrow forehead braided tight

As if for taming accidental thoughts
From possible pulses; brown hair pricked with gray
By frigid use of life, (she was not old
Although my father's elder by a year)
A nose drawn sharply, yet in delicate lines;
A close mild mouth, a little soured about
The ends, through speaking unrequited loves
Or peradventure niggardly half-truths;
Eyes of no colour,—once they might have smiled,
But never, never have forgot themselves
In smiling; cheeks, in which was yet a rose
Of perished summers, like a rose in a book,
Kept more for ruth than pleasure,—if past bloom,
Past fading also.
     She had lived, we'll say,
A harmless life, she called a virtuous life,
A quiet life, which was not life at all,
(But that, she had not lived enough to know)
Between the vicar and the county squires,
The lord-lieutenant looking down sometimes
From the empyrean to assure their souls
Against chance-vulgarisms, and, in the abyss
The apothecary, looked on once a year
To prove their soundness of humility.
The poor-club exercised her Christian gifts
Of knitting stockings, stitching petticoats,
Because we are of one flesh after all
And need one flannel (with a proper sense
Of difference in the quality)—and still
The book-club, guarded from your modern trick
Of shaking dangerous questions from the crease
Preserved her intellectual. She had lived
A sort of cage-bird life, born in a cage,
Accounting that to leap from perch to perch
Was act and joy enough for any bird.
Dear heaven, how silly are the things that live
In thickets, and eat berries!

                          I, alas,
A wild bird scarcely fledged, was brought to her cage,
And she was there to meet me.   Very kind.
Bring the clean water, give out the fresh seed.

She stood upon the steps to welcome me,
Calm, in black garb.   I clung about her neck,—
Young babes, who catch at every shred of wool
To draw the new light closer, catch and cling
Less blindly.   In my ears, my father's word
Hummed ignorantly, as the sea in shells,
"Love, love, my child."   She, black there with my grief,
Might feel my love—she was his sister once,
I clung to her.   A moment she seemed moved,
Kissed me with cold lips, suffered me to cling,
And drew me feebly through the hall into
The room she sate in.
                          There, with some strange spasm
Of pain and passion, she wrung loose my hands
Imperiously, and held me at arm's length,
And with two gray-steel naked-bladed eyes
Searched through my face,—ay, stabbed it through and
              through,
Through brows and cheeks and chin, as if to find
A wicked murderer in my innocent face,
If not here, there perhaps.   Then, drawing breath,
She struggled for her ordinary calm—
And missed it rather,—told me not to shrink,
As if she had told me not to lie or swear,—
"She loved my father and would love me too
As long as I deserved it."   Very kind.

I understood her meaning afterward;
She thought to find my mother in my face,
And questioned it for that.   For she, my aunt,
Had loved my father truly, as she could,
And hated, with the gall of gentle souls,

My Tuscan mother who had fooled away
A wise man from wise courses, a good man
From obvious duties, and, depriving her,
His sister, of the household precedence,
Had wronged his tenants, robbed his native land,
And made him mad, alike by life and death,
In love and sorrow. She had pored for years
What sort of woman could be suitable
To her son of hate, to entertain it with,
And so, her very curiosity
Became hate too, and all the idealism
She ever used in life, was used for hate,
Till hate, so nourished, did exceed at last
The love from which it grew, in strength and heat,
And wrinkled her smooth conscience with a sense
Of disputable virtue (say not, sin)
When Christian doctrine was enforced at church.

And thus my father's sister was to me
My mother's hater. From that day, she did
Her duty to me, (I appreciate it
In her own word as spoken to herself)
Her duty, in large measure, well-pressed out,
But measured always. She was generous, bland,
More courteous than was tender, gave me still
The first place,—as if fearful that God's saints
Would look down suddenly and say, "Herein
You missed a point, I think, through lack of love."
Alas, a mother never is afraid
Of speaking angerly to any child,
Since love, she knows, is justified of love.

And I, I was a good child on the whole,
A meek and manageable child. Why not?
I did not live, to have the faults of life:
There seemed more true life in my father's grave
Than in all England. Since *that* threw me off

Who fain would cleave, (his latest will, they say,
Consigned me to his land) I only thought
Of lying quiet there where I was thrown
Like sea-weed on the rocks, and suffering her
To prick me to a pattern with her pin
Fibre from fibre, delicate leaf from leaf,
And dry out from my drowned anatomy
The last sea-salt left in me.
      So it was.
I broke the copious curls upon my head
In braids, because she liked smooth-ordered hair.
I left off saying my sweet Tuscan words
Which still at any stirring of the heart
Came up to float across the English phrase
As lilies, (*Bene* or *Che che*,) because
She liked my father's child to speak his tongue,
I learnt the collects and the catechism,
The creeds, from Athanasius back to Nice,
The Articles, the Tracts *against* the times,
(By no means Buonaventure's "Prick of Love,")
And various popular synopses of
Inhuman doctrines never taught by John,
Because she liked instructed piety.
I learnt my complement of classic French
(Kept pure of Balzac and neologism)
And German also, since she liked a range
Of liberal education,—tongues, not books.
I learnt a little algebra, a little
Of the mathematics,—brushed with extreme flounce
The circle of the sciences, because
She misliked women who are frivolous.
I learnt the royal genealogies
Of Oviedo, the internal laws
Of the Burmese empire,—by how many feet
Mount Chimborazo outsoars Teneriffe,
What navigable river joins itself
To Lara; and what census of the year five

Was taken at Klagenfurt,—because she liked
A general insight into useful facts.
I learnt much music,—such as would have been
As quite impossible in Johnson's day
As still it might be wished—fine sleights of hand
And unimagined fingering, shuffling off
The hearer's soul through hurricanes of notes
To a noisy Tophet; and I drew .. costumes
From French engravings, nereids neatly draped,
(With smirks of simmering godship): I washed in
Landscapes from nature (rather say, washed out).
I danced the polka and Cellarius,
Spun glass, stuffed birds, and modelled flowers in wax,
Because she liked accomplishments in girls.
I read a score of books on womanhood
To prove, if women do not think at all,
They may teach thinking, (to a maiden-aunt
Or else the author)—books that boldly assert
Their right of comprehending husband's talk
When not too deep, and even of answering
With pretty "may it please you," or "so it is,"—
Their rapid insight and fine aptitude,
Particular worth and general missionariness,
As long as they keep quiet by the fire
And never say "no" when the world says "ay,"
For that is fatal,—their angelic reach
Of virtue, chiefly used to sit and darn,
And fatten household sinners,—their, in brief,
Potential faculty in everything
Of abdicating power in it: she owned
She liked a woman to be womanly,
And English women, she thanked God and sighed,
(Some people always sigh in thanking God)
Were models to the universe. And last
I learnt cross-stitch, because she did not like
To see me wear the night with empty hands
A-doing nothing. So, my shepherdess

Was something after all, (the pastoral saints
Be praised for't) leaning lovelorn with pink eyes
To match her shoes, when I mistook the silks;
Her head uncrushed by that round weight of hat
So strangely similar to the tortoise-shell
Which slew the tragic poet.
                     By the way,
The works of women are symbolical.
We sew, sew, prick our fingers, dull our sight,
Producing what? A pair of slippers, sir,
To put on when you 're weary— or a stool
To stumble over and vex you .. "curse that stool!"
Or else at best, a cushion, where you lean
And sleep, and dream of something we are not
But would be for your sake. Alas, alas!
This hurts most, this—that, after all, we are paid
The worth of our work, perhaps.
                         In looking down
Those years of education (to return)
I wonder if Brinvilliers suffered more
In the water-torture,.. flood succeeding flood
To drench the incapable throat and split the veins ..
Than I did. Certain of your feebler souls
Go out in such a process; many pine
To a sick, inodorous light; my own endured:
I had relations in the Unseen, and drew
The elemental nutriment and heat
From nature, as earth feels the sun at nights,
Or as a babe sucks surely in the dark.
I kept the life thrust on me, on the outside
Of the inner life with all its ample room
For heart and lungs, for will and intellect,
Inviolable by conventions. God,
I thank thee for that grace of thine!
                             At first
I felt no life which was not patience,—did
The thing she bade me, without heed to a thing

Beyond it, sate in just the chair she placed,
With back against the window, to exclude
The sight of the great lime-tree on the lawn,
Which seemed to have come on purpose from the woods
To bring the house a message,—ay, and walked
Demurely in her carpeted low rooms,
As if I should not, harkening my own steps,
Misdoubt I was alive. I read her books,
Was civil to her cousin, Romney Leigh,
Gave ear to her vicar, tea to her visitors,
And heard them whisper, when I changed a cup,
(I blushed for joy at that)—"The Italian child,
For all her blue eyes and her quiet ways,
Thrives ill in England: she is paler yet
Than when we came the last time; she will die."

"Will die." My cousin, Romney Leigh, blushed too,
With sudden anger, and approaching me
Said low between his teeth, "You 're wicked now!
You wish to die and leave the world a-dusk
For others, with your naughty light blown out?"
I looked into his face defyingly;
He might have known that, being what I was,
'Twas natural to like to get away
As far as dead folk can: and then indeed
Some people make no trouble when they die.
He turned and went abruptly, slammed the door
And shut his dog out.
      Romney, Romney Leigh.
I have not named my cousin hitherto,
And yet I used him as a sort of friend;
My elder by few years, but cold and shy
And absent .. tender, when he thought of it,
Which scarcely was imperative, grave betimes,
As well as early master of Leigh Hall,
Whereof the nightmare sate upon his youth
Repressing all its seasonable delights

And agonising with a ghastly sense
Of universal hideous want and wrong
To incriminate possession. When he came
From college to the country, very oft
He crossed the hill on visits to my aunt,
With gifts of blue grapes from the hothouses,
A book in one hand,—mere statistics,—(if
I chanced to lift the cover,) count of all
The goats whose beards grow sprouting down toward hell
Against God's separative judgment-hour.
And she, she almost loved him,—even allowed
That sometimes he should seem to sigh my way;
It made him easier to be pitiful,
And sighing was his gift. So, undisturbed
At whiles she let him shut my music up
And push my needles down, and lead me out
To see in that south angle of the house
The figs grow black as if by a Tuscan rock,
On some light pretext. She would turn her head
At other moments, go to fetch a thing,
And leave me breath enough to speak with him,
For his sake; it was simple.
     Sometimes too
He would have saved me utterly, it seemed,
He stood and looked so.
     Once, he stood so near
He dropped a sudden hand upon my head
Bent down on woman's work, as soft as rain—
But then I rose and shook it off as fire,
The stranger's touch that took my father's place
Yet dared seem soft.
     I used him for a friend
Before I ever knew him for a friend.
'Twas better, 'twas worse also, afterward:
We came so close, we saw our differences
Too intimately. Always Romney Leigh
Was looking for the worms, I for the gods.

A godlike nature his; the gods look down,
Incurious of themselves; and certainly
'Tis well I should remember, how, those days,
I was a worm too and he looked on me.

A little by his act perhaps, yet more
By something in me, surely not my will,
I did not die. But slowly, as one in swoon,
To whom life creeps back in the form of death,
With a sense of separation, a blind pain
Of blank obstruction, and a roar i' the ears
Of visionary chariots which retreat
As earth grows clearer . . slowly, by degrees,
I woke, rose up . . where was I? in the world;
For uses therefore I must count worth while.

I had a little chamber in the house,
As green as any privet-hedge a bird
Might choose to build in, though the nest itself
Could show but dead-brown sticks and straws; the walls
Were green, the carpet was pure green, the straight
Small bed was curtained greenly, and the folds
Hung green about the window which let in
The out-door world with all its greenery.
You could not push your head out and escape
A dash of dawn-dew from the honeysuckle,
But so you were baptized into the grace
And privilege of seeing . . .
                              First, the lime,
(I had enough there, of the lime, be sure, —
My morning-dream was often hummed away
By the bees in it;) past the lime, the lawn,
Which, after sweeping broadly round the house,
Went trickling through the shrubberies in a stream
Of tender turf, and wore and lost itself
Among the acacias, over which you saw
The irregular line of elms by the deep lane

Which stopped the grounds and dammed the overflow
Of arbutus and laurel. Out of sight
The lane was; sunk so deep, no foreign tramp
Nor drover of wild ponies out of Wales
Could guess if lady's hall or tenant's lodge
Dispensed such odours,—though his stick well-crooked
Might reach the lowest trail of blossoming briar
Which dipped upon the wall. Behind the elms,
And through their tops, you saw the folded hills
Striped up and down with hedges, (burly oaks
Projecting from the line to show themselves)
Through which my cousin Romney's chimneys smoked
As still as when a silent mouth in frost
Breathes, showing where the woodlands hid Leigh Hall;
While, far above, a jut of table-land,
A promontory without water, stretched,—
You could not catch it if the days were thick,
Or took it for a cloud; but, otherwise,
The vigorous sun would catch it up at eve
And use it for an anvil till he had filled
The shelves of heaven with burning thunderbolts,
Protesting against night and darkness:—then,
When all his setting trouble was resolved
To a trance of passive glory, you might see
In apparition on the golden sky
(Alas, my Giotto's background!) the sheep run
Along the fine clear outline, small as mice
That run along a witch's scarlet thread.

Not a grand nature. Not my chesnut-woods
Of Vallombrosa, cleaving by the spurs
To the precipices. Not my headlong leaps
Of waters, that cry out for joy or fear
In leaping through the palpitating pines,
Like a white soul tossed out to eternity
With thrills of time upon it. Not indeed
My multitudinous mountains, sitting in

The magic circle, with the mutual touch
Electric, panting from their full deep hearts
Beneath the influent heavens, and waiting for
Communion and commission. Italy
Is one thing, England one.
      On English ground
You understand the letter,—ere the fall
How Adam lived in a garden. All the fields
Are tied up fast with hedges, nosegay-like;
The hills are crumpled plains, the plains parterres,
The trees, round, woolly, ready to be clipped,
And if you seek for any wilderness
You find, at best, a park. A nature tamed
And grown domestic like a barn-door fowl,
Which does not awe you with its claws and beak
Nor tempt you to an eyrie too high up,
But which, in cackling, sets you thinking of
Your eggs to-morrow at breakfast, in the pause
Of finer meditation.
    Rather say,
A sweet familiar nature, stealing in
As a dog might, or child, to touch your hand
Or pluck your gown, and humbly mind you so
Of presence and affection, excellent
For inner uses, from the things without.

I could not be unthankful, I who was
Entreated thus and holpen. In the room
I speak of, ere the house was well awake,
And also after it was well asleep,
I sate alone, and drew the blessing in
Of all that nature. With a gradual step,
A stir among the leaves, a breath, a ray,
It came in softly, while the angels made
A place for it beside me. The moon came,
And swept my chamber clean of foolish thoughts.
The sun came, saying, "Shall I lift this light

Against the lime-tree, and you will not look?
I make the birds sing—listen! but, for you,
God never hears your voice, excepting when
You lie upon the bed at nights and weep."

Then, something moved me. Then, I wakened up
More slowly than I verily write now,
But wholly, at last, I wakened, opened wide
The window and my soul, and let the airs
And out-door sights sweep gradual gospels in,
Regenerating what I was. O Life,
How oft we throw it off and think,—"Enough,
Enough of life in so much!—here's a cause
For rupture;—herein we must break with Life,
Or be ourselves unworthy; here we are wronged,
Maimed, spoiled for aspiration: farewell Life!"
And so, as froward babes, we hide our eyes
And think all ended.—Then, Life calls to us
In some transformed, apocalyptic voice,
Above us, or below us, or around:
Perhaps we name it Nature's voice, or Love's,
Tricking ourselves, because we are more ashamed
To own our compensations than our griefs:
Still, Life's voice!—still, we make our peace with Life.

And I, so young then, was not sullen. Soon
I used to get up early, just to sit
And watch the morning quicken in the gray,
And hear the silence open like a flower
Leaf after leaf,—and stroke with listless hand
The woodbine through the window, till at last
I came to do it with a sort of love,
At foolish unaware: whereat I smiled,—
A melancholy smile, to catch myself
Smiling for joy.
    Capacity for joy
Admits temptation. It seemed, next, worth while

To dodge the sharp sword set against my life;
To slip down stairs through all the sleepy house,
As mute as any dream there, and escape
As a soul from the body, out of doors,
Glide through the shrubberies, drop into the lane,
And wander on the hills an hour or two,
Then back again before the house should stir.

Or else I sate on in my chamber green,
And lived my life, and thought my thoughts, and prayed
My prayers without the vicar; read my books,
Without considering whether they were fit
To do me good. Mark, there. We get no good
By being ungenerous, even to a book,
And calculating profits, so much help
By so much reading. It is rather when
We gloriously forget ourselves and plunge
Soul-forward, headlong, into a book's profound,
Impassioned for its beauty and salt of truth—
'Tis then we get the right good from a book.

I read much. What my father taught before
From many a volume, Love re-emphasised
Upon the self-same pages: Theophrast
Grew tender with the memory of his eyes,
And Ælian made mine wet. The trick of Greek
And Latin, he had taught me, as he would
Have taught me wrestling or the game of fives
If such he had known,—most like a shipwrecked man
Who heaps his single platter with goats' cheese
And scarlet berries; or like any man
Who loves but one, and so gives all at once,
Because he has it, rather than because
He counts it worthy. Thus, my father gave;
And thus, as did the women formerly
By young Achilles, when they pinned a veil
Across the boy's audacious front, and swept

With tuneful laughs the silver-fretted rocks,
He wrapt his little daughter in his large
Man's doublet, careless did it fit or no.

But, after I had read for memory,
I read for hope. The path my father's foot
Had trod me out, (which suddenly broke off
What time he dropped the wallet of the flesh
And passed) alone I carried on, and set
My child-heart 'gainst the thorny underwood,
To reach the grassy shelter of the trees.
Ah babe i' the wood, without a brother-babe!
My own self-pity, like the red-breast bird,
Flies back to cover all that past with leaves.

Sublimest danger, over which none weeps,
When any young wayfaring soul goes forth
Alone, unconscious of the perilous road,
The day-sun dazzling in his limpid eyes,
To thrust his own way, he an alien, through
The world of books! Ah, you!—you think it fine,
You clap hands—"A fair day!"—you cheer him on,
As if the worst, could happen, were to rest
Too long beside a fountain. Yet, behold,
Behold!—the world of books is still the world,
And worldlings in it are less merciful
And more puissant. For the wicked there
Are winged like angels; every knife that strikes
Is edged from elemental fire to assail
A spiritual life; the beautiful seems right
By force of beauty, and the feeble wrong
Because of weakness; power is justified
Though armed against Saint Michael; many a crown
Covers bald foreheads. In the book-world, true,
There's no lack, neither, of God's saints and kings,
That shake the ashes of the grave aside
From their calm locks and undiscomfited

Look stedfast truths against Time's changing mask.
True, many a prophet teaches in the roads;
True, many a seer pulls down the flaming heavens
Upon his own head in strong martyrdom
In order to light men a moment's space.
But stay!—who judges?—who distinguishes
'Twixt Saul and Nahash justly, at first sight,
And leaves king Saul precisely at the sin,
To serve king David? who discerns at once
The sound of the trumpets, when the trumpets blow
For Alaric as well as Charlemagne?
Who judges wizards, and can tell true seers
From conjurors? the child, there? Would you leave
That child to wander in a battle-field
And push his innocent smile against the guns;
Or even in a catacomb,—his torch
Grown ragged in the fluttering air, and all
The dark a-mutter round him? not a child.

I read books bad and good—some bad and good
At once; (good aims not always make good books:
Well-tempered spades turn up ill-smelling soils
In digging vineyards even) books that prove
God's being so definitely, that man's doubt
Grows self-defined the other side the line,
Made atheist by suggestion; moral books,
Exasperating to license; genial books,
Discounting from the human dignity;
And merry books, which set you weeping when
The sun shines,—ay, and melancholy books,
Which make you laugh that any one should weep
In this disjointed life for one wrong more.

The world of books is still the world, I write,
And both worlds have God's providence, thank God,
To keep and hearten: with some struggle, indeed,
Among the breakers, some hard swimming through

The deeps—I lost breath in my soul sometimes
And cried, "God save me if there's any God,"
But, even so, God saved me; and, being dashed
From error on to error, every turn
Still brought me nearer to the central truth.

I thought so. All this anguish in the thick
Of men's opinions .. press and counterpress,
Now up, now down, now underfoot, and now
Emergent .. all the best of it, perhaps,
But throws you back upon a noble trust
And use of your own instinct,—merely proves
Pure reason stronger than bare inference
At strongest. Try it,—fix against heaven's wall
The scaling-ladders of school logic—mount
Step by step!—sight goes faster; that still ray
Which strikes out from you, how, you cannot tell,
And why, you know not, (did you eliminate,
That such as you indeed should analyse?)
Goes straight and fast as light, and high as God.

The cygnet finds the water, but the man
Is born in ignorance of his element
And feels out blind at first, disorganised
By sin i' the blood, his spirit-insight dulled
And crossed by his sensations. Presently
He feels it quicken in the dark sometimes,
When, mark, be reverent, be obedient,
For such dumb motions of imperfect life
Are oracles of vital Deity
Attesting the Hereafter. Let who says
"The soul's a clean white paper," rather say,
A palimpsest, a prophet's holograph
Defiled, erased and covered by a monk's,—
The apocalypse, by a Longus! poring on
Which obscene text, we may discern perhaps
Some fair, fine trace of what was written once,

Some upstroke of an alpha and omega
Expressing the old scripture.
                    Books, books, books!
I had found the secret of a garret-room
Piled high with cases in my father's name,
Piled high, packed large,—where, creeping in and out
Among the giant fossils of my past,
Like some small nimble mouse between the ribs
Of a mastodon, I nibbled here and there
At this or that box, pulling through the gap,
In heats of terror, haste, victorious joy,
The first book first. And how I felt it beat
Under my pillow, in the morning's dark,
An hour before the sun would let me read!
My books! At last because the time was ripe,
I chanced upon the poets.
                    As the earth
Plunges in fury, when the internal fires
Have reached and pricked her heart, and, throwing flat
The marts and temples, the triumphal gates
And towers of observation, clears herself
To elemental freedom—thus, my soul,
At poetry's divine first finger-touch,
Let go conventions and sprang up surprised,
Convicted of the great eternities
Before two worlds.
                    What's this, Aurora Leigh,
You write so of the poets, and not laugh?
Those virtuous liars, dreamers after dark,
Exaggerators of the sun and moon,
And soothsayers in a tea-cup?
                    I write so
Of the only truth-tellers now left to God,
The only speakers of essential truth,
Opposed to relative, comparative,
And temporal truths; the only holders by
His sun-skirts, through conventional gray glooms;

The only teachers who instruct mankind
From just a shadow on a charnel-wall
To find man's veritable stature out
Erect, sublime, the measure of a man,
And that's the measure of an angel, says
The apostle. Ay, and while your common men
Lay telegraphs, gauge railroads, reign, reap, dine,
And dust the flaunty carpets of the world
For kings to walk on, or our president,
The poet suddenly will catch them up
With his voice like a thunder,—"This is soul,
This is life, this word is being said in heaven,
Here's God down on us! what are you about?"
How all those workers start amid their work,
Look round, look up, and feel, a moment's space,
That carpet-dusting, though a pretty trade,
Is not the imperative labour after all.

My own best poets, am I one with you,
That thus I love you,—or but one through love?
Does all this smell of thyme about my feet
Conclude my visit to your holy hill
In personal presence, or but testify
The rustling of your vesture through my dreams
With influent odours? When my joy and pain,
My thought and aspiration, like the stops
Of pipe or flute, are absolutely dumb
Unless melodious, do you play on me
My pipers,—and if, sooth, you did not blow,
Would no sound come? or is the music mine,
As a man's voice or breath is called his own,
Inbreathed by the Life-breather? There's a doubt
For cloudy seasons!
      But the sun was high
When first I felt my pulses set themselves
For concord; when the rhythmic turbulence
Of blood and brain swept outward upon words,

As wind upon the alders, blanching them
By turning up their under-natures till
They trembled in dilation.   O delight
And triumph of the poet, who would say
A man's mere "yes," a woman's common "no,"
A little human hope of that or this,
And says the word so that it burns you through
With a special revelation, shakes the heart
Of all the men and women in the world,
As if one came back from the dead and spoke,
With eyes too happy, a familiar thing
Become divine i' the utterance! while for him
The poet, speaker, he expands with joy;
The palpitating angel in his flesh
Thrills inly with consenting fellowship
To those innumerous spirits who sun themselves
Outside of time.
                    O life, O poetry,
—Which means life in life! cognisant of life
Beyond this blood-beat, passionate for truth
Beyond these senses!—poetry, my life,
My eagle, with both grappling feet still hot
From Zeus's thunder, who hast ravished me
Away from all the shepherds, sheep, and dogs,
And set me in the Olympian roar and round
Of luminous faces for a cup-bearer,
To keep the mouths of all the godheads moist
For everlasting laughters,—I myself
Half drunk across the beaker with their eyes!
How those gods look!
                    Enough so, Ganymede,
We shall not bear above a round or two.
We drop the golden cup at Heré's foot
And swoon back to the earth,—and find ourselves
Face-down among the pine-cones, cold with dew,
While the dogs bark, and many a shepherd scoffs,
"What's come now to the youth?"   Such ups and downs

Have poets.
                    Am I such indeed?   The name
Is royal, and to sign it like a queen,
Is what I dare not,—though some royal blood
Would seem to tingle in me now and then,
With sense of power and ache,—with imposthumes
And manias usual to the race.   Howbeit
I dare not: 'tis too easy to go mad
And ape a Bourbon in a crown of straws;
The thing's too common.
                            Many fervent souls
Strike rhyme on rhyme, who would strike steel on steel
If steel had offered, in a restless heat
Of doing something.   Many tender souls
Have strung their losses on a rhyming thread,
As children, cowslips:—the more pains they take,
The work more withers.   Young men, ay, and maids,
Too often sow their wild oats in tame verse,
Before they sit down under their own vine
And live for use.   Alas, near all the birds
Will sing at dawn,—and yet we do not take
The chaffering swallow for the holy lark.

In those days, though, I never analysed,
Not even myself.   Analysis comes late.
You catch a sight of Nature, earliest,
In full front sun-face, and your eyelids wink
And drop before the wonder of 't; you miss
The form, through seeing the light.   I lived, those days,
And wrote because I lived—unlicensed else;
My heart beat in my brain.   Life's violent flood
Abolished bounds,—and, which my neighbour's field,
Which mine, what mattered? it is thus in youth!
We play at leap-frog over the god Term;
The love within us and the love without
Are mixed, confounded; if we are loved or love,
We scarce distinguish: thus, with other power;

Being acted on and acting seem the same:
In that first onrush of life's chariot-wheels,
We know not if the forests move or we.

And so, like most young poets, in a flush
Of individual life I poured myself
Along the veins of others, and achieved
Mere lifeless imitations of live verse,
And made the living answer for the dead,
Profaning nature. "Touch not, do not taste,
Nor handle,"—we're too legal, who write young:
We beat the phorminx till we hurt our thumbs,
As if still ignorant of counterpoint;
We call the Muse,—"O Muse, benignant Muse,"—·
As if we had seen her purple-braided head,
With the eyes in it, start between the boughs
As often as a stag's. What make-believe,
With so much earnest! what effete results
From virile efforts! what cold wire-drawn odes,
From such white heats!—bucolics, where the cows
Would scare the writer if they splashed the mud
In lashing off the flies,—didactics, driven
Against the heels of what the master said;
And counterfeiting epics, shrill with trumps
A babe might blow between two straining cheeks
Of bubbled rose, to make his mother laugh;
And elegiac griefs, and songs of love,
Like cast-off nosegays picked up on the road,
The worse for being warm: all these things, writ
On happy mornings, with a morning heart,
That leaps for love, is active for resolve,
Weak for art only. Oft, the ancient forms
Will thrill, indeed, in carrying the young blood.
The wine-skins, now and then, a little warped,
Will crack even, as the new wine gurgles in.
Spare the old bottles!—spill not the new wine.

By Keats's soul, the man who never stepped
In gradual progress like another man,
But, turning grandly on his central self,
Ensphered himself in twenty perfect years
And died, not young, (the life of a long life
Distilled to a mere drop, falling like a tear
Upon the world's cold cheek to make it burn
For ever;) by that strong excepted soul,
I count it strange and hard to understand
That nearly all young poets should write old,
That Pope was sexagenary at sixteen,
And beardless Byron academical,
And so with others. It may be perhaps
Such have not settled long and deep enough
In trance, to attain to clairvoyance,—and still
The memory mixes with the vision, spoils,
And works it turbid.
                    Or perhaps, again,
In order to discover the Muse-Sphinx,
The melancholy desert must sweep round,
Behind you as before.—
                       For me, I wrote
False poems, like the rest, and thought them true
Because myself was true in writing them.
I peradventure have writ true ones since
With less complacence.
                       But I could not hide
My quickening inner life from those at watch.
They saw a light at a window now and then,
They had not set there: who had set it there?
My father's sister started when she caught
My soul agaze in my eyes. She could not say
I had no business with a sort of soul,
But plainly she objected,—and demurred
That souls were dangerous things to carry straight
Through all the spilt saltpetre of the world.
She said sometimes, "Aurora, have you done

Your task this morning? have you read that book?
And are you ready for the crochet here?"—
As if she said, "I know there's something wrong;
I know I have not ground you down enough
To flatten and bake you to a wholesome crust
For household uses and proprieties,
Before the rain has got into my barn
And set the grains a-sprouting. What, you're green
With out-door impudence? you almost growl?"
To which I answered, "Would she hear my task,
And verify my abstract of the book?
Or should I sit down to the crochet work?
Was such her pleasure?" Then I sate and teased
The patient needle till it spilt the thread,
Which oozed off from it in meandering lace
From hour to hour. I was not, therefore, sad;
My soul was singing at a work apart
Behind the wall of sense, as safe from harm
As sings the lark when sucked up out of sight
In vortices of glory and blue air.

And so, through forced work and spontaneous work,
The inner life informed the outer life,
Reduced the irregular blood to a settled rhythm,
Made cool the forehead with fresh-sprinkling dreams,
And, rounding to the spheric soul the thin,
Pined body, struck a colour up the cheeks
Though somewhat faint. I clenched my brows across
My blue eyes greatening in the looking-glass,
And said, "We'll live, Aurora! we'll be strong.
The dogs are on us—but we will not die."

Whoever lives true life, will love true love.
I learnt to love that England. Very oft,
Before the day was born, or otherwise
Through secret windings of the afternoons,
I threw my hunters off and plunged myself

Among the deep hills, as a hunted stag
Will take the waters, shivering with the fear
And passion of the course. And when at last
Escaped, so many a green slope built on slope
Betwixt me and the enemy's house behind,
I dared to rest, or wander, in a rest
Made sweeter for the step upon the grass,
And view the ground's most gentle dimplement,
(As if God's finger touched but did not press
In making England) such an up and down
Of verdure,—nothing too much up or down,
A ripple of land; such little hills, the sky
Can stoop to tenderly and the wheatfields climb;
Such nooks of valleys lined with orchises,
Fed full of noises by invisible streams;
And open pastures where you scarcely tell
White daisies from white dew,—at intervals
The mythic oaks and elm-trees standing out
Self-poised upon their prodigy of shade,—
I thought my father's land was worthy too
Of being my Shakspeare's.
      Very oft alone,
Unlicensed: not unfrequently with leave
To walk the third with Romney and his friend
The rising painter, Vincent Carrington,
Whom men judge hardly as bee-bonneted,
Because he holds that, paint a body well,
You paint a soul by implication, like
The grand first Master. Pleasant walks! for if
He said, "When I was last in Italy,"
It sounded as an instrument that's played
Too far off for the tune—and yet it's fine
To listen.
    Ofter we walked only two
If cousin Romney pleased to walk with me.
We read, or talked, or quarrelled, as it chanced.
We were not lovers, nor even friends well-matched:

Say rather, scholars upon different tracks,
And thinkers disagreed, he, overfull
Of what is, and I, haply, overbold
For what might be.
                But then the thrushes sang,
And shook my pulses and the elms' new leaves;
At which I turned, and held my finger up,
And bade him mark that, howsoe'er the world
Went ill, as he related, certainly
The thrushes still sang in it. At the word
His brow would soften,—and he bore with me
In melancholy patience, not unkind,
While breaking into voluble ecstasy
I flattered all the beauteous country round,
As poets use, the skies, the clouds, the fields,
The happy violets hiding from the roads
The primroses run down to, carrying gold;
The tangled hedgerows, where the cows push out
Impatient horns and tolerant churning mouths
'Twixt dripping ash-boughs,—hedgerows all alive
With birds and gnats and large white butterflies
Which look as if the May-flower had caught life
And palpitated forth upon the wind;
Hills, vales, woods, netted in a silver mist,
Farms, granges, doubled up among the hills;
And cattle grazing in the watered vales,
And cottage-chimneys smoking from the woods,
And cottage-gardens smelling everywhere,
Confused with smell of orchards. "See," I said,
"And see! is God not with us on the earth?
And shall we put Him down by aught we do?
Who says there's nothing for the poor and vile
Save poverty and wickedness? behold!"
And ankle-deep in English grass I leaped
And clapped my hands, and called all very fair.

In the beginning when God called all good,

Even then was evil near us, it is writ;
But we indeed who call things good and fair,
The evil is upon us while we speak;
Deliver us from evil, let us pray.

SECOND BOOK.

Times followed one another. Came a morn
I stood upon the brink of twenty years,
And looked before and after, as I stood
Woman and artist,—either incomplete,
Both credulous of completion. There I held
The whole creation in my little cup,
And smiled with thirsty lips before I drank
"Good health to you and me, sweet neighbour mine,
And all these peoples."
                  I was glad, that day;
The June was in me, with its multitudes
Of nightingales all singing in the dark,
And rosebuds reddening where the calyx split.
I felt so young, so strong, so sure of God!
So glad, I could not choose be very wise!
And, old at twenty, was inclined to pull
My childhood backward in a childish jest
To see the face of 't once more, and farewell!
In which fantastic mood I bounded forth
At early morning,—would not wait so long
As even to snatch my bonnet by the strings,
But, brushing a green trail across the lawn
With my gown in the dew, took will and way
Among the acacias of the shrubberies,
To fly my fancies in the open air
And keep my birthday, till my aunt awoke
To stop good dreams. Meanwhile I murmured on
As honeyed bees keep humming to themselves,
"The worthiest poets have remained uncrowned

Till death has bleached their foreheads to the bone;
And so with me it must be unless I prove
Unworthy of the grand adversity,
And certainly I would not fail so much.
What, therefore, if I crown myself to-day,
In sport, not pride, to learn the feel of it,
Before my brows be numbed as Dante's own
To all the tender pricking of such leaves?
Such leaves! what leaves?"

                I pulled the branches down
To choose from.

              "Not the bay! I choose no bay,
(The fates deny us if we are overbold)
Nor myrtle—which means chiefly love; and love
Is something awful which one dares not touch
So early o' mornings. This verbena strains
The point of passionate fragrance; and hard by,
This guelder-rose, at far too slight a beck
Of the wind, will toss about her flower-apples.
Ah—there's my choice,—that ivy on the wall,
That headlong ivy! not a leaf will grow
But thinking of a wreath. Large leaves, smooth leaves,
Serrated like my vines, and half as green.
I like such ivy, bold to leap a height
'Twas strong to climb; as good to grow on graves
As twist about a thyrsus; pretty too,
(And that's not ill) when twisted round a comb."

Thus speaking to myself, half singing it,
Because some thoughts are fashioned like a bell
To ring with once being touched, I drew a wreath
Drenched, blinding me with dew, across my brow,
And fastening it behind so, turning faced
. . My public!—cousin Romney—with a mouth
Twice graver than his eyes.

                I stood there fixed,—
My arms up, like the caryatid, sole

Of some abolished temple, helplessly
Persistent in a gesture which derides
A former purpose.   Yet my blush was flame,
As if from flax, not stone.
                            "Aurora Leigh,
The earliest of Auroras!"
                            Hand stretched out
I clasped, as shipwrecked men will clasp a hand,
Indifferent to the sort of palm.   The tide
Had caught me at my pastime, writing down
My foolish name too near upon the sea
Which drowned me with a blush as foolish.   "You,
My cousin!"
            The smile died out in his eyes
And dropped upon his lips, a cold dead weight,
For just a moment, "Here's a book I found!
No name writ on it—poems, by the form;
Some Greek upon the margin,—lady's Greek
Without the accents.   Read it?   Not a word.
I saw at once the thing had witchcraft in 't,
Whereof the reading calls up dangerous spirits:
I rather bring it to the witch."
                                "My book.
You found it". .
                "In the hollow by the stream
That beech leans down into—of which you said
The Oread in it has a Naiad's heart
And pines for waters."
                    "Thank you."
                                "Thanks to *you*
My cousin! that I have seen you not too much
Witch, scholar, poet, dreamer, and the rest,
To be a woman also."
                    With a glance
The smile rose in his eyes again and touched
The ivy on my forehead, light as air.
I answered gravely, "Poets needs must be

Or men or women— more 's the pity."
                                    "Ah,
But men, and still less women, happily,
Scarce need be poets. Keep to the green wreath,
Since even dreaming of the stone and bronze
Brings headaches, pretty cousin, and defiles
The clean white morning dresses."
                               "So you judge!
Because I love the beautiful I must
Love pleasure chiefly, and be overcharged
For ease and whiteness! well, you know the world,
And only miss your cousin, 'tis not much.
But learn this; I would rather take my part
With God's Dead, who afford to walk in white
Yet spread His glory, than keep quiet here
And gather up my feet from even a step
For fear to soil my gown in so much dust.
I choose to walk at all risks.—Here, if heads
That hold a rhythmic thought, must ache perforce,
For my part I choose headaches,—and to-day 's
My birthday."
             "Dear Aurora, choose instead
To cure them. You have balsams."
                                "I perceive.
The headache is too noble for my sex.
You think the heartache would sound decenter,
Since that's the woman's special, proper ache,
And altogether tolerable, except
To a woman."
            Saying which, I loosed my wreath,
And swinging it beside me as I walked,
Half petulant, half playful, as we walked,
I sent a sidelong look to find his thought,—
As falcon set on falconer's finger may,
With sidelong head, and startled, braving eye,
Which means, "You'll see—you'll see! I'll soon take flight
You shall not hinder." He, as shaking out

His hand and answering "Fly then," did not speak,
Except by such a gesture. Silently
We paced, until, just coming into sight
Of the house-windows, he abruptly caught
At one end of the swinging wreath, and said
"Aurora!" There I stopped short, breath and all.

"Aurora let's be serious, and throw by
This game of head and heart. Life means, be sure,
Both heart and head,—both active, both complete,
And both in earnest. Men and women make
The world, as head and heart make human life.
Work man, work woman, since there's work to do
In this beleaguered earth, for head and heart,
And thought can never do the work of love:
But work for ends, I mean for uses, not
For such sleek fringes (do you call them ends,
Still less God's glory?) as we sew ourselves
Upon the velvet of those baldaquins
Held 'twixt us and the sun. That book of yours,
I have not read a page of; but I toss
A rose up—it falls calyx down, you see!
The chances are that, being a woman, young
And pure, with such a pair of large, calm eyes,
You write as well .. and ill,.. upon the whole,
As other women. If as well, what then?
If even a little better,... still, what then?
We want the Best in art now, or no art.
The time is done for facile settings up
Of minnow gods, nymphs here and tritons there;
The polytheists have gone out in God,
That unity of Bests. No best, no God!
And so with art, we say. Give arts divine,
Direct, indubitable, real as grief,
Or leave us to the grief we grow ourselves
Divine by overcoming with mere hope
And most prosaic patience. You, you are young

As Eve with nature's daybreak on her face,
But this same world you are come to, dearest coz,
Has done with keeping birthdays, saves her wreaths
To hang upon her ruins,—and forgets
To rhyme the cry with which she still beats back
Those savage, hungry dogs that hunt her down
To the empty grave of Christ. The world's hard pressed:
The sweat of labour in the early curse
Has (turning acrid in six thousand years)
Become the sweat of torture. Who has time,
An hour's time . . think!—to sit upon a bank
And hear the cymbal tinkle in white hands?
When Egypt's slain, I say, let Miriam sing!—
Before—where's Moses?"
       "Ah, exactly that.
Where's Moses?—is a Moses to be found?
You'll seek him vainly in the bulrushes,
While I in vain touch cymbals. Yet concede,
Such sounding brass has done some actual good
(The application in a woman's hand,
If that were credible, being scarcely spoilt,)
In colonising beehives."
       "There it is!—
You play beside a death-bed like a child,
Yet measure to yourself a prophet's place
To teach the living. None of all these things,
Can women understand. You generalise
Oh, nothing,—not even grief! Your quick-breathed hearts,
So sympathetic to the personal pang,
Close on each separate knife-stroke, yielding up
A whole life at each wound, incapable
Of deepening, widening a large lap of life
To hold the world-full woe. The human race
To you means, such a child, or such a man,
You saw one morning waiting in the cold,
Beside that gate, perhaps. You gather up
A few such cases, and when strong sometimes

Will write of factories and of slaves, as if
Your father were a negro, and your son
A spinner in the mills. All's yours and you,
All, coloured with your blood, or otherwise
Just nothing to you. Why, I call you hard
To general suffering. Here's the world half blind
With intellectual light, half brutalised
With civilisation, having caught the plague
In silks from Tarsus, shrieking east and west
Along a thousand railroads, mad with pain
And sin too!.. does one woman of you all
(You who weep easily) grow pale to see
This tiger shake his cage?—does one of you
Stand still from dancing, stop from stringing pearls,
And pine and die because of the great sum
Of universal anguish!—Show me a tear
Wet as Cordelia's, in eyes bright as yours,
Because the world is mad. You cannot count,
That you should weep for this account, not you!
You weep for what you know. A red-haired child
Sick in a fever, if you touch him once,
Though but so little as with a finger-tip,
Will set you weeping; but a million sick ..
You could as soon weep for the rule of three
Or compound fractions. Therefore, this same world
Uncomprehended by you, must remain
Uninfluenced by you.—Women as you are,
Mere women, personal and passionate,
You give us doating mothers, and perfect wives,
Sublime Madonnas, and enduring saints!
We get no Christ from you,—and verily
We shall not get a poet, in my mind."

"With which conclusion you conclude"..
                                                "But this:
That you, Aurora, with the large live brow
And steady eyelids, cannot condescend

To play at art, as children play at swords,
To show a pretty spirit, chiefly admired
Because true action is impossible.
You never can be satisfied with praise
Which men give women when they judge a book
Not as mere work but as mere woman's work,
Expressing the comparative respect
Which means the absolute scorn. "Oh, excellent!
"What grace, what facile turns, what fluent sweeps,
"What delicate discernment .. almost thought!
"The book does honour to the sex, we hold.
"Among our female authors we make room
"For this fair writer, and congratulate
"The country that produces in these times
"Such women, competent to .. spell."
                                        "Stop there,"
I answered, burning through his thread of talk
With a quick flame of emotion,—"You have read
My soul, if not my book, and argue well
I would not condescend .. we will not say
To such a kind of praise, (a worthless end
Is praise of all kinds) but to such a use
Of holy art and golden life. I am young,
And peradventure weak—you tell me so—
Through being a woman. And, for all the rest,
Take thanks for justice. I would rather dance
At fairs on tight-rope, till the babies dropped
Their gingerbread for joy,—than shift the types
For tolerable verse, intolerable
To men who act and suffer. Better far
Pursue a frivolous trade by serious means,
Than a sublime art frivolously."
                                        "You,
Choose nobler work than either, O moist eyes
And hurrying lips and heaving heart! We are young
Aurora, you and I. The world,—look round,—
The world, we're come to late, is swollen hard

With perished generations and their sins:
The civiliser's space grinds horribly
On dead men's bones, and cannot turn up soil
That's otherwise than fetid. All success
Proves partial failure; all advance implies
What's left behind; all triumph, something crushed
At the chariot-wheels; all government, some wrong:
And rich men make the poor, who curse the rich,
Who agonise together, rich and poor,
Under and over, in the social spasm
And crisis of the ages. Here's an age
That makes its own vocation! here we have stepped
Across the bounds of time! here's nought to see,
But just the rich man and just Lazarus,
And both in torments, with a mediate gulph,
Though not a hint of Abraham's bosom. Who
Being man, Aurora, can stand calmly by
And view these things, and never tease his soul
For some great cure? No physic for this grief,
In all the earth and heavens too?"

                                          "You believe
In God, for your part?—ay? that He who makes,
Can make good things from ill things, best from worst,
As men plant tulips upon dunghills when
They wish them finest?"

                          "True. A death-heat is
The same as life-heat, to be accurate,
And in all nature is no death at all,
As men account of death, so long as God
Stands witnessing for life perpetually,
By being just God. That's abstract truth, I know,
Philosophy, or sympathy with God:
But I, I sympathise with man, not God,
(I think I was a man for chiefly this)
And when I stand beside a dying bed,
'Tis death to me. Observe,—it had not much
Consoled the race of mastodons to know,

Before they went to fossil, that anon
Their place would quicken with the elephant:
They were not elephants but mastodons;
And I, a man, as men are now and not
As men may be hereafter, feel with men
In the agonising present."
                              "Is it so,"
I said, "my cousin? is the world so bad,
While I hear nothing of it through the trees?
The world was always evil,—but so bad?"

"So bad, Aurora. Dear, my soul is gray
With poring over the long sum of ill;
So much for vice, so much for discontent,
So much for the necessities of power,
So much for the connivances of fear,
Coherent in statistical despairs
With such a total of distracted life, ..
To see it down in figures on a page,
Plain, silent, clear, as God sees through the earth
The sense of all the graves,—that's terrible
For one who is not God, and cannot right
The wrong he looks on. May I choose indeed
But vow away my years, my means, my aims,
Among the helpers, if there's any help
In such a social strait? The common blood
That swings along my veins, is strong enough
To draw me to this duty."
                              Then I spoke.
"I have not stood long on the strand of life,
And these salt waters have had scarcely time
To creep so high up as to wet my feet:
I cannot judge these tides—I shall, perhaps.
A woman's always younger than a man
At equal years, because she is disallowed
Maturing by the outdoor sun and air,
And kept in long-clothes past the age to walk.

Ah well, I know you men judge otherwise!
You think a woman ripens as a peach,
In the cheeks, chiefly. Pass it to me now;
I'm young in age, and younger still, I think,
As a woman. But a child may say amen
To a bishop's prayer and feel the way it goes,
And I, incapable to loose the knot
Of social questions, can approve, applaud
August compassion, christian thoughts that shoot
Beyond the vulgar white of personal aims.
Accept my reverence."
                    There he glowed on me
With all his face and eyes. "No other help?"
Said he—"no more than so?"
                        "What help?" I asked.
"You'd scorn my help,—as Nature's self, you say,
Has scorned to put her music in my mouth
Because a woman's. Do you now turn round
And ask for what a woman cannot give?"

"For what she only can, I turn and ask,"
He answered, catching up my hands in his,
And dropping on me from his high-eaved brow
The full weight of his soul,—"I ask for love,
And that, she can; for life in fellowship
Through bitter duties—that, I know she can;
For wifehood—will she?"
                      "Now," I said, "may God
Be witness 'twixt us two!" and with the word,
Meseemed I floated into a sudden light
Above his stature,—"am I proved too weak
To stand alone, yet strong enough to bear
Such leaners on my shoulder? poor to think,
Yet rich enough to sympathise with thought?
Incompetent to sing, as blackbirds can,
Yet competent to love, like HIM?"
                            I paused;

Perhaps I darkened, as the light-house will
That turns upon the sea. "It's always so.
Anything does for a wife."

"Aurora, dear,
And dearly honoured,"—he pressed in at once
With eager utterance,—"you translate me ill.
I do not contradict my thought of you
Which is most reverent, with another thought
Found less so. If your sex is weak for art,
(And I who said so, did but honour you
By using truth in courtship) it is strong
For life and duty. Place your fecund heart
In mine, and let us blossom for the world
That wants love's colour in the gray of time.
My talk, meanwhile, is arid to you, ay,
Since all my talk can only set you where
You look down coldly on the arena-heaps
Of headless bodies, shapeless, indistinct!
The Judgment-Angel scarce would find his way
Through such a heap of generalised distress
To the individual man with lips and eyes,
Much less Aurora. Ah my sweet, come down,
And hand in hand we'll go where yours shall touch
These victims, one by one! till, one by one,
The formless, nameless trunk of every man
Shall seem to wear a head with hair you know,
And every woman catch your mother's face
To melt you into passion."

"I am a girl,"
I answered slowly; "you do well to name
My mother's face. Though far too early, alas,
God's hand did interpose 'twixt it and me,
I know so much of love as used to shine
In that face and another. Just so much;
No more indeed at all. I have not seen
So much love since, I pray you pardon me,
As answers even to make a marriage with

In this cold land of England. What you love,
Is not a woman, Romney, but a cause:
You want a helpmate, not a mistress, sir,
A wife to help your ends—in her no end.
Your cause is noble, your ends excellent,
But I, being most unworthy of these and that,
Do otherwise conceive of love.   Farewell."

"Farewell, Aurora? you reject me thus?"
He said.
   "Sir, you were married long ago.
You have a wife already whom you love,
Your social theory.   Bless you both, I say.
For my part, I am scarcely meek enough
To be the handmaid of a lawful spouse.
Do I look a Hagar, think you?"
       "So you jest."

"Nay, so, I speak in earnest," I replied.
"You treat of marriage too much like, at least,
A chief apostle: you would bear with you
A wife .. a sister .. shall we speak it out?
A sister of charity."
      "Then, must it be
Indeed farewell? And was I so far wrong
In hope and in illusion, when I took
The woman to be nobler than the man,
Yourself the noblest woman, in the use
And comprehension of what love is,—love,
That generates the likeness of itself
Through all heroic duties? so far wrong,
In saying bluntly, venturing truth on love,
'Come, human creature, love and work with me,'—
Instead of, 'Lady, thou art wondrous fair,
'And, where the Graces walk before, the Muse
'Will follow at the lightning of their eyes,

'And where the Muse walks, lovers need to creep:
'Turn round and love me, or I die of love.'"

With quiet indignation I broke in.
"You misconceive the question like a man,
Who sees a woman as the complement
Of his sex merely. You forget too much
That every creature, female as the male,
Stands single in responsible act and thought
As also in birth and death. Whoever says
To a loyal woman, 'Love and work with me,'
Will get fair answers if the work and love,
Being good themselves, are good for her—the best
She was born for. Women of a softer mood,
Surprised by men when scarcely awake to life,
Will sometimes only hear the first word, love,
And catch up with it any kind of work,
Indifferent, so that dear love go with it.
I do not blame such women, though, for love,
They pick much oakum; earth's fanatics make
Too frequently heaven's saints. But *me* your work
Is not the best for,—nor your love the best,
Nor able to commend the kind of work
For love's sake merely. Ah, you force me, sir,
To be over-bold in speaking of myself:
I too have my vocation,—work to do.
The heavens and earth have set me since I changed
My father's face for theirs, and, though your world
Were twice as wretched as you represent,
Most serious work, most necessary work
As any of the economists'. Reform,
Make trade a Christian possibility,
And individual right no general wrong;
Wipe out earth's furrows of the Thine and Mine,
And leave one green for men to play at bowls,
With innings for them all! .. what then, indeed,

If mortals are not greater by the head
Than any of their prosperities? what then,
Unless the artist keep up open roads
Betwixt the seen and unseen,—bursting through
The best of your conventions with his best,
The speakable, imaginable best
God bids him speak, to prove what lies beyond
Both speech and imagination? A starved man
Exceeds a fat beast: we'll not barter, sir,
The beautiful for barley.—And, even so,
I hold you will not compass your poor ends
Of barley-feeding and material ease,
Without a poet's individualism
To work your universal. It takes a soul,
To move a body: it takes a high-souled man,
To move the masses, even to a cleaner stye:
It takes the ideal, to blow a hair's-breadth off
The dust of the actual.—Ah, your Fouriers failed,
Because not poets enough to understand
That life develops from within.——For me,
Perhaps I am not worthy, as you say,
Of work like this: perhaps a woman's soul
Aspires, and not creates: yet we aspire,
And yet I'll try out your perhapses, sir,
And if I fail .. why, burn me up my straw
Like other false works—I'll not ask for grace;
Your scorn is better, cousin Romney. I
Who love my art, would never wish it lower
To suit my stature. I may love my art.
You'll grant that even a woman may love art,
Seeing that to waste true love on anything
Is womanly, past question."
      I retain
The very last word which I said that day,
As you the creaking of the door, years past,
Which let upon you such disabling news
You ever after have been graver. He,

His eyes, the motions in his silent mouth,
Were fiery points on which my words were caught,
Transfixed for ever in my memory
For his sake, not their own. And yet I know
I did not love him .. nor he me .. that's sure ..
And what I said, is unrepented of,
As truth is always. Yet .. a princely man!—
If hard to me, heroic for himself!
He bears down on me through the slanting years,
The stronger for the distance. If he had loved,
Ay, loved me, with that retributive face, ..
I might have been a common woman now
And happier, less known and less left alone,
Perhaps a better woman after all,
With chubby children hanging on my neck
To keep me low and wise. Ah me, the vines
That bear such fruit, are proud to stoop with it.
The palm stands upright in a realm of sand.

And I, who spoke the truth then, stand upright,
Still worthy of having spoken out the truth,
By being content I spoke it though it set
Him there, me here.—O woman's vile remorse,
To hanker after a mere name, a show,
A supposition, a potential love!
Does every man who names love in our lives,
Become a power for that? is love's true thing
So much best to us, that what personates love
Is next best? A potential love, forsooth!
I'm not so vile. No, no—he cleaves, I think,
This man, this image,—chiefly for the wrong
And shock he gave my life, in finding me
Precisely where the devil of my youth
Had set me, on those mountain-peaks of hope
All glittering with the dawn-dew, all erect
And famished for the noon,—exclaiming, while
I looked for empire and much tribute, "Come,

I have some worthy work for thee below.
Come, sweep my barns and keep my hospitals,
And I will pay thee with a current coin
Which men give women."
                          As we spoke, the grass
Was trod in haste beside us, and my aunt,
With smile distorted by the sun,—face, voice
As much at issue with the summer-day
As if you brought a candle out of doors,
Broke in with, "Romney, here!—My child, entreat
Your cousin to the house, and have your talk,
If girls must talk upon their birthdays. Come."

He answered for me calmly, with pale lips
That seemed to motion for a smile in vain.
"The talk is ended, madam, where we stand.
Your brother's daughter has dismissed me here;
And all my answer can be better said
Beneath the trees, than wrong by such a word
Your house's hospitalities. Farewell."

With that he vanished. I could hear his heel
Ring bluntly in the lane, as down he leapt
The short way from us.—Then a measured speech
Withdrew me. "What means this, Aurora Leigh?
My brother's daughter has dismissed my guests!"

The lion in me felt the keeper's voice
Through all its quivering dewlaps; I was quelled
Before her,—meekened to the child she knew:
I prayed her pardon, said, "I had little thought
To give dismissal to a guest of hers,
In letting go a friend of mine who came
To take me into service as a wife,—
No more than that, indeed."
                          "No more, no more!
Pray Heaven," she answered, "that I was not mad.

I could not mean to tell her to her face
That Romney Leigh had asked me for a wife,
And I refused him?"
                    "Did he ask?" I said;
"I think he rather stooped to take me up
For certain uses which he found to do
For something called a wife. He never asked."

"What stuff!" she answered; "are they queens, these girls?
They must have mantles, stitched with twenty silks,
Spread out upon the ground, before they'll step
One footstep for the noblest lover born."

"But I am born," I said with firmness, "I,
To walk another way than his, dear aunt."

"You walk, you walk! A babe at thirteen months
Will walk as well as you," she cried in haste,
"Without a steadying finger. Why, you child,
God help you, you are groping in the dark,
For all this sunlight. You suppose, perhaps,
That you, sole offspring of an opulent man,
Are rich and free to choose a way to walk?
You think, and it's a reasonable thought,
That I, beside, being well to do in life,
Will leave my handful in my niece's hand
When death shall paralyse these fingers? Pray,
Pray, child, albeit I know you love me not,
As if you loved me, that I may not die!
For when I die and leave you, out you go,
(Unless I make room for you in my grave)
Unhoused, unfed, my dear, poor brother's lamb,
(Ah heaven,— that pains!)—without a right to crop
A single blade of grass beneath these trees,
Or cast a lamb's small shadow on the lawn,
Unfed, unfolded! Ah, my brother, here's
The fruit you planted in your foreign loves!—

Ay, there's the fruit he planted! never look
Astonished at me with your mother's eyes,
For it was they who set you where you are,
An undowered orphan. Child, your father's choice
Of that said mother, disinherited
His daughter, his and hers. Men do not think
Of sons and daughters, when they fall in love,
So much more than of sisters; otherwise
He would have paused to ponder what he did,
And shrunk before that clause in the entail
Excluding offspring by a foreign wife,
(The clause set up a hundred years ago
By a Leigh who wedded a French dancing-girl
And had his heart danced over in return);
But this man shrank at nothing, never thought
Of you, Aurora, any more than me—
Your mother must have been a pretty thing,
For all the coarse Italian blacks and browns,
To make a good man, which my brother was,
Unchary of the duties to his house;
But so it fell indeed. Our cousin Vane,
Vane Leigh, the father of this Romney, wrote
Directly on your birth, to Italy,
'I ask your baby daughter for my son
In whom the entail now merges by the law.
Betroth her to us out of love, instead
Of colder reasons, and she shall not lose
By love or law from henceforth'—so he wrote;
A generous cousin, was my cousin Vane.
Remember how he drew you to his knee
The year you came here, just before he died,
And hollowed out his hands to hold your cheeks,
And wished them redder,—you remember Vane.
And now his son who represents our house
And holds the fiefs and manors in his place,
To whom reverts my pittance when I die,
(Except a few books and a pair of shawls)

The boy is generous like him, and prepared
To carry out his kindest word and thought
To you, Aurora. Yes, a fine young man
Is Romney Leigh; although the sun of youth
Has shone too straight upon his brain, I know,
And fevered him with dreams of doing good
To good-for-nothing people. But a wife
Will put all right, and stroke his temples cool
With healthy touches" . .
      I broke in at that.
I could not lift my heavy heart to breathe
Till then, but then I raised it, and it fell
In broken words like these—"No need to wait:
The dream of doing good to . . me, at least,
Is ended, without waiting for a wife
To cool the fever for him. We've escaped
That danger,—thank Heaven for it."
       "You," she cried,
"Have got a fever. What, I talk and talk
An hour long to you,—I instruct you how
You cannot eat or drink or stand or sit
Or even die, like any decent wretch
In all this unroofed and unfurnished world,
Without your cousin,—and you still maintain
There's room 'twixt him and you, for flirting fans
And running knots in eyebrows? You must have
A pattern lover sighing on his knee?
You do not count enough, a noble heart
(Above book-patterns) which this very morn
Unclosed itself in two dear fathers' names
To embrace your orphaned life? fie, fie! But stay,
I write a word, and counteract this sin."

She would have turned to leave me, but I clung.
"O sweet my father's sister, hear my word
Before you write yours. Cousin Vane did well,
And cousin Romney well,—and I well too,

In casting back with all my strength and will
The good they meant me. O my God, my God!
God meant me good, too, when he hindered me
From saying 'yes' this morning. If you write
A word, it shall be 'no.' I say no, no!
I tie up 'no' upon His altar-horns,
Quite out of reach of perjury! At least
My soul is not a pauper; I can live
At least my soul's life, without alms from men;
And if it must be in heaven instead of earth,
Let heaven look to it,—I am not afraid."

She seized my hands with both hers, strained them fast,
And drew her probing and unscrupulous eyes
Right through me, body and heart. "Yet, foolish Sweet,
You love this man. I've watched you when he came,
And when he went, and when we've talked of him:
I am not old for nothing; I can tell
The weather-signs of love: you love this man."

Girls blush sometimes because they are alive,
Half wishing they were dead to save the shame.
The sudden blush devours them, neck and brow;
They have drawn too near the fire of life, like gnats
And flare up bodily, wings and all. What then?
Who's sorry for a gnat .. or girl?
       I blushed.
I feel the brand upon my forehead now
Strike hot, sear deep, as guiltless men may feel
The felon's iron, say, and scorn the mark
Of what they are not. Most illogical
Irrational nature of our womanhood,
That blushes one way, feels another way,
And prays, perhaps, another! After all,
We cannot be the equal of the male
Who rules his blood a little.
      For although

I blushed indeed, as if I loved the man,
And her incisive smile, accrediting
That treason of false witness in my blush,
Did bow me downward like a swathe of grass
Below its level that struck me,—I attest
The conscious skies and all their daily suns,
I think I loved him not,—nor then, nor since,
Nor ever. Do we love the schoolmaster,
Being busy in the woods? much less, being poor,
The overseer of the parish? Do we keep
Our love to pay our debts with?
       White and cold
I grew next moment. As my blood recoiled
From that imputed ignominy, I made
My heart great with it. Then, at last, I spoke,
Spoke veritable words but passionate,
Too passionate perhaps .. ground up with sobs
To shapeless endings. She let fall my hands
And took her smile off, in sedate disgust,
As peradventure she had touched a snake,—
A dead snake, mind!—and turning round, replied,
"We'll leave Italian manners, if you please.
I think you had an English father, child,
And ought to find it possible to speak
A quiet 'yes' or 'no' like English girls,
Without convulsions. In another month
We'll take another answer—no, or yes."
With that, she left me in the garden-walk.

I had a father! yes, but long ago—
How long it seemed that moment. Oh, how far,
How far and safe, God, dost thou keep thy saints
When once gone from us! We may call against
The lighted windows of thy fair June-heaven
Where all the souls are happy,—and not one,
Not even my father, look from work or play
To ask, "Who is it that cries after us,

Below there, in the dusk?" Yet formerly
He turned his face upon me quick enough,
If I said "father." Now I might cry loud;
The little lark reached higher with his song
Than I with crying. Oh, alone, alone,—
Not troubling any in heaven, nor any on earth,
I stood there in the garden, and looked up
The deaf blue sky that brings the roses out
On such June mornings.
     You who keep account
Of crisis and transition in this life,
Set down the first time Nature says plain "no"
To some "yes" in you, and walks over you
In gorgeous sweeps of scorn. We all begin
By singing with the birds, and running fast
With June-days, hand in hand: but once, for all,
The birds must sing against us, and the sun
Strike down upon us like a friend's sword caught
By an enemy to slay us, while we read
The dear name on the blade which bites at us!—
That's bitter and convincing: after that,
We seldom doubt that something in the large
Smooth order of creation, though no more
Than haply a man's footstep, has gone wrong.
Some tears fell down my cheeks, and then I smiled,
As those smile who have no face in the world
To smile back to them. I had lost a friend
In Romney Leigh; the thing was sure—a friend,
Who had looked at me most gently now and then,
And spoken of my favourite books, "our books,"
With such a voice! Well, voice and look were now
More utterly shut out from me I felt,
Than even my father's. Romney now was turned
To a benefactor, to a generous man,
Who had tied himself to marry .. me, instead
Of such a woman, with low timorous lids
He lifted with a sudden word one day,

And left, perhaps, for my sake.—Ah, self-tied
By a contract, male Iphigenia bound
At a fatal Aulis for the winds to change,
(But loose him, they'll not change), he well might seem
A little cold and dominant in love!
He had a right to be dogmatical,
This poor, good Romney. Love, to him, was made
A simple law-clause. If I married him,
I should not dare to call my soul my own
Which so he had bought and paid for: every thought
And every heart-beat down there in the bill;
Not one found honestly deductible
From any use that pleased him! He might cut
My body into coins to give away
Among his other paupers; change my sons,
While I stood dumb as Griseld, for black babes
Or piteous foundlings; might unquestioned set
My right hand teaching in the Ragged Schools,
My left hand washing in the Public Baths,
What time my angel of the Ideal stretched
Both his to me in vain. I could not claim
The poor right of a mouse in a trap, to squeal,
And take so much as pity from myself.

Farewell, good Romney! if I loved you even,
I could but ill afford to let you be
So generous to me. Farewell, friend, since friend
Betwixt us two, forsooth, must be a word
So heavily overladen. And, since help
Must come to me from those who love me not,
Farewell, all helpers—I must help myself,
And am alone from henceforth.—Then I stooped
And lifted the soiled garland from the earth,
And set it on my head as bitterly
As when the Spanish monarch crowned the bones
Of his dead love. So be it. I preserve
That crown still,—in the drawer there! 'twas the first,

The rest are like it;—those Olympian crowns,
We run for, till we lose sight of the sun
In the dust of the racing chariots!
                              After that,
Before the evening fell, I had a note,
Which ran,—" Aurora, sweet Chaldean, you read
My meaning backward like your eastern books,
While I am from the west, dear. Read me now
A little plainer. Did you hate me quite
But yesterday? I loved you for my part;
I love you. If I spoke untenderly
This morning, my beloved, pardon it;
And comprehend me that I loved you so
I set you on the level of my soul,
And overwashed you with the bitter brine
Of some habitual thoughts. Henceforth, my flower,
Be planted out of reach of any such,
And lean the side you please, with all your leaves!
Write woman's verses and dream woman's dreams;
But let me feel your perfume in my home
To make my sabbath after working-days.
Bloom out your youth beside me,—be my wife."

I wrote in answer—"We Chaldeans discern
Still farther than we read. I know your heart,
And shut it like the holy book it is,
Reserved for mild-eyed saints to pore upon
Betwixt their prayers at vespers. Well, you 're right,
I did not surely hate you yesterday;
And yet I do not love you enough to-day
To wed you, cousin Romney. Take this word,
And let it stop you as a generous man
From speaking farther. You may tease, indeed,
And blow about my feelings, or my leaves,
And here's my aunt will help you with east winds
And break a stalk, perhaps, tormenting me;
But certain flowers grow near as deep as trees,

And, cousin, you'll not move my root, not you,
With all your confluent storms. Then let me grow
Within my wayside hedge, and pass your way!
This flower has never as much to say to you
As the antique tomb which said to travellers, 'Pause,'
'Siste, viator.'" Ending thus, I sighed.

The next week passed in silence, so the next,
And several after: Romney did not come
Nor my aunt chide me. I lived on and on,
As if my heart were kept beneath a glass,
And everybody stood, all eyes and ears,
To see and hear it tick. I could not sit,
Nor walk, nor take a book, nor lay it down,
Nor sew on steadily, nor drop a stitch,
And a sigh with it, but I felt her looks
Still cleaving to me, like the sucking asp
To Cleopatra's breast, persistently
Through the intermittent pantings. Being observed,
When observation is not sympathy,
Is just being tortured. If she said a word,
A "thank you," or an "if it please you, dear,"
She meant a commination, or, at best,
An exorcism against the devildom
Which plainly held me. So with all the house.
Susannah could not stand and twist my hair,
Without such glancing at the looking-glass
To see my face there, that she missed the plait.
And John,—I never sent my plate for soup,
Or did not send it, but the foolish John
Resolved the problem, 'twixt his napkined thumbs,
Of what was signified by taking soup
Or choosing mackerel. Neighbours who dropped in
On morning visits, feeling a joint wrong,
Smiled admonition, sate uneasily,
And talked with measured, emphasised reserve,
Of parish news, like doctors to the sick,

When not called in,—as if, with leave to speak,
They might say something. Nay, the very dog
Would watch me from his sun-patch on the floor,
In alternation with the large black fly
Not yet in reach of snapping. So I lived.

A Roman died so; smeared with honey, teased
By insects, stared to torture by the noon:
And many patient souls 'neath English roofs
Have died like Romans. I, in looking back,
Wish only, now, I had borne the plague of all
With meeker spirits than were rife at Rome.

For, on the sixth week, the dead sea broke up,
Dashed suddenly through beneath the heel of Him
Who stands upon the sea and earth and swears
Time shall be nevermore. The clock struck nine
That morning too,—no lark was out of tune,
The hidden farms among the hills breathed straight
Their smoke toward heaven, the lime-tree scarcely stirred
Beneath the blue weight of the cloudless sky,
Though still the July air came floating through
The woodbine at my window, in and out,
With touches of the out-door country-news
For a bending forehead. There I sate, and wished
That morning-truce of God would last till eve,
Or longer. "Sleep," I thought, "late sleepers,—sleep,
And spare me yet the burden of your eyes."

Then, suddenly, a single ghastly shriek
Tore upward from the bottom of the house.
Like one who wakens in a grave and shrieks,
The still house seemed to shriek itself alive,
And shudder through its passages and stairs
With slam of doors and clash of bells.—I sprang,
I stood up in the middle of the room,

And there confronted at my chamber-door,
A white face,—shivering, ineffectual lips.

"Come, come," they tried to utter, and I went:
As if a ghost had drawn me at the point
Of a fiery finger through the uneven dark,
I went with reeling footsteps down the stair,
Nor asked a question.
                     There she sate, my aunt,—
Bolt upright in the chair beside her bed,
Whose pillow had no dint! she had used no bed
For that night's sleeping, yet slept well. My God,
The dumb derision of that gray, peaked face
Concluded something grave against the sun,
Which filled the chamber with its July burst
When Susan drew the curtains ignorant
Of who sate open-eyed behind her. There
She sate .. it sate .. we said "she" yesterday ..
And held a letter with unbroken seal
As Susan gave it to her hand last night:
All night she had held it. If its news referred
To duchies or to dunghills, not an inch
She'd budge, 'twas obvious, for such worthless odds:
Nor, though the stars were suns and overburned
Their spheric limitations, swallowing up
Like wax the azure spaces, could they force
Those open eyes to wink once. What last sight
Had left them blank and flat so,—drawing out
The faculty of vision from the roots,
As nothing more, worth seeing, remained behind?

Were those the eyes that watched me, worried me?
That dogged me up and down the hours and days,
A beaten, breathless, miserable soul?
And did I pray, a half-hour back, but so,
To escape the burden of those eyes .. those eyes?
"Sleep late" I said?—

                    Why now, indeed, they sleep.
God answers sharp and sudden on some prayers,
And thrusts the thing we have prayed for in our face
A gauntlet with a gift in 't. Every wish
Is like a prayer, with God.
                            I had my wish,
To read and meditate the thing I would,
To fashion all my life upon my thought,
And marry or not marry. Henceforth none
Could disapprove me, vex me, hamper me.
Full ground-room, in this desert newly made,
For Babylon or Balbec,—when the breath,
Now choked with sand, returns for building towns.
The heir came over on the funeral day,
And we two cousins met before the dead,
With two pale faces. Was it death or life
That moved us?. When the will was read and done,
The official guests and witnesses withdrawn,
We rose up in a silence almost hard,
And looked at one another. Then I said,
"Farewell, my cousin."
                    But he touched, just touched,
My hatstrings tied for going, (at the door
The carriage stood to take me) and said low,
His voice a little unsteady through his smile,
"Siste, viator."
            "Is there time," I asked,
"In these last days of railroads, to stop short
Like Cæsar's chariot (weighing half a ton)
On the Appian road, for morals?"
                            "There is time,"
He answered grave, "for necessary words,
Inclusive, trust me, of no epitaph
On man or act, my cousin. We have read
A will, which gives you all the personal goods
And funded monies of your aunt."
                            "I thank

Her memory for it. With three hundred pounds
We buy in England even, clear standing-room
To stand and work in. Only two hours since,
I fancied I was poor."

"And, cousin, still
You're richer than you fancy. The will says,
*Three hundred pounds, and any other sum
Of which the said testatrix dies possessed.*
I say she died possessed of other sums."

"Dear Romney, need we chronicle the pence?
I'm richer than I thought—that's evident.
Enough so."

"Listen rather. You've to do
With business and a cousin," he resumed,
"And both, I fear, need patience. Here's the fact.
The other sum (there *is* another sum,
Unspecified in any will which dates
After possession, yet bequeathed as much
And clearly as those said three hundred pounds)
Is thirty thousand. You will have it paid
When?.. where? My duty troubles you with words."

He struck the iron when the bar was hot;
No wonder if my eyes sent out some sparks.
"Pause there! I thank you. You are delicate
In glosing gifts;—but I, who share your blood,
Am rather made for giving, like yourself,
Than taking, like your pensioners. Farewell."

He stopped me with a gesture of calm pride.
"A Leigh," he said, "gives largesse and gives love,
But gloses never: if a Leigh could glose,
He would not do it, moreover, to a Leigh,
With blood trained up along nine centuries
To hound and hate a lie from eyes like yours.
And now we'll make the rest as clear; your aunt

Possessed these moneys."
                    "You will make it clear,
My cousin, as the honour of us both,
Or one of us speaks vainly! that's not I.
My aunt possessed this sum,—inherited
From whom, and when? bring documents, prove dates.

"Why now indeed you throw your bonnet off
As if you had time left for a logarithm!
The faith's the want. Dear cousin, give me faith,
And you shall walk this road with silken shoes,
As clean as any lady of our house
Supposed the proudest. Oh, I comprehend
The whole position from your point of sight.
I oust you from your father's halls and lands
And make you poor by getting rich—that's law,
Considering which, in common circumstance,
You would not scruple to accept from me
Some compensation, some sufficiency
Of income—that were justice; but, alas,
I love you,—that's mere nature; you reject
My love,—that's nature also; and at once,
You cannot, from a suitor disallowed,
A hand thrown back as mine is, into yours
Receive a doit, a farthing,—not for the world!
That's woman's etiquette, and obviously
Exceeds the claim of nature, law, and right,
Unanswerable to all. I grant, you see,
The case as you conceive it,—leave you room
To sweep your ample skirts of womanhood,
While, standing humbly squeezed against the wall,
I own myself excluded from being just,
Restrained from paying indubitable debts,
Because denied from giving you my soul.
That's my misfortune!—I submit to it
As if, in some more reasonable age,
'Twould not be less inevitable. Enough.

You'll trust me, cousin, as a gentleman,
To keep your honour, as you count it, pure,
Your scruples (just as if I thought them wise)
Safe and inviolate from gifts of mine."

I answered mild but earnest. "I believe
In no one's honour which another keeps,
Nor man's nor woman's. As I keep, myself,
My truth and my religion, I depute
No father, though I had one this side death,
Nor brother, though I had twenty, much less you,
Though twice my cousin, and once Romney Leigh,
To keep my honour pure. You face, to-day,
A man who wants instruction, mark me, not
A woman who wants protection. As to a man,
Show manhood, speak out plainly, be precise
With facts and dates. My aunt inherited
This sum, you say—"
      "I said she died possessed
Of this, dear cousin."
      "Not by heritage.
Thank you: we're getting to the facts at last.
Perhaps she played at commerce with a ship
Which came in heavy with Australian gold?
Or touched a lottery with her finger-end,
Which tumbled on a sudden into her lap
Some old Rhine tower or principality?
Perhaps she had to do with a marine
Sub-transatlantic railroad, which pre-pays
As well as pre-supposes? or perhaps
Some stale ancestral debt was after-paid
By a hundred years, and took her by surprise?—
You shake your head, my cousin; I guess ill."

"You need not guess, Aurora, nor deride;
The truth is not afraid of hurting you.
You'll find no cause, in all your scruples, why

Your aunt should cavil at a deed of gift
'Twixt her and me."
                    "I thought so—ah! a gift."

"You naturally thought so," he resumed.
"A very natural gift."
                    "A gift, a gift!
Her individual life being stranded high
Above all want, approaching opulence,
Too haughty was she to accept a gift
Without some ultimate aim: ah, ah, I see,—
A gift intended plainly for her heirs,
And so accepted .. if accepted .. ah,
Indeed that might be; I am snared perhaps
Just so. But, cousin, shall I pardon you,
If thus you have caught me with a cruel springe?"

He answered gently, "Need you tremble and pant
Like a netted lioness? is 't my fault, mine,
That you're a grand wild creature of the woods
And hate the stall built for you? Any way,
Though triply netted, need you glare at me?
I do not hold the cords of such a net;
You're free from me, Aurora!"
                    "Now may God
Deliver me from this strait! This gift of yours
Was tendered .. when? accepted .. when?" I asked.
"A month .. a fortnight since? Six weeks ago
It was not tendered; by a word she dropped
I know it was not tendered nor received.
When was it? bring your dates."
                    "What matters when?
A half-hour ere she died, or a half-year,
Secured the gift, maintains the heritage
Inviolable with law. As easy pluck
The golden stars from heaven's embroidered stole
To pin them on the gray side of this earth,

As make you poor again, thank God."
                              "Not poor
Nor clean again from henceforth, you thank God?
Well, sir—I ask you—I insist at need,—
Vouchsafe the special date, the special date."

"The day before her death-day," he replied,
"The gift was in her hands. We'll find that deed,
And certify that date to you."
                              As one
Who has climbed a mountain-height and carried up
His own heart climbing, panting in his throat
With the toil of the ascent, takes breath at last,
Looks back in triumph—so I stood and looked.
"Dear cousin Romney, we have reached the top
Of this steep question, and may rest, I think.
But first,—I pray you pardon, that the shock
And surge of natural feeling and event
Has made me oblivious of acquainting you
That this, this letter, (unread, mark, still sealed)
Was found enfolded in the poor dead hand:
That spirit of hers had gone beyond the address,
Which could not find her though you wrote it clear,—
I know your writing, Romney,—recognise
The open-hearted *A*, the liberal sweep
Of the *G*. Now listen,—let us understand:
You will not find that famous deed of gift,
Unless you find it in the letter here,
Which not being mine, I give you back.—Refuse
To take the letter? well then—you and I,
As writer and as heiress, open it
Together, by your leave.——Exactly so:
The words in which the noble offering 's made,
Are nobler still, my cousin; and, I own,
The proudest and most delicate heart alive,
Distracted from the measure of the gift
By such a grace in giving, might accept

Your largesse without thinking any more
Of the burthen of it, than King Solomon
Considered, when he wore his holy ring
Charactered over with the ineffable spell,
How many carats of fine gold made up
Its money-value: so, Leigh gives to Leigh!
Or rather, might have given, observe,—for that's
The point we come to. Here's a proof of gift,
But here's no proof, sir, of acceptancy,
But rather, disproof. Death's black dust, being blown,
Infiltrated through every secret fold
Of this sealed letter by a puff of fate,
Dried up for ever the fresh-written ink,
Annulled the gift, disutilised the grace,
And left these fragments."
      As I spoke, I tore
The paper up and down, and down and up
And crosswise, till it fluttered from my hands,
As forest-leaves, stripped suddenly and rapt
By a whirlwind on Valdarno, drop again,
Drop slow, and strew the melancholy ground
Before the amazèd hills . . . why, so, indeed,
I'm writing like a poet, somewhat large
In the type of the image, and exaggerate
A small thing with a great thing, topping it:—
But then I'm thinking how his eyes looked, his,
With what despondent and surprised reproach!
I think the tears were in them as he looked;
I think the manly mouth just trembled. Then
He broke the silence.
     "I may ask, perhaps,
Although no stranger .. only Romney Leigh,
Which means still less .. than Vincent Carrington,
Your plans in going hence, and where you go.
This cannot be a secret."
      "All my life
Is open to you, cousin. I go hence

To London, to the gathering-place of souls,
To live mine straight out, vocally, in books;
Harmoniously for others, if indeed
A woman's soul, like man's, be wide enough
To carry the whole octave (that's to prove)
Or, if I fail, still purely for myself.
Pray God be with me, Romney."
                              "Ah, poor child,
Who fight against the mother's 'tiring hand,
And choose the headsman's! May God change his world
For your sake, sweet, and make it mild as heaven,
And juster than I have found you."
                                    But I paused.
"And you, my cousin?"—
                       "I," he said,—"you ask?
You care to ask? Well, girls have curious minds
And fain would know the end of everything,
Of cousins therefore with the rest. For me,
Aurora, I've my work; you know my work;
And, having missed this year some personal hope,
I must beware the rather that I miss
No reasonable duty. While you sing
Your happy pastorals of the meads and trees,
Bethink you that I go to impress and prove
On stifled brains and deafened ears, stunned deaf,
Crushed dull with grief, that nature sings itself,
And needs no mediate poet, lute or voice,
To make it vocal. While you ask of men
Your audience, I may get their leave perhaps
For hungry orphans to say audibly
"We're hungry, see,"—for beaten and bullied wives
To hold their unweaned babies up in sight,
Whom orphanage would better, and for all
To speak and claim their portion .. by no means
Of the soil, .. but of the sweat in tilling it;
Since this is now-a-days turned privilege,
To have only God's curse on us, and not man's.

Such work I have for doing, elbow-deep
In social problems,—as you tie your rhymes,
To draw my uses to cohere with needs
And bring the uneven world back to its round,
Or, failing so much, fill up, bridge at least
To smoother issues some abysmal cracks
And feuds of earth, intestine heats have made
To keep men separate,—using sorry shifts
Of hospitals, almshouses, infant schools,
And other practical stuff of partial good
You lovers of the beautiful and whole
Despise by system."

      "*I* despise? The scorn
Is yours, my cousin. Poets become such
Through scorning nothing. You decry them for
The good of beauty sung and taught by them,
While they respect your practical partial good
As being a part of beauty's self. Adieu!
When God helps all the workers for his world,
The singers shall have help of Him, not last."

He smiled as men smile when they will not speak
Because of something bitter in the thought;
And still I feel his melancholy eyes
Look judgment on me. It is seven years since:
I know not if 'twas pity or 'twas scorn
Has made them so far-reaching: judge it ye
Who have had to do with pity more than love
And scorn than hatred. I am used, since then,
To other ways, from equal men. But so,
Even so, we let go hands, my cousin and I,
And in between us, rushed the torrent-world
To blanch our faces like divided rocks.
And bar for ever mutual sight and touch
Except through swirl of spray and all that roar.

THIRD BOOK.

"To-DAY thou girdest up thy loins thyself
And goest where thou wouldest: presently
Others shall gird thee," said the Lord, "to go
Where thou would'st not." He spoke to Peter thus,
To signify the death which he should die
When crucified head downward.
      If He spoke
To Peter then, He speaks to us the same;
The word suits many different martyrdoms,
And signifies a multiform of death,
Although we scarcely die apostles, we,
And have mislaid the keys of heaven and earth.

For 'tis not in mere death that men die most,
And, after our first girding of the loins
In youth's fine linen and fair broidery
To run up hill and meet the rising sun,
We are apt to sit tired, patient as a fool,
While others gird us with the violent bands
Of social figments, feints, and formalisms,
Reversing our straight nature, lifting up
Our base needs, keeping down our lofty thoughts,
Head downward on the cross-sticks of the world.

Yet He can pluck us from that shameful cross.
God, set our feet low and our forehead high,
And show us how a man was made to walk!

Leave the lamp, Susan, and go up to bed.
The room does very well; I have to write

Beyond the stroke of midnight. Get away;
Your steps, for ever buzzing in the room,
Tease me like gnats. Ah, letters! throw them down
At once, as I must have them, to be sure,
Whether I bid you never bring me such
At such an hour, or bid you. No excuse;
You choose to bring them, as I choose perhaps
To throw them in the fire. Now get to bed,
And dream, if possible, I am not cross.

Why what a pettish, petty thing I grow,—
A mere, mere woman, a mere flaccid nerve,
A kerchief left out all night in the rain,
Turned soft so,—overtasked and overstrained
And overlived in this close London life!
And yet I should be stronger.
                         Never burn
Your letters, poor Aurora! for they stare
With red seals from the table, saying each,
"Here's something that you know not." Out alas,
'Tis scarcely that the world's more good and wise
Or even straighter and more consequent
Since yesterday at this time—yet, again,
If but one angel spoke from Ararat
I should be very sorry not to hear:
So open all the letters! let me read.
Blanche Ord, the writer in the "Lady's Fan,"
Requests my judgment on .. that, afterwards.
Kate Ward desires the model of my cloak,
And signs, "Elisha to you." Pringle Sharpe
Presents his work on "Social Conduct," craves
A little money for his pressing debts .. •
From me, who scarce have money for my needs;
Art's fiery chariot which we journey in
Being apt to singe our singing-robes to holes
Although you ask me for my cloak, Kate Ward!
Here's Rudgely knows it,—editor and scribe;

He's "forced to marry where his heart is not,
Because the purse lacks where he lost his heart."
Ah,——lost it because no one picked it up;
That's really loss,—(and passable impudence.)
My critic Hammond flatters prettily,
And wants another volume like the last.
My critic Belfair wants another book
Entirely different, which will sell, (and live?)
A striking book, yet not a startling book,
The public blames originalities,
(You must not pump spring-water unawares
Upon a gracious public full of nerves:)
Good things, not subtle, new yet orthodox,
As easy reading as the dog-eared page
That's fingered by said public fifty years,
Since first taught spelling by its grandmother,
And yet a revelation in some sort:
That's hard, my critic Belfair. So—what next?
My critic Stokes objects to abstract thoughts;
"Call a man, John, a woman, Joan," says he,
"And do not prate so of *humanities:*"
Whereat I call my critic simply, Stokes.
My critic Jobson recommends more mirth
Because a cheerful genius suits the times,
And all true poets laugh unquenchably
Like Shakspeare and the gods. That's very hard.
The gods may laugh, and Shakspeare; Dante smiled
With such a needy heart on two pale lips
We cry, "Weep rather, Dante." Poems are
Men, if true poems: and who dares exclaim
At any man's door, "Here, 'tis understood
The thunder fell last week and killed a wife
And scared a sickly husband—what of that?
Get up, be merry, shout and clap your hands,
Because a cheerful genius suits the times—"?
None says so to the man, and why indeed
Should any to the poem? A ninth seal;

'The apocalypse is drawing to a close.
Ha,—this from Vincent Carrington,—"Dear friend,
I want good counsel. Will you lend me wings
To raise me to the subject, in a sketch
I'll bring to-morrow—may I? at eleven?
A poet's only born to turn to use:
So save you! for the world .. and Carrington."
"(Writ after.) Have you heard of Romney Leigh,
Beyond what's said of him in newspapers,
His phalansteries there, his speeches here,
His pamphlets, pleas, and statements, everywhere?
He dropped *me* long ago, but no one drops
A golden apple—though indeed one day
You hinted that, but jested. Well, at least
You know Lord Howe who sees him .. whom he sees
And *you* see and I hate to see,—for Howe
Stands high upon the brink of theories,
Observes the swimmers and cries 'Very fine,'
But keeps dry linen equally,—unlike
That gallant breaster, Romney. Strange it is,
Such sudden madness seizing a young man
To make earth over again,—while I'm content
To make the pictures. Let me bring the sketch.
A tiptoe Danae, overbold and hot,
Both arms a-flame to meet her wishing Jove
Halfway, and burn him faster down; the face
And breasts upturned and straining, the loose locks
All glowing with the anticipated gold.
Or here's another on the self-same theme.
She lies here—flat upon her prison-floor,
The long hair swathed about her to the heel
Like wet sea-weed. You dimly see her through
The glittering haze of that prodigious rain,
Half blotted out of nature by a love
As heavy as fate. I'll bring you either sketch.
I think, myself, the second indicates
More passion."

                    Surely. Self is put away,
And calm with abdication. She is Jove,
And no more Danae—greater thus. Perhaps
The painter symbolises unaware
Two states of the recipient artist-soul,
One, forward, personal, wanting reverence,
Because aspiring only. We'll be calm,
And know that, when indeed our Joves come down,
We all turn stiller than we have ever been.

Kind Vincent Carrington. I'll let him come.
He talks of Florence,—and may say a word
Of something as it chanced seven years ago,
A hedgehog in the path, or a lame bird,
In those green country walks, in that good time
When certainly I was so miserable . .
I seem to have missed a blessing ever since.

The music soars within the little lark,
And the lark soars. It is not thus with men.
We do not make our places with our strains,—
Content, while they rise, to remain behind
Alone on earth instead of so in heaven.
No matter; I bear on my broken tale.

When Romney Leigh and I had parted thus,
I took a chamber up three flights of stairs
Not far from being as steep as some larks climb,
And there, in a certain house in Kensington,
Three years I lived and worked. Get leave to work
In this world—'tis the best you get at all;
For God, in cursing, gives us better gifts
Than men in benediction. God says, "Sweat
For foreheads," men say "crowns," and so we are crowned,
Ay, gashed by some tormenting circle of steel
Which snaps with a secret spring. Get work, get work;
Be sure 'tis better than what you work to get.

Serene and unafraid of solitude
I worked the short days out,—and watched the sun
On lurid morns or monstrous afternoons
(Like some Druidic idol's fiery brass
With fixed unflickering outline of dead heat,
From which the blood of wretches pent inside
Seems oozing forth to incarnadine the air)
Push out through fog with his dilated disk,
And startle the slant roofs and chimney-pots
With splashes of fierce colour.   Or I saw
Fog only, the great tawny weltering fog,
Involve the passive city, strangle it
Alive, and draw it off into the void,
Spires, bridges, streets, and squares, as if a spunge
Had wiped out London,—or as noon and night
Had clapped together and utterly struck out
The intermediate time, undoing themselves
In the act.   Your city poets see such things
Not despicable.   Mountains of the south,
When drunk and mad with elemental wines
They rend the seamless mist and stand up bare,
Make fewer singers, haply.   No one sings,
Descending Sinai: on Parnassus-mount
You take a mule to climb and not a muse
Except in fable and figure: forests chant
Their anthems to themselves, and leave you dumb.
But sit in London at the day's decline,
And view the city perish in the mist
Like Pharaoh's armaments in the deep Red Sea,
The chariots, horsemen, footmen, all the host,
Sucked down and choked to silence—then, surprised
By a sudden sense of vision and of tune,
You feel as conquerors though you did not fight,
And you and Israel's other singing girls,
Ay, Miriam with them, sing the song you choose.

I worked with patience, which means almost power:
I did some excellent things indifferently,
Some bad things excellently. Both were praised,
The latter loudest. And by such a time
That I myself had set them down as sins
Scarce worth the price of sackcloth, week by week
Arrived some letter through the sedulous post,
Like these I've read, and yet dissimilar,
With pretty maiden seals,—initials twined
Of lilies, or a heart marked *Emily*
(Convicting Emily of being all heart);
Or rarer tokens from young bachelors,
Who wrote from college with the same goosequill,
Suppose, they had just been plucked of, and a snatch
From Horace, "Collegisse juvat," set
Upon the first page. Many a letter, signed
Or unsigned, showing the writers at eighteen
Had lived too long, although a muse should help
Their dawn by holding candles,—compliments
To smile or sigh at. Such could pass with me
No more than coins from Moscow circulate
At Paris: would ten roubles buy a tag
Of ribbon on the boulevard, worth a sou?
I smiled that all this youth should love me,—sighed
That such a love could scarcely raise them up
To love what was more worthy than myself;
Then sighed again, again, less generously,
To think the very love they lavished so,
Proved me inferior. The strong loved me not,
And he .. my cousin Romney .. did not write.
I felt the silent finger of his scorn
Prick every bubble of my frivolous fame
As my breath blew it, and resolve it back
To the air it came from. Oh, I justified
The measure he had taken of my height:

The thing was plain—he was not wrong a line;
I played at art, made thrusts with a toy-sword,
Amused the lads and maidens.
                              Came a sigh
Deep, hoarse with resolution,—I would work
To better ends, or play in earnest. "Heavens,
I think I should be almost popular
If this went on!"—I ripped my verses up,
And found no blood upon the rapier's point;
The heart in them was just an embryo's heart
Which never yet had beat, that it should die;
Just gasps of make-believe galvanic life;
Mere tones, inorganised to any tune.

And yet I felt it in me where it burnt,
Like those hot fire-seeds of creation held
In Jove's clenched palm before the worlds were sown,—
But I—I was not Juno even! my hand
Was shut in weak convulsion, woman's ill,
And when I yearned to loose a finger— lo,
The nerve revolted. 'Tis the same even now;
This hand may never, haply, open large,
Before the spark is quenched, or the palm charred,
To prove the power not else than by the pain.

It burnt, it burns—my whole life burnt with it,
And light, not sunlight and not torchlight, flashed
My steps out through the slow and difficult road.
I had grown distrustful of too forward Springs,
The season's books in drear significance
Of morals, dropping round me. Lively books!
The ash has livelier verdure than the yew;
And yet the yew's green longer, and alone
Found worthy of the holy Christmas time:
We'll plant more yews if possible, albeit
We plant the graveyards with them.
                                   Day and night

I worked my rhythmic thought, and furrowed up
Both watch and slumber with long lines of life
Which did not suit their season. The rose fell
From either cheek, my eyes globed luminous
Through orbits of blue shadow, and my pulse
Would shudder along the purple-veinèd wrist
Like a shot bird. Youth's stern, set face to face
With youth's ideal: and when people came
And said, "You work too much, you are looking ill."
I smiled for pity of them who pitied me,
And thought I should be better soon perhaps
For those ill looks. Observe—"I," means in youth
Just *I*, the conscious and eternal soul
With all its ends, and not the outside life,
The parcel-man, the doublet of the flesh,
The so much liver, lung, integument,
Which make the sum of "I" hereafter when
World-talkers talk of doing well or ill.
I prosper if I gain a step, although
A nail then pierced my foot: although my brain
Embracing any truth froze paralysed,
I prosper: I but change my instrument;
I break the spade off, digging deep for gold,
And catch the mattock up.
      I worked on, on.
Through all the bristling fence of nights and days
Which hedges time in from the eternities,
I struggled,—never stopped to note the stakes
Which hurt me in my course. The midnight oil
Would stink sometimes; there came some vulgar needs:
I had to live that therefore I might work,
And, being but poor, I was constrained, for life,
To work with one hand for the booksellers
While working with the other for myself
And art: you swim with feet as well as hands,
Or make small way. I apprehended this,—
In England no one lives by verse that lives;

And, apprehending, I resolved by prose
To make a space to sphere my living verse.
I wrote for cyclopædias, magazines,
And weekly papers, holding up my name
To keep it from the mud. I learnt the use
Of the editorial "we" in a review
As courtly ladies the fine trick of trains,
And swept it grandly through the open doors
As if one could not pass through doors at all
Save so encumbered. I wrote tales beside,
Carved many an article on cherry-stones
To suit light readers,—something in the lines
Revealing, it was said, the mallet-hand,
But that, I'll never vouch for: what you do
For bread, will taste of common grain, not grapes,
Although you have a vineyard in Champagne;
Much less in Nephelococcygia
As mine was, peradventure.
                                    Having bread
For just so many days, just breathing-room
For body and verse, I stood up straight and worked
My veritable work. And as the soul
Which grows within a child makes the child grow,—
Or as the fiery sap, the touch from God,
Careering through a tree, dilates the bark
And roughs with scale and knob, before it strikes
The summer foliage out in a green flame—
So life, in deepening with me, deepened all
The course I took, the work I did. Indeed
The academic law convinced of sin;
The critics cried out on the falling off,
Regretting the first manner. But I felt
My heart's life throbbing in my verse to show
It lived, it also—certes incomplete,
Disordered with all Adam in the blood,
But even its very tumours, warts and wens
Still organised by and implying life.

A lady called upon me on such a day.
She had the low voice of your English dames,
Unused, it seems, to need rise half a note
To catch attention,—and their quiet mood,
As if they lived too high above the earth
For that to put them out in anything:
So gentle, because verily so proud;
So wary and afraid of hurting you,
By no means that you are not really vile,
But that they would not touch you with their foot
To push you to your place; so self-possessed
Yet gracious and conciliating, it takes
An effort in their presence to speak truth:
You know the sort of woman,—brilliant stuff,
And out of nature. "Lady Waldemar."
She said her name quite simply, as if it meant
Not much indeed, but something,—took my hands,
And smiled as if her smile could help my case,
And dropped her eyes on me and let them melt.
"Is this," she said, "the Muse?"
        "No sybil even,"
I answered, "since she fails to guess the cause
Which taxed you with this visit, madam."
           "Good,"
She said, "I value what's sincere at once.
Perhaps if I had found a literal Muse,
The visit might have taxed me. As it is,
You wear your blue so chiefly in your eyes,
My fair Aurora, in a frank good way,
It comforts me entirely for your fame,
As well as for the trouble of ascent
To this Olympus."
      There, a silver laugh
Ran rippling through her quickened little breaths
The steep stair somewhat justified.
          "But still

Your ladyship has left me curious why
You dared the risk of finding the said Muse?"

"Ah,—keep me, notwithstanding, to the point,
Like any pedant? Is the blue in eyes
As awful as in stockings after all,
I wonder, that you'd have my business out
Before I breathe—exact the epic plunge
In spite of gasps? Well, naturally you think
I've come here, as the lion-hunters go
To deserts, to secure you with a trap
For exhibition in my drawing-rooms
On zoologic soirées? not in the least.
Roar softly at me; I am frivolous, .
I dare say; I have played at wild-beast shows
Like other women of my class,—but now
I meet my lion simply as Androcles
Met his . . when at his mercy."

                              So, she bent
Her head, as queens may mock,—then lifting up
Her eyelids with a real grave queenly look,
Which ruled and would not spare, not even herself,—
"I think you have a cousin:—Romney Leigh."

"You bring a word from *him?*"—my eyes leapt up
To the very height of hers,—"a word from *him?*"

"I bring a word about him, actually.
But first," (she pressed me with her urgent eyes)
You do not love him,—you?"
                              "You're frank at least
In putting questions, madam," I replied,
"I love my cousin cousinly—no more."

"I guessed as much. I'm ready to be frank
In answering also, if you'll question me,
Or even for something less. You stand outside,

You artist women, of the common sex;
You share not with us, and exceed us so
Perhaps by what you're mulcted in, your hearts
Being starved to make your heads: so run the old
Traditions of you. I can therefore speak
Without the natural shame which creatures feel
When speaking on their level, to their like.
There's many a papist she, would rather die
Than own to her maid she put a ribbon on
To catch the indifferent eye of such a man,
Who yet would count adulteries on her beads
At holy Mary's shrine and never blush;
Because the saints are so far off, we lose
All modesty before them. Thus, to-day,
'Tis *I*, love Romney Leigh."
                              "Forbear," I cried.
"If here's no Muse, still less is any saint;
Nor even a friend, that Lady Waldemar
Should make confessions" ..
                              "That's unkindly said
If no friend, what forbids to make a friend
To join to our confession ere we have done?
I love your cousin. If it seems unwise
To say so, it's still foolisher (we're frank)
To feel so. My first husband left me young,
And pretty enough, so please you, and rich enough,
To keep my booth in May-fair with the rest
To happy issues. There are marquises
Would serve seven years to call me wife, I know,
And, after seven, I might consider it,
For there's some comfort in a marquisate
When all's said,—yes, but after the seven years;
I, now, love Romney. You put up your lip,
So like a Leigh! so like him!—Pardon me,
I'm well aware I do not derogate
In loving Romney Leigh. The name is good,
The means are excellent, but the man, the man—

Heaven help us both,—I am near as mad as he,
In loving such an one."
                          She slowly swung
Her heavy ringlets till they touched her smile,
As reasonably sorry for herself,
And thus continued.
                    "Of a truth, Miss Leigh,
I have not, without struggle, come to this.
I took a master in the German tongue,
I gamed a little, went to Paris twice;
But, after all, this love! . . . you eat of love,
And do as vile a thing as if you ate
Of garlic—which, whatever else you eat,
Tastes uniformly acrid, till your peach
Reminds you of your onion. Am I coarse?
Well, love's coarse, nature's coarse—ah, there's the rub!
We fair fine ladies, who park out our lives
From common sheep-paths, cannot help the crows
From flying over,—we're as natural still
As Blowsalinda. Drape us perfectly
In Lyons' velvet,—we are not, for that,
Lay-figures, look you: we have hearts within,
Warm, live, improvident, indecent hearts,
As ready for outrageous ends and acts
As any distressed sempstress of them all
That Romney groans and toils for. We catch love
And other fevers, in the vulgar way:
Love will not be outwitted by our wit,
Nor outrun by our equipages:—mine
Persisted, spite of efforts. All my cards
Turned up but Romney Leigh; my German stopped
At germane Wertherism; my Paris rounds
Returned me from the Champs Elysées just
A ghost, and sighing like Dido's. I came home
Uncured,—convicted rather to myself
Of being in love . . . in love! That's coarse you'll say:
I'm talking garlic."

                        Coldly I replied.
"Apologise for atheism, not love!
For me, I do believe in love, and God.
I know my cousin: Lady Waldemar
I know not: yet I say as much as this;
Whoever loves him, let her not excuse
But cleanse herself, that, loving such a man,
She may not do it with such unworthy love
He cannot stoop and take it."
                        "That is said
Austerely, like a youthful prophetess,
Who knits her brows across her pretty eyes
To keep them back from following the gray flight
Of doves between the temple-columns. Dear,
Be kinder with me; let us two be friends.
I'm a mere woman,—the more weak perhaps
Through being so proud; you're better; as for him,
He's best. Indeed he builds his goodness up
So high, it topples down to the other side
And makes a sort of badness; there's the worst
I have to say against your cousin's best!
And so be mild, Aurora, with my worst
For his sake, if not mine."
                        "I own myself
Incredulous of confidence like this
Availing him or you."
                        "And I, myself,
Of being worthy of him with any love:
In your sense I am not so—let it pass.
And yet I save him if I marry him;
Let that pass too."
                        "Pass, pass! we play police
Upon my cousin's life, to indicate
What may or may not pass?" I cried. "He knows
What's worthy of him; the choice remains with *him;*
And what he chooses, act or wife, I think
I shall not call unworthy, I, for one."

"'Tis somewhat rashly said," she answered slow;
"Now let's talk reason, though we talk of love.
Your cousin Romney Leigh's a monster; there,
The word's out fairly, let me prove the fact.
We'll take, say, that most perfect of antiques
They call the Genius of the Vatican,
(Which seems too beauteous to endure itself
In this mixed world,) and fasten it for once
Upon the torso of the Dancing Fawn,
(Who might limp surely, if he did not dance,)
Instead of Buonarroti's mask: what then?
We show the sort of monster Romney is,
With god-like virtues and heroic aims
Subjoined to limping possibilities
Of mismade human nature. Grant the man
Twice godlike, twice heroic,—still he limps,
And here's the point we come to."
       "Pardon me,
But, Lady Waldemar, the point's the thing
We never come to."
     "Caustic, insolent
At need! I like you"—(there, she took my hands)
"And now my lioness, help Androcles,
For all your roaring. Help me! for myself
I would not say so—but for him. He limps
So certainly, he'll fall into the pit
A week hence,—so I lose him—so he is lost!
For when he's fairly married, he a Leigh,
To a girl of doubtful life, undoubtful birth,
Starved out in London till her coarse-grained hands
Are whiter than her morals,—even you
May call his choice unworthy."
      "Married! lost!
He, ... Romney!"
     "Ah, you're moved at last," she said.
"These monsters, set out in the open sun,

Of course throw monstrous shadows: those who think
Awry, will scarce act straightly. Who but he?
And who but you can wonder? He has been mad,
The whole world knows, since first, a nominal man,
He soured the proctors, tried the gownsmen's wits,
With equal scorn of triangles and wine,
And took no honours, yet was honourable.
They'll tell you he lost count of Homer's ships
In Melbourne's poor-bills, Ashley's factory bills,—
Ignored the Aspasia we all dare to praise,
For other women, dear, we could not name
Because we're decent. Well, he had some right
On his side probably; men always have,
Who go absurdly wrong. The living boor
Who brews your ale, exceeds in vital worth
Dead Cæsar who 'stops bungholes,' in the cask;
And also, to do good is excellent,
For persons of his income, even to boors:
I sympathise with all such things. But he
Went mad upon them .. madder and more mad
From college times to these,—as, going down hill,
The faster still, the farther. You must know
Your Leigh by heart: he has sown his black young curls
With bleaching cares of half a million men
Already. If you do not starve, or sin,
You're nothing to him: pay the income-tax
And break your heart upon 't, he'll scarce be touched;
But come upon the parish, qualified
For the parish stocks, and Romney will be there
To call you brother, sister, or perhaps
A tenderer name still. Had I any chance
With Mister Leigh, who am Lady Waldemar
And never committed felony?"
                              "You speak
Too bitterly," I said, "for the literal truth."

"The truth is bitter. Here's a man who looks

For ever on the ground! you must be low,
Or else a pictured ceiling overhead,
Good painting thrown away. For me, I've done
What women may, we're somewhat limited,
We modest women, but I've done my best.
—How men are perjured when they swear our eyes
Have meaning in them! they're just blue or brown,
They just can drop their lids a little. And yet
Mine did more, for I read half Fourier through,
Proudhon, Considerant, and Louis Blanc,
With various others of his socialists,
And, if I had been a fathom less in love,
Had cured myself with gaping. As it was,
I quoted from them prettily enough
Perhaps, to make them sound half rational
To a saner man than he whene'er we talked,
(For which I dodged occasion)—learnt by heart
His speeches in the Commons and elsewhere
Upon the social question; heaped reports
Of wicked women and penitentiaries
On all my tables, (with a place for Sue)
And gave my name to swell subscription-lists
Toward keeping up the sun at nights in heaven,
And other possible ends. All things I did,
Except the impossible .. such as wearing gowns
Provided by the Ten Hours' movement: there,
I stopped—we must stop somewhere. He, meanwhile,
Unmoved as the Indian tortoise 'neath the world,
Let all that noise go on upon his back:
He would not disconcert or throw me out,
'Twas well to see a woman of my class
With such a dawn of conscience. For the heart,
Made firewood for his sake, and flaming up
To his face,—he merely warmed his feet at it:
Just deigned to let my carriage stop him short
In park or street,—he leaning on the door

With news of the committee which sate last
On pickpockets at suck."

       "You jest—you jest."

"As martyrs jest, dear, (if you read their lives)
Upon the axe which kills them. When all's done
By me, .. for him—you'll ask him presently
The colour of my hair—he cannot tell,
Or answers 'dark' at random; while, be sure,
He's absolute on the figure, five or ten,
Of my last subscription. Is it bearable,
And I a woman?"
      "Is it reparable,
Though *I* were a man?"
      "I know not. That's to prove.
But first, this shameful marriage?"
      "Ay?" I cried,
"Then really there's a marriage?"
      "Yesterday
I held him fast upon it. 'Mister Leigh,'
Said I, 'shut up a thing, it makes more noise.
'The boiling town keeps secrets ill; I've known
'Yours since last week. Forgive my knowledge so:
'You feel I'm not the woman of the world
'The world thinks; you have borne with me before,
'And used me in your noble work, our work,
'And now you shall not cast me off because
'You're at the difficult point, the *join*. 'Tis true
'Even I can scarce admit the cogency
'Of such a marriage .. where you do not love,
'(Except the class) yet marry and throw your name
'Down to the gutter, for a fire-escape
'To future generations! 'tis sublime,
'A great example, a true Genesis
'Of the opening social era. But take heed,
'This virtuous act must have a patent weight,

'Or loses half its virtue. Make it tell,
'Interpret it, and set in the light,
'And do not muffle it in a winter-cloak
'As a vulgar bit of shame, as if, at best,
'A Leigh had made a misalliance and blushed
'A Howard should know it.' Then, I pressed him more:
'He would not choose,' I said, 'that even his kin, ..
'Aurora Leigh, even .. should conceive his act
'Less sacrifice, more fantasy.' At which
He grew so pale, dear, .. to the lips, I knew
I had touched him. 'Do you know her,' he inquired,
'My cousin Aurora?' 'Yes,' I said, and lied,
(But truly we all know you by your books)
And so I offered to come straight to you,
Explain the subject, justify the cause,
And take you with me to St. Margaret's Court
To see this miracle, this Marian Erle,
This drover's daughter (she's not pretty, he swears)
Upon whose finger, exquisitely pricked
By a hundred needles, we're to hang the tie
'Twixt class and class in England,—thus indeed
By such a presence, yours and mine, to lift
The match up from the doubtful place. At once
He thanked me sighing, murmured to himself
'She'll do it perhaps, she's noble,'—thanked me twice,
And promised, as my guerdon, to put off
His marriage for a month."
       I answered then.
"I understand your drift imperfectly.
You wish to lead me to my cousin's betrothed,
To touch her hand if worthy, and hold her hand
If feeble, thus to justify his match.
So be it then. But how this serves your ends,
And how the strange confession of your love
Serves this, I have to learn—I cannot see."

She knit her restless forehead. "Then, despite,

Aurora, that most radiant morning name,
You're dull as any London afternoon.
I wanted time, and gained it,—wanted *you*,
And gain you! you will come and see the girl
In whose most prodigal eyes the lineal pearl
And pride of all your lofty race of Leighs
Is destined to solution. Authorised
By sight and knowledge, then, you'll speak your mind,
And prove to Romney, in your brilliant way,
He'll wrong the people and posterity,
(Say such a thing is bad for me and you,
And you fail utterly,) by concluding thus
An execrable marriage. Break it up,
Disroot it—peradventure presently
We'll plant a better fortune in its place.
Be good to me, Aurora, scorn me less
For saying the thing I should not. Well I know
I should not. I have kept, as others have,
The iron rule of womanly reserve
In lip and life, till now: I wept a week
Before I came here."—Ending, she was pale;
The last words, haughtily said, were tremulous.
This palfrey pranced in harness, arched her neck,
And, only by the foam upon the bit,
You saw she champed against it.
                                    Then I rose.
"I love love: truth's no cleaner thing than love.
I comprehend a love so fiery hot
It burns its natural veil of august shame,
And stands sublimely in the nude, as chaste
As Medicean Venus. But I know,
A love that burns through veils will burn through masks
And shrivel up treachery. What, love and lie!
Nay—go to the opera! your love's curable."

"I love and lie?" she said—"I lie, forsooth?"
And beat her taper foot upon the floor,

And smiled against the shoe,—"You're hard, Miss Leigh,
Unversed in current phrases.—Bowling-greens
Of poets are fresher than the world's highways:
Forgive me that I rashly blew the dust
Which dims our hedges even, in your eyes,
And vexed you so much. You find, probably,
No evil in this marriage,—rather good
Of innocence, to pastoralise in song:
You'll give the bond your signature, perhaps,
Beneath the lady's mark,—indifferent
That Romney chose a wife, could write her name,
In witnessing he loved her."
      "Loved!" I cried;
"Who tells you that he wants a wife to love?
He gets a horse to use, not love, I think:
There's work for wives as well,—and after, straw,
When men are liberal. For myself, you err
Supposing power in me to break this match.
I could not do it, to save Romney's life,
And would not, to save mine."
      "You take it so."
She said, "farewell then. Write your books in peace,
As far as may be for some secret stir
Now obvious to me,—for, most obviously,
In coming hither I mistook the way."
Whereat she touched my hand and bent her head,
And floated from me like a silent cloud
That leaves the sense of thunder.
      I drew breath,
Oppressed in my deliverance. After all
This woman breaks her social system up
For love, so counted—the love possible
To such,—and lilies are still lilies, pulled
By smutty hands, though spotted from their white;
And thus she is better haply, of her kind,
Than Romney Leigh, who lives by diagrams,
And crosses out the spontaneities

Of all his individual, personal life
With formal universals. As if man
Were set upon a high stool at a desk
To keep God's books for Him in red and black,
And feel by millions! What, if even God
Were chiefly God by living out Himself
To an individualism of the Infinite,
Eterne, intense, profuse,—still throwing up
The golden spray of multitudinous worlds
In measure to the proclive weight and rush
Of His inner nature,—the spontaneous love
Still proof and outflow of spontaneous life?
Then live, Aurora.
      Two hours afterward,
Within St. Margaret's Court I stood alone,
Close-veiled. A sick child, from an ague-fit,
Whose wasted right hand gambled 'gainst his left
With an old brass button in a blot of sun,
Jeered weakly at me as I passed across
The uneven pavement; while a woman, rouged
Upon the angular cheek-bones, kerchief torn,
Thin dangling locks, and flat lascivious mouth,
Cursed at a window both ways, in and out,
By turns some bed-rid creature and myself,—
"Lie still there, mother! liker the dead dog
You'll be to-morrow. What, we pick our way,
Fine madam, with those damnable small feet!
We cover up our face from doing good,
As if it were our purse! What brings you here,
My lady? is 't to find my gentleman
Who visits his tame pigeon in the eaves?
Our cholera catch you with its cramps and spasms,
And tumble up your good clothes, veil and all,
And turn your whiteness dead-blue." I looked up;
I think I could have walked through hell that day,
And never flinched. "The dear Christ comfort you,"
I said, "you must have been most miserable,

To be so cruel,"—and I emptied out
My purse upon the stones: when, as I had cast
The last charm in the cauldron, the whole court
Went boiling, bubbling up, from all its doors
And windows, with a hideous wail of laughs
And roar of oaths, and blows perhaps .. I passed
Too quickly for distinguishing .. and pushed
A little side-door hanging on a hinge,
And plunged into the dark, and groped and climbed
The long, steep, narrow stair 'twixt broken rail
And mildewed wall that let the plaster drop
To startle me in the blackness. Still, up, up!
So high lived Romney's bride. I paused at last
Before a low door in the roof, and knocked;
There came an answer like a hurried dove—
"So soon? can that be Mister Leigh? so soon?"
And, as I entered, an ineffable face
Met mine upon the threshold. "Oh, not you,
Not you!"—the dropping of the voice implied,
"Then, if not you, for me not any one."
I looked her in the eyes, and held her hands,
And said, "I am his cousin,—Romney Leigh's;
And here I come to see my cousin too."
She touched me with her face and with her voice,
This daughter of the people. Such soft flowers,
From such rough roots? the people, under there,
Can sin so, curse so, look so, smell so ... faugh!
Yet have such daughters?

                No wise beautiful
Was Marian Erle. She was not white nor brown,
But could look either, like a mist that changed
According to being shone on more or less:
The hair, too, ran its opulence of curls
In doubt 'twixt dark and bright, nor left you clear
To name the colour. Too much hair perhaps
(I'll name a fault here) for so small a head,
Which seemed to droop on that side and on this,

As a full-blown rose uneasy with its weight
Though not a wind should trouble it. Again,
The dimple in the cheek had better gone
With redder, fuller rounds; and somewhat large
The mouth was, though the milky little teeth
Dissolved it to so infantine a smile.
For soon it smiled at me; the eyes smiled too,
But 'twas as if remembering they had wept,
And knowing they should, some day, weep again.

We talked. She told me all her story out,
Which I'll re-tell with fuller utterance,
As coloured and confirmed in aftertimes
By others and herself too. Marian Erle
Was born upon the ledge of Malvern Hill,
To eastward, in a hut built up at night
To evade the landlord's eye, of mud and turf,
Still liable, if once he looked that way,
To being straight levelled, scattered by his foot,
Like any other anthill. Born, I say;
God sent her to his world, commissioned right,
Her human testimonials fully signed,
Not scant in soul—complete in lineaments;
But others had to swindle her a place
To wail in when she had come. No place for her,
By man's law! born an outlaw, was this babe;
Her first cry in our strange and strangling air,
When cast in spasms out by the shuddering womb,
Was wrong against the social code,—forced wrong:—
What business had the baby to cry there?

I tell her story and grow passionate.
She, Marian, did not tell it so, but used
Meek words that made no wonder of herself
For being so sad a creature. "Mister Leigh
"Considered truly that such things should change.
"They *will*, in heaven—but meantime, on the earth,

"There's none can like a nettle as a pink,
"Except himself. We're nettles, some of us,
"And give offence by the act of springing up;
"And, if we leave the damp side of the wall,
"The hoes, of course, are on us." So she said.
Her father earned his life by random jobs
Despised by steadier workmen—keeping swine
On commons, picking hops, or hurrying on
The harvest at wet seasons, or, at need,
Assisting the Welsh drovers, when a drove
Of startled horses plunged into the mist
Below the mountain-road, and sowed the wind
With wandering neighings. In between the gaps
Of such irregular work, he drank and slept,
And cursed his wife because, the pence being out,
She could not buy more drink. At which she turned,
(The worm) and beat her baby in revenge
For her own broken heart. There's not a crime
But takes its proper change out still in crime
If once rung on the counter of this world:
Let sinners look to it.
                         Yet the outcast child,
For whom the very mother's face forewent
The mother's special patience, lived and grew;
Learnt early to cry low, and walk alone,
With that pathetic vacillating roll
Of the infant body on the uncertain feet,
(The earth being felt unstable ground so soon)
At which most women's arms unclose at once
With irrepressive instinct. Thus, at three,
This poor weaned kid would run off from the fold,
This babe would steal off from the mother's chair,
And, creeping through the golden walls of gorse,
Would find some keyhole toward the secresy
Of Heaven's high blue, and, nestling down, peer out—
Oh, not to catch the angels at their games,
She had never heard of angels,—but to gaze

She knew not why, to see she knew not what,
A-hungering outward from the barren earth
For something like a joy. She liked, she said,
To dazzle black her sight against the sky,
For then, it seemed, some grand blind Love came down
And groped her out, and clasped her with a kiss;
She learnt God that way, and was beat for it
Whenever she went home,—yet came again,
As surely as the trapped hare, getting free,
Returns to his form. This grand blind Love, she said,
This skyey father and mother both in one,
Instructed her and civilised her more
Than even Sunday-school did afterward,
To which a lady sent her to learn books
And sit upon a long bench in a row
With other children. Well, she laughed sometimes
To see them laugh and laugh and maul their texts;
But ofter she was sorrowful with noise
And wondered if their mothers beat them hard
That ever they should laugh so. There was one
She loved indeed,—Rose Bell, a seven years' child
So pretty and clever, who read syllables
When Marian was at letters; *she* would laugh
At nothing—hold your finger up, she laughed,
Then shook her curls down over eyes and mouth
To hide her make-mirth from the schoolmaster:
And Rose's pelting glee, as frank as rain
On cherry-blossoms, brightened Marian too,
To see another merry whom she loved.
She whispered once (the children side by side,
With mutual arms entwined about their necks)
"Your mother lets you laugh so?" "Ay," said Rose,
"She lets me. She was dug into the ground
Six years since, I being but a yearling wean.
Such mothers let us play and lose our time,
And never scold nor beat us! don't you wish
You had one like that?" There, Marian breaking off

Looked suddenly in my face. "Poor Rose," said she,
"I heard her laugh last night in Oxford Street.
I'd pour out half my blood to stop that laugh.
Poor Rose, poor Rose!" said Marian.
                                    She resumed.
It tried her, when she had learnt at Sunday-school
What God was, what he wanted from us all,
And how in choosing sin we vexed the Christ,
To go straight home and hear her father pull
The Name down on us from the thunder-shelf
Then drink away his soul into the dark
From seeing judgment. Father, mother, home,
Were God and heaven reversed to her: the more
She knew of Right, the more she guessed their wrong;
Her price paid down for knowledge, was to know
The vileness of her kindred: through her heart,
Her filial and tormented heart, henceforth,
They struck their blows at virtue. Oh, 'tis hard
To learn you have a father up in heaven
By a gathering certain sense of being, on earth,
Still worse than orphaned: 'tis too heavy a grief,
The having to thank God for such a joy!

And so passed Marian's life from year to year.
Her parents took her with them when they tramped,
Dodged lanes and heaths, frequented towns and fairs,
And once went farther and saw Manchester,
And once the sea, that blue end of the world,
That fair scroll-finis of a wicked book,—
And twice a prison,— back at intervals,
Returning to the hills. Hills draw like heaven,
And stronger sometimes, holding out their hands
To pull you from the vile flats up to them.
And though perhaps these strollers still strolled back,
As sheep do, simply that they knew the way,
They certainly felt bettered unaware
Emerging from the social smut of towns

To wipe their feet clean on the mountain turf,
In which long wanderings, Marian lived and learned,
Endured and learned. The people on the roads
Would stop and ask her why her eyes outgrew
Her cheeks, and if she meant to lodge the birds
In all that hair; and then they lifted her,
The miller in his cart, a mile or twain,
The butcher's boy on horseback. Often too
The pedlar stopped, and tapped her on the head
With absolute forefinger, brown and ringed,
And asked if peradventure she could read,
And when she answered "ay," would toss her down
Some stray odd volume from his heavy pack,
A Thomson's Seasons, mulcted of the Spring,
Or half a play of Shakspeare's, torn across,
(She had to guess the bottom of a page
By just the top sometimes,—as difficult,
As, sitting on the moon, to guess the earth!)
Or else a sheaf of leaves (for that small Ruth's
Small gleanings) torn out from the heart of books,
From Churchyard Elegies and Edens Lost,
From Burns, and Bunyan, Selkirk, and Tom Jones,—
'Twas somewhat hard to keep the things distinct,
And oft the jangling influence jarred the child
Like looking at a sunset full of grace
Through a pothouse window while the drunken oaths
Went on behind her. But she weeded out
Her book-leaves, threw away the leaves that hurt,
(First tore them small, that none should find a word)
And made a nosegay of the sweet and good
To fold within her breast, and pore upon
At broken moments of the noontide glare,
When leave was given her to untie her cloak
And rest upon the dusty highway's bank
From the road's dust: or oft, the journey done,
Some city friend would lead her by the hand
To hear a lecture at an institute.

And thus she had grown, this Marian Erle of ours,
To no book-learning,—she was ignorant
Of authors,—not in earshot of the things
Out-spoken o'er the heads of common men
By men who are uncommon,—but within
The cadenced hum of such, and capable
Of catching from the fringes of the wind
Some fragmentary phrases, here and there,
Of that fine music,—which, being carried in
To her soul, had reproduced itself afresh
In finer motions of the lips and lids.

She said, in speaking of it, "If a flower
Were thrown you out of heaven at intervals,
You'd soon attain to a trick of looking up,—
And so with her." She counted me her years,
Till *I* felt old; and then she counted me
Her sorrowful pleasures, till I felt ashamed.
She told me she was fortunate and calm
On such and such a season, sate and sewed,
With no one to break up her crystal thoughts,
While rhymes from lovely poems span around
Their ringing circles of ecstatic tune,
Beneath the moistened finger of the Hour.
Her parents called her a strange, sickly child,
Not good for much, and given to sulk and stare,
And smile into the hedges and the clouds,
And tremble if one shook her from her fit
By any blow, or word even. Out-door jobs
Went ill with her, and household quiet work
She was not born to. Had they kept the north,
They might have had their pennyworth out of her
Like other parents, in the factories,
(Your children work for you, not you for them,
Or else they better had been choked with air
The first breath drawn;) but, in this trampling life,
Was nothing to be done with such a child.

But tramp and tramp. And yet she knitted hose
Not ill, and was not dull at needlework;
And all the country people gave her pence
For darning stockings past their natural age,
And patching petticoats from old to new,
And other light work done for thrifty wives.

One day, said Marian,—the sun shone that day—
Her mother had been badly beat, and felt
The bruises sore about her wretched soul,
(That must have been): she came in suddenly,
And snatching in a sort of breathless rage
Her daughter's headgear comb, let down the hair
Upon her like a sudden waterfall,
Then drew her drenched and passive by the arm
Outside the hut they lived in. When the child
Could clear her blinded face from all that stream
Of tresses .. there, a man stood, with beast's eyes
That seemed as they would swallow her alive
Complete in body and spirit, hair and all,—
And burning stertorous breath that hurt her cheek,
He breathed so near. The mother held her tight,
Saying hard between her teeth—"Why wench, why wench,
The squire speaks to you now—the squire's too good;
He means to set you up, and comfort us.
Be mannerly at least." The child turned round
And looked up piteous in the mother's face,
(Be sure that mother's death-bed will not want
Another devil to damn, than such a look)
"Oh mother!" then, with desperate glance to heaven,
"God, free me from my mother," she shrieked out,
"These mothers are too dreadful." And, with force
As passionate as fear, she tore her hands
Like lilies from the rocks, from hers and his
And sprang down, bounded headlong down the steep,
Away from both—away, if possible,
As far as God,—away! They yelled at her,

As famished hounds at a hare. She heard them yell;
She felt her name hiss after her from the hills,
Like shot from guns. On, on. And now she had cast
The voices off with the uplands. On. Mad fear
Was running in her feet and killing the ground;
The white roads curled as if she burnt them up,
The green fields melted, wayside trees fell back
To make room for her. Then her head grew vexed;
Trees, fields, turned on her and ran after her;
She heard the quick pants of the hills behind,
Their keen air pricked her neck: she had lost her feet,
Could run no more, yet somehow went as fast,
The horizon red 'twixt steeples in the east
So sucked her forward, forward, while her heart
Kept swelling, swelling, till it swelled so big
It seemed to fill her body,—when it burst
And overflowed the world and swamped the light;
"And now I am dead and safe," thought Marian Erle—.
She had dropped, she had fainted.
                                        As the sense returned,
The night had passed—not life's night. She was 'ware
Of heavy tumbling motions, creaking wheels,
The driver shouting to the lazy team
That swung their rankling bells against her brain,
While, through the waggon's coverture and chinks,
The cruel yellow morning pecked at her
Alive or dead upon the straw inside,—
At which her soul ached back into the dark
And prayed, "no more of that." A waggoner
Had found her in a ditch beneath the moon,
As white as moonshine save for the oozing blood.
At first he thought her dead; but when he had wiped
The mouth and heard it sigh, he raised her up,
And laid her in his waggon in the straw,
And so conveyed her to the distant town
To which his business called himself, and left
That heap of misery at the hospital.

She stirred;—the place seemed new and strange as death
The white strait bed, with others strait and white,
Like graves dug side by side at measured lengths,
And quiet people walking in and out
With wonderful low voices and soft steps
And apparitional equal care for each,
Astonished her with order, silence, law.
And when a gentle hand held out a cup,
She took it, as you do at sacrament,
Half awed, half melted,—not being used, indeed,
To so much love as makes the form of love
And courtesy of manners. Delicate drinks
And rare white bread, to which some dying eyes
Were turned in observation. O my God,
How sick we must be, ere we make men just!
I think it frets the saints in heaven to see
How many desolate creatures on the earth
Have learnt the simple dues of fellowship
And social comfort, in a hospital,
As Marian did. She lay there, stunned, half tranced,
And wished, at intervals of growing sense,
She might be sicker yet, if sickness made
The world so marvellous kind, the air so hushed,
And all her wake-time quiet as a sleep;
For now she understood (as such things were)
How sickness ended very oft in heaven
Among the unspoken raptures:—yet more sick,
And surelier happy. Then she dropped her lids,
And, folding up her hands as flowers at night,
Would lose no moment of the blessed time.

She lay and seethed in fever many weeks,
But youth was strong and overcame the test;
Revolted soul and flesh were reconciled
And fetched back to the necessary day
And daylight duties. She could creep about

The long bare rooms, and stare out drearily
From any narrow window on the street,
'Till some one who had nursed her as a friend
Said coldly to her, as an enemy,
"She had leave to go next week, being well enough,"
(While only her heart ached.) "Go next week," thought she,
"Next week! how would it be with her next week,
Let out into that terrible street alone
Among the pushing people, .. to go .. where*"

One day, the last before the dreaded last,
Among the convalescents, like herself
Prepared to go next morning, she sate dumb,
And heard half absently the women talk,—
How one was famished for her baby's cheeks,
"The little wretch would know her! a year old
And lively, like his father!"—one was keen
To get to work, and fill some clamorous mouths;
And one was tender for her dear goodman
Who had missed her sorely,--and one, querulous ..
"Would pay backbiting neighbours who had dared
To talk about her as already dead,"—
And one was proud .. "and if her sweetheart Luke
Had left her for a ruddier face than hers,
(The gossip would be seen through at a glance)
Sweet riddance of such sweethearts—let him hang!
'Twere good to have been sick for such an end."

And while they talked, and Marian felt the worse
For having missed the worst of all their wrongs,
A visitor was ushered through the wards
And paused among the talkers. "When he looked
It was as if he spoke, and when he spoke
He sang perhaps," said Marian; "could she tell?
She only knew" (so much she had chronicled,

As seraphs might the making of the sun)
"That he who came and spake, was Romney Leigh,
And then and there she saw and heard him first."

And when it was her turn to have the face
Upon her, all those buzzing pallid lips
Being satisfied with comfort—when he changed
To Marian, saying "And *you?* you're going, where?"—
She, moveless as a worm beneath a stone
Which some one's stumbling foot has spurned aside,
Writhed suddenly astonished with the light,
And breaking into sobs cried, "Where I go?
None asked me till this moment. Can I say
Where *I* go,—when it has not seemed worth while
To God himself, who thinks of every one,
To think of me and fix where I shall go?"

"So young," he gently asked her, "you have lost
Your father and your mother?"
       "Both," she said,
"Both lost! my father was burnt up with gin
Or ever I sucked milk, and so is lost.
My mother sold me to a man last month,
And so my mother's lost, 'tis manifest.
And I, who fled from her for miles and miles,
As if I had caught sight of the fire of hell
Through some wild gap, (she was my mother, sir)
It seems I shall be lost too, presently,
And so we end, all three of us."
       "Poor child,"
He said,—with such a pity in his voice,
It soothed her more than her own tears,—"poor child!
'Tis simple that betrayal by mother's love
Should bring despair of God's too. Yet be taught,
He's better to us than many mothers are,
And children cannot wander beyond reach
Of the sweep of his white raiment. Touch and hold!

And if you weep still, weep where John was laid
While Jesus loved him."
                         "She could say the words,"
She told me, "exactly as he uttered them
A year back, since in any doubt or dark
They came out like the stars, and shone on her
With just their comfort. Common words, perhaps;
The ministers in church might say the same;
But *he*, he made the church with what he spoke,—
The difference was the miracle," said she.

Then catching up her smile to ravishment,
She added quickly, "I repeat his words,
But not his tones: can any one repeat
The music of an organ, out of church?
And when he said "poor child," I shut my eyes
To feel how tenderly his voice broke through,
As the ointment-box broke on the Holy feet
To let out the rich medicative nard."

She told me how he had raised and rescued her
With reverent pity, as, in touching grief,
He touched the wounds of Christ,—and made her feel
More self-respecting. Hope, he called, belief
In God,—work, worship,—therefore let us pray!
And thus, to snatch her soul from atheism,
And keep it stainless from her mother's face,
He sent her to a famous sempstress-house
Far off in London, there to work and hope.

With that, they parted. She kept sight of Heaven,
But not of Romney. He had good to do
To others: through the days and through the nights
She sewed and sewed and sewed. She drooped sometimes,
And wondered, while along the tawny light
She struck the new thread into her needle's eye,
How people without mothers on the hills

Could choose the town to live in!—then she drew
The stitch, and mused how Romney's face would look,
And if 't were likely he'd remember hers
When they two had their meeting after death.

FOURTH BOOK.

THEY met still sooner. 'Twas a year from thence
That Lucy Gresham, the sick sempstress girl,
Who sewed by Marian's chair so still and quick,
And leant her head upon its back to cough
More freely, when, the mistress turning round,
The others took occasion to laugh out,
Gave up at last. Among the workers, spoke
A bold girl with black eyebrows and red lips;
"You know the news? Who's dying, do you think?
Our Lucy Gresham. I expected it
As little as Nell Hart's wedding. Blush not, Nell,
Thy curls be red enough without thy cheeks,
And, some day, there'll be found a man to dote
On red curls.—Lucy Gresham swooned last night,
Dropped sudden in the street while going home;
And now the baker says, who took her up
And laid her by her grandmother in bed,
He'll give her a week to die in. Pass the silk.
Let's hope he gave her a loaf too, within reach,
For otherwise they'll starve before they die,
That funny pair of bedfellows! Miss Bell,
I'll thank you for the scissors. The old crone
Is paralytic—that's the reason why
Our Lucy's thread went faster than her breath,
Which went too quick, we all know. Marian Erle!
Why, Marian Erle, you're not the fool to cry?
Your tears spoil Lady Waldemar's new dress,
You piece of pity!"
                    Marian rose up straight,

And, breaking through the talk and through the work,
Went outward, in the face of their surprise,
To Lucy's home, to nurse her back to life
Or down to death. She knew, by such an act,
All place and grace were forfeit in the house,
Whose mistress would supply the missing hand
With necessary, not inhuman haste,
And take no blame. But pity, too, had dues:
She could not leave a solitary soul
To founder in the dark, while she sate still
And lavished stitches on a lady's hem
As if no other work were paramount.
"Why, God," thought Marian, "has a missing hand
This moment; Lucy wants a drink, perhaps.
Let others miss me! never miss me, God!"

So Marian sate by Lucy's bed, content
With duty, and was strong, for recompense,
To hold the lamp of human love arm-high,
To catch the death-strained eyes and comfort them,
Until the angels, on the luminous side
Of death, had got theirs ready. And she said,
If Lucy thanked her sometimes, called her kind,
It touched her strangely. "Marian Erle, called kind!
What, Marian, beaten and sold, who could not die!
'Tis verily good fortune to be kind.
Ah you," she said, "who are born to such a grace,
Be sorry for the unlicensed class, the poor,
Reduced to think the best good fortune means
That others, simply, should be kind to them."

From sleep to sleep when Lucy had slid away
So gently, like the light upon a hill,
Of which none names the moment that it goes
Though all see when 't is gone,—a man came in
And stood beside the bed. The old idiot wretch
Screamed feebly, like a baby overlain,

"Sir, sir, you won't mistake me for the corpse?
Don't look at *me*, sir! never bury *me!*
Although I lie here I'm alive as you,
Except my legs and arms,—I eat and drink
And understand,—(that you're the gentleman
Who fits the funerals up, Heaven speed you, sir,)
And certainly I should be livelier still
If Lucy here .. sir, Lucy is the corpse ..
Had worked more properly to buy me wine;
But Lucy, sir, was always slow at work,
I shan't lose much by Lucy.   Marian Erle,
Speak up and show the gentleman the corpse."

And then a voice said, " Marian Erle."   She rose;
It was the hour for angels—there, stood hers!
She scarcely marvelled to see Romney Leigh.
As light November snows to empty nests,
As grass to graves, as moss to mildewed stones,
As July suns to ruins, through the rents,
As ministering spirits to mourners, through a loss,
As Heaven itself to men, through pangs of death,
He came uncalled wherever grief had come.
"And so," said Marian Erle, "we met anew,"
And added softly, "so, we shall not part."

He was not angry that she had left the house
Wherein he placed her.   Well—she had feared it might
Have vexed him.   Also, when he found her set
On keeping, though the dead was out of sight,
That half-dead, half-live body left behind
With cankerous heart and flesh, which took your best
And cursed you for the little good it did,
(Could any leave the bedrid wretch alone,
So joyless she was thankless even to God,
Much more to you?) he did not say 'twas well,
Yet Marian thought he did not take it ill,—
Since day by day he came, and every day

She felt within his utterance and his eyes
A closer, tenderer presence of the soul,
Until at last he said, "We shall not part."

On that same day, was Marian's work complete:
She had smoothed the empty bed, and swept the floor
Of coffin sawdust, set the chairs anew
The dead had ended gossip in, and stood
In that poor room so cold and orderly,
The door-key in her hand, prepared to go
As *they* had, howbeit not their way.   He spoke.

"Dear Marian, of one clay God made us all,
And though men push and poke and paddle in't
(As children play at fashioning dirt-pies)
And call their fancies by the name of facts,
Assuming difference, lordship, privilege,
When all's plain dirt,—they come back to it at last,
The first grave-digger proves it with a spade,
And pats all even.   Need we wait for this,
You, Marian, and I, Romney?"
                                She, at that,
Looked blindly in his face, as when one looks
Through driving autumn-rains to find the sky.
He went on speaking.
                        "Marian, I being born
What men call noble, and you, issued from
The noble people,—though the tyrannous sword
Which pierced Christ's heart, has cleft the world in twain
'Twixt class and class, opposing rich to poor,
Shall we keep parted?   Not so.   Let us lean
And strain together rather, each to each,
Compress the red lips of this gaping wound
As far as two souls can,—ay, lean and league,
I from my superabundance,—from your want
You,—joining in a protest 'gainst the wrong
On both sides."

All the rest, he held her hand
In speaking, which confused the sense of much.
Her heart against his words beat out so thick,
They might as well be written on the dust
Where some poor bird, escaping from hawk's beak,
Has dropped and beats its shuddering wings,—the lines
Are rubbed so, yet 'twas something like to this,
—"That they two, standing at the two extremes
Of social classes, had received one seal,
Been dedicate and drawn beyond themselves
To mercy and ministration,—he, indeed,
Through what he knew, and she, through what she felt,
He, by man's conscience, she, by woman's heart,
Relinquishing their several 'vantage posts
Of wealthy ease and honourable toil,
To work with God at love. And since God willed
That putting out his hand to touch this ark
He found a woman's hand there, he'd accept
The sign too, hold the tender fingers fast,
And say, 'My fellow-worker, be my wife!'"

She told the tale with simple, rustic turns,—
Strong leaps of meaning in her sudden eyes
That took the gaps of any imperfect phrase
Of the unschooled speaker: I have rather writ
The thing I understood so, than the thing
I heard so. And I cannot render right
Her quick gesticulation, wild yet soft,
Self-startled from the habitual mood she used,
Half sad, half languid,—like dumb creatures (now
A rustling bird, and now a wandering deer,
Or squirrel 'gainst the oak-gloom flashing up
His sidelong burnished head, in just her way
Of savage spontaneity,) that stir
Abruptly the green silence of the woods,
And make it stranger, holier, more profound;

As Nature's general heart confessed itself
Of life, and then fell backward on repose.

I kissed the lips that ended.—"So indeed
He loves you, Marian?"
                        "Loves me!" She looked up
With a child's wonder when you ask him first
Who made the sun—a puzzled blush, that grew,
Then broke off in a rapid radiant smile
Of sure solution. "Loves me! he loves all,—
And me, of course. He had not asked me else
To work with him for ever and be his wife."

Her words reproved me. This perhaps was love—
To have its hands too full of gifts to give,
For putting out a hand to take a gift;
To love so much, the perfect round of love
Includes, in strict conclusion, being loved;
As Eden-dew went up and fell again,
Enough for watering Eden. Obviously
She had not thought about his love at all:
The cataracts of her soul had poured themselves,
And risen self-crowned in rainbow: would she ask
Who crowned her?—it sufficed that she was crowned.
With women of my class 'tis otherwise:
We haggle for the small change of our gold,
And so much love accord for so much love,
Rialto-prices. Are we therefore wrong?
If marriage be a contract, look to it then,
Contracting parties should be equal, just,
But if, a simple fealty on one side,
A mere religion,—right to give, is all,
And certain brides of Europe duly ask
To mount the pile as Indian widows do,
The spices of their tender youth heaped up,
The jewels of their gracious virtues worn,

More gems, more glory,—to consume entire
For a living husband: as the man's alive,
Not dead, the woman's duty by so much,
Advanced in England beyond Hindostan.

I sate there musing, till she touched my hand
With hers, as softly as a strange white bird
She feared to startle in touching. "You are kind
But are you, peradventure, vexed at heart
Because your cousin takes me for a wife?
I know I am not worthy—nay, in truth,
I'm glad on't, since, for that, he chooses me.
He likes the poor things of the world the best;
I would not therefore, if I could, be rich.
It pleasures him to stoop for buttercups;
I would not be a rose upon the wall
A queen might stop at, near the palace-door,
To say to a courtier, 'Pluck that rose for me,
It's prettier than the rest.' O Romney Leigh!
I'd rather far be trodden by his foot,
Than lie in a great queen's bosom."
                        Out of breath
She paused.
            "Sweet Marian, do you disavow
The roses with that face?"
                        She dropt her head
As if the wind had caught that flower of her
And bent it in the garden,—then looked up
With grave assurance. "Well, you think me bold!
But so we all are, when we're praying God.
And if I'm bold—yet, lady, credit me,
That, since I know myself for what I am,
Much fitter for his handmaid than his wife,
I'll prove the handmaid and the wife at once,
Serve tenderly, and love obediently,
And be a worthier mate, perhaps, than some

Who are wooed in silk among their learned books;
While I shall set myself to read his eyes,
Till such grow plainer to me than the French
To wisest ladies. Do you think I'll miss
A letter, in the spelling of his mind?
No more than they do when they sit and write
Their flying words with flickering wild-fowl tails,
Nor ever pause to ask how many *i*s,
Should that be *y* or *i*, they know 't so well:
I've seen them writing, when I brought a dress
And waited,—floating out their soft white hands
On shining paper. But they're hard sometimes,
For all those hands!—we've used out many nights,
And worn the yellow daylight into shreds
Which flapped and shivered down our aching eyes
Till night appeared more tolerable, just
That pretty ladies might look beautiful,
Who said at last .. "You're lazy in that house!
"You're slow in sending home the work,—I count
"I've waited near an hour for 't." Pardon me,
I do not blame them, madam, nor misprize;
They are fair and gracious; ay, but not like you,
Since none but you has Mister Leigh's own blood
Both noble and gentle,—and, without it .. well,
They are fair, I said; so fair, it scarce seems strange
That, flashing out in any looking-glass
The wonder of their glorious brows and breasts,
They're charmed so, they forget to look behind
And mark how pale we've grown we pitiful
Remainders of the world. And so perhaps
If Mister Leigh had chosen a wife from these,
She might, although he's better than her best
And dearly she would know it, steal a thought
Which should be all his, an eye-glance from his face,
To plunge into the mirror opposite
In search of her own beauty's pearl; while *I* ..

Ah, dearest lady, serge will outweigh silk
For winter-wear when bodies feel a-cold,
And I'll be a true wife to your cousin Leigh."

Before I answered he was there himself.
I think he had been standing in the room
And listened probably to half her talk,
Arrested, turned to stone,—as white as stone.
Will tender sayings make men look so white?
He loves her then profoundly.
       "You are here,
Aurora? Here I meet you!"—We clasped hands.

"Even so, dear Romney. Lady Waldemar
Has sent me in haste to find a cousin of mine
Who shall be."
    "Lady Waldemar is good."

"Here's one, at least, who is good," I sighed, and touched
Poor Marian's happy head, as doglike she
Most passionately patient, waited on,
A-tremble for her turn of greeting words;
"I've sate a full hour with your Marian Erle,
And learnt the thing by heart,—and from my heart
Am therefore competent to give you thanks
For such a cousin."
     "You accept at last
A gift from me, Aurora, without scorn?
At last I please you?"—How his voice was changed.

"You cannot please a woman against her will,
And once you vexed me. Shall we speak of that?
We'll say, then, you were noble in it all
And I not ignorant—let it pass! And now
You please me, Romney, when you please yourself;
So, please you, be fanatical in love,

And I'm well pleased.   Ah, cousin! at the old hall
Among the gallery portraits of our Leighs,
We shall not find a sweeter signory
Than this pure forehead's."
                            Not a word he said.
How arrogant men are!—Even philanthropists,
Who try to take a wife up in the way
They put down a subscription-cheque,—if once
She turns and says, "I will not tax you so,
Most charitable sir,"—feel ill at ease
As though she had wronged them somehow.   I suppose
We women should remember what we are,
And not throw back an obolus inscribed
With Cæsar's image, lightly.   I resumed.

"It strikes me, some of those sublime Vandykes
Were not too proud to make good saints in heaven;
And if so, then they're not too proud to-day,
To bow down (now the ruffs are off their necks)
And own this good, true, noble Marian, yours,
And mine, I'll say!—For poets (bear the word)
Half-poets even, are still whole democrats,—
Oh, not that we're disloyal to the high,
But loyal to the low, and cognisant
Of the less scrutable majesties.   For me,
I comprehend your choice, I justify
Your right in choosing."
                         "No, no, no," he sighed,
With a sort of melancholy impatient scorn,
As some grown man who never had a child
Puts by some child who plays at being a man,
"You did not, do not, cannot comprehend
My choice, my ends, my motives, nor myself:
No matter now: we'll let it pass, you say.
I thank you for your generous cousinship
Which helps this present; I accept for her
Your favourable thoughts.   We're fallen on days,

We two who are not poets, when to wed
Requires less mutual love than common love
For two together to bear out at once
Upon the loveless many. Work in pairs,
In galley-couplings or in marriage-rings,
The difference lies in the honour, not the work,—
And such we're bound to, I and she. But love,
(You poets are benighted in this age,
The hour's too late for catching even moths,
You've gnats instead,) love!—love's fool-paradise
Is out of date, like Adam's. Set a swan
To swim the Trenton, rather than true love
To float its fabulous plumage safely down
The cataracts of this loud transition-time,—
Whose roar for ever henceforth in my ears
Must keep me deaf to music."
       There, I turned
And kissed poor Marian, out of discontent.
The man had baffled, chafed me, till I flung
For refuge to the woman,—as, sometimes,
Impatient of some crowded room's close smell,
You throw a window open and lean out
To breathe a long breath in the dewy night
And cool your angry forehead. She, at least,
Was not built up as walls are, brick by brick,
Each fancy squared, each feeling ranged by line,
The very heat of burning youth applied
To indurate form and system! excellent bricks,
A well-built wall,—which stops you on the road,
And, into which, you cannot see an inch
Although you beat your head against it—pshaw!

"Adieu," I said, "for this time, cousins both,
And, cousin Romney, pardon me the word,
Be happy!—oh, in some esoteric sense
Of course!—I mean no harm in wishing well.
Adieu, my Marian:—may she come to me,

Dear Romney, and be married from my house?
It is not part of your philosophy
To keep your bird upon the blackthorn?"

"Ay,
He answered, "but it is. I take my wife
Directly from the people,—and she comes,
As Austria's daughter to imperial France,
Betwixt her eagles, blinking not her race,
From Margaret's Court at garret-height, to meet
And wed me at St. James's, nor put off
Her gown of serge for that. The things we do,
We do: we'll wear no mask, as if we blushed."

"Dear Romney, you're the poet," I replied,
But felt my smile too mournful for my word,
And turned and went. Ay, masks, I thought,—beware
Of tragic masks we tie before the glass,
Uplifted on the cothurn half a yard
Above the natural stature! we would play
Heroic parts to ourselves,—and end, perhaps,
As impotently as Athenian wives
Who shrieked in fits at the Eumenides.

His foot pursued me down the stair. "At least
You'll suffer me to walk with you beyond
These hideous streets, these graves, where men alive
Packed close with earthworms, burr unconsciously
About the plague that slew them; let me go.
The very women pelt their souls in mud
At any woman who walks here alone.
How came you here alone?—you are ignorant."

We had a strange and melancholy walk:
The night came drizzling downward in dark rain,
And, as we walked, the colour of the time,
The act, the presence, my hand upon his arm,
His voice in my ear, and mine to my own sense,

AURORA LEIGH.

Appeared unnatural. We talked modern books
And daily papers, Spanish marriage-schemes
And English climate—was 't so cold last year?
And will the wind change by to-morrow morn?
Can Guizot stand? is London full? is trade
Competitive? has Dickens turned his hinge
A-pinch upon the fingers of the great?
And are potatoes to grow mythical
Like moly? will the apple die out too?
Which way is the wind to-night? south-east? due east?
We talked on fast, while every common word
Seemed tangled with the thunder at one end,
And ready to pull down upon our heads
A terror out of sight. And yet to pause
Were surelier mortal: we tore greedily up
All silence, all the innocent breathing-points,
As if, like pale conspirators in haste,
We tore up papers where our signatures
Imperilled us to an ugly shame or death.

I cannot tell you why it was. 'Tis plain
We had not loved nor hated: wherefore dread
To spill gunpowder on ground safe from fire?
Perhaps we had lived too closely, to diverge
So absolutely: leave two clocks, they say,
Wound up to different hours, upon one shelf,
And slowly, through the interior wheels of each,
The blind mechanic motion sets itself
A-throb to feel out for the mutual time.
It was not so with us, indeed: while he
Struck midnight, I kept striking six at dawn,
While he marked judgment, I, redemption-day;
And such exception to a general law
Imperious upon inert matter even,
Might make us, each to either, insecure,
A beckoning mystery or a troubling fear.

I mind me, when we parted at the door,
How strange his good-night sounded,—like good-night
Beside a deathbed, where the morrow's sun
Is sure to come too late for more good-days.
And all that night I thought .. "Good-night," said he.

And so, a month passed. Let me set it down
At once,—I have been wrong, I have been wrong.
We are wrong always when we think too much
Of what we think or are: albeit our thoughts
Be verily bitter as self-sacrifice,
We're no less selfish. If we sleep on rocks
Or roses, sleeping past the hour of noon
We're lazy. This I write against myself.
I had done a duty in the visit paid
To Marian, and was ready otherwise
To give the witness of my presence and name
Whenever she should marry.—Which, I thought,
Sufficed. I even had cast into the scale
An overweight of justice toward the match;
The Lady Waldemar had missed her tool,
Had broken it in the lock as being too straight
For a crooked purpose, while poor Marian Erle
Missed nothing in my accents or my acts:
I had not been ungenerous on the whole,
Nor yet untender; so, enough. I felt
Tired, overworked: this marriage somewhat jarred;
Or, if it did not, all the bridal noise,
The pricking of the map of life with pins,
In schemes of .. "Here we'll go," and "There we'll stay,"
And "Everywhere we'll prosper in our love,"
Was scarce my business: let them order it;
Who else should care? I threw myself aside,
As one who had done her work and shuts her eyes
To rest the better.
              I, who should have known,

Forereckoned mischief! Where we disavow
Being keeper to our brother we're his Cain.

I might have held that poor child to my heart
A little longer! 'twould have hurt me much
To have hastened by its beats the marriage day,
And kept her safe meantime from tampering hands
Or, peradventure, traps. What drew me back
From telling Romney plainly the designs
Of Lady Waldemar, as spoken out
To me .. me? had I any right, ay, right,
With womanly compassion and reserve
To break the fall of woman's impudence?—
To stand by calmly, knowing what I knew,
And hear him call her *good?*

                      Distrust that word.
"There is none good save God," said Jesus Christ.
If He once, in the first creation-week,
Called creatures good,—for ever, afterward,
The Devil only has done it, and his heirs,
The knaves who win so, and the fools who lose;
The word's grown dangerous. In the middle age,
I think they called malignant fays and imps
Good people. A good neighbour, even in this,
Is fatal sometimes,—cuts your morning up
To mince-meat of the very smallest talk,
Then helps to sugar her bohea at night
With your reputation. I have known good wives,
As chaste, or nearly so, as Potiphar's;
And good, good mothers, who would use a child
To better an intrigue; good friends, beside,
(Very good) who hung succinctly round your neck
And sucked your breath, as cats are fabled to do
By sleeping infants. And we all have known
Good critics who have stamped out poet's hope,
Good statesmen who pulled ruin on the state,
Good patriots who for a theory risked a cause,

Good kings who disembowelled for a tax,
Good popes who brought all good to jeopardy,
Good Christians who sate still in easy chairs
And damned the general world for standing up.—
Now may the good God pardon all good men!

How bitterly I speak,—how certainly
The innocent white milk in us is turned,
By much persistent shining of the sun!—
Shake up the sweetest in us long enough
With men, it drops to foolish curd, too sour
To feed the most untender of Christ's lambs.

I should have thought,—a woman of the world
Like her I'm meaning, centre to herself,
Who has wheeled on her own pivot half a life
In isolated self-love and self-will,
As a windmill seen at distance radiating
Its delicate white vans against the sky,
So soft and soundless, simply beautiful,
Seen nearer,—what a roar and tear it makes,
How it grinds and bruises!—if she loves at last,
Her love 's a re-adjustment of self-love,
No more,—a need felt of another's use
To her one advantage, as the mill wants grain,
The fire wants fuel, the very wolf wants prey,
And none of these is more unscrupulous
Than such a charming woman when she loves.
She'll not be thwarted by an obstacle
So trifling as .. her soul is, .. much less yours!
Is God a consideration?—she loves you,
Not God; she will not flinch for Him indeed:
She did not for the Marchioness of Perth,
When wanting tickets for the fancy ball.
She loves you, sir, with passion, to lunacy,
She loves you like her diamonds .. almost.
                                          Well,

A month passed so, and then the notice came,
On such a day the marriage at the church.
I was not backward.
     Half Saint Giles in frieze
Was bidden to meet Saint James in cloth of gold,
And, after contract at the altar, pass
To eat a marriage-feast on Hampstead Heath.
Of course the people came in uncompelled,
Lame, blind, and worse—sick, sorrowful, and worse—
The humours of the peccant social wound
All pressed out, poured down upon Pimlico,
Exasperating the unaccustomed air
With a hideous interfusion. You'd suppose
A finished generation, dead of plague,
Swept outward from their graves into the sun,
The moil of death upon them. What a sight!
A holiday of miserable men
Is sadder than a burial-day of kings.

They clogged the streets, they oozed into the church
In a dark slow stream, like blood. To see that sight,
The noble ladies stood up in their pews,
Some pale for fear, a few as red for hate,
Some simply curious, some just insolent,
And some in wondering scorn,—"What next? what next?"
These crushed their delicate rose-lips from the smile
That misbecame them in a holy place,
With broidered hems of perfumed handkerchiefs;
Those passed the salts, with confidence of eyes
And simultaneous shiver of moiré silk;
While all the aisles, alive and black with heads,
Crawled slowly toward the altar from the street,
As bruised snakes crawl and hiss out of a hole
With shuddering involution, swaying slow
From right to left, and then from left to right,
In pants and pauses. What an ugly crest

Of faces rose upon you everywhere
From that crammed mass! you did not usually
See faces like them in the open day:
They hide in cellars, not to make you mad
As Romney Leigh is.—Faces!—O my God,
We call those, faces? men's and women's .. ay,
And children's;—babies, hanging like a rag
Forgotten on their mother's neck,—poor mouths,
Wiped clean of mother's milk by mother's blow
Before they are taught her cursing. Faces? .. phew,
We'll call them vices, festering to despairs,
Or sorrows, petrifying to vices: not
A finger-touch of God left whole on them,
All ruined, lost—the countenance worn out
As the garment, the will dissolute as the act,
The passions loose and draggling in the dirt
To trip a foot up at the first free step!
Those, faces? 'twas as if you had stirred up hell
To heave its lowest dreg-fiends uppermost
In fiery swirls of slime,—such strangled fronts,
Such obdurate jaws were thrown up constantly
To twit you with your race, corrupt your blood,
And grind to devilish colours all your dreams
Henceforth,—though, haply, you should drop asleep
By clink of silver waters, in a muse
On Raffael's mild Madonna of the Bird.

I've waked and slept through many nights and days
Since then,—but still that day will catch my breath
Like a nightmare. There are fatal days, indeed,
In which the fibrous years have taken root
So deeply, that they quiver to their tops
Whene'er you stir the dust of such a day.
My cousin met me with his eyes and hand,
And then, with just a word, .. that "Marian Erle
Was coming with her bridesmaids presently,"

Made haste to place me by the altar-stair
Where he and other noble gentlemen
And high-born ladies, waited for the bride.

We waited. It was early: there was time
For greeting and the morning's compliment,
And gradually a ripple of women's talk
Arose and fell and tossed about a spray
Of English *s*s, soft as a silent hush,
And, notwithstanding, quite as audible
As louder phrases thrown out by the men.
—"Yes, really, if we need to wait in church
We need to talk there."—"She? 'tis Lady Ayr,
In blue—not purple! that's the dowager."
—"She looks as young"—"She flirts as young, you mean.
Why if you had seen her upon Thursday night,
You'd call Miss Norris modest."—"*You* again!
I waltzed with you three hours back. Up at six,
Up still at ten; scarce time to change one's shoes;
I feel as white and sulky as a ghost.
So pray don't speak to me, Lord Belcher."—"No,
I'll look at you instead, and it's enough
While you have that face." "In church, my lord! fie, fie!
—"Adair, you stayed for the Division?"—"Lost
By one." "The devil it is! I'm sorry for 't.
And if I had not promised Mistress Grove" ..
"You might have kept your word to Liverpool."
—"Constituents must remember, after all,
We're mortal."—"We remind them of it,"—"Hark,
The bride comes! here she comes, in a stream of milk!"
—"There? Dear, you are asleep still; don't you know
The five Miss Granvilles? always dressed in white
To show they're ready to be married."—"Lower!
The aunt is at your elbow."—"Lady Maud,
Did Lady Waldemar tell you she had seen
This girl of Leigh's?" "No, –wait! 'twas Mistress Brookes,
Who told me Lady Waldemar told her—

No, 'twasn't Mistress Brookes."—"She's pretty?"—"Who?
Mistress Brookes? Lady Waldemar?"—"How hot!
Pray is't the law to-day we're not to breathe?
You're treading on my shawl—I thank you, sir."
—"They say the bride's a mere child, who can't read,
But knows the things she shouldn't, with wide-awake
Great eyes. I'd go through fire to look at her."
—"You do, I think."—"And Lady Waldemar
(You see her; sitting close to Romney Leigh.
How beautiful she looks, a little flushed!)
Has taken up the girl, and methodised
Leigh's folly. Should I have come here, you suppose,
Except she'd asked me?"—"She'd have served him more
By marrying him herself."
     "Ah—there she comes,
The bride, at last!"
     "Indeed, no. Past eleven.
She puts off her patched petticoat to-day
And puts on May-fair manners, so begins
By setting us to wait."—"Yes, yes, this Leigh
Was always odd; it's in the blood, I think;
His father's uncle's cousin's second son
Was, was .. you understand me; and for him,
He's stark,—has turned quite lunatic upon
This modern question of the poor—the poor.
An excellent subject when you're moderate;
You've seen Prince Albert's model lodging-house?
Does honour to his Royal Highness. Good!
But would he stop his carriage in Cheapside
To shake a common fellow by the fist
Whose name was .. Shakspeare? no. We draw a line,
And if we stand not by our order, we
In England, we fall headlong. Here's a sight,—
A hideous sight, a most indecent sight!
My wife would come, sir, or I had kept her back.
By heaven, sir, when poor Damiens' trunk and limbs
Were torn by horses, women of the court

Stood by and stared, exactly as to-day
On this dismembering of society,
With pretty, troubled faces."
                         "Now, at last.
She comes now."
                  "Where? who sees? you push me, sir,
Beyond the point of what is mannerly.
You're standing, madam, on my second flounce.
I do beseech you ..."
                    "No—it's not the bride.
Half-past eleven. How late. The bridegroom, mark,
Gets anxious and goes out."
                         "And as I said
These Leighs! our best blood running in the rut!
It's something awful. We had pardoned him
A simple misalliance got up aside
For a pair of sky-blue eyes; the House of Lords
Has winked at such things, and we've all been young
But here's an inter-marriage reasoned out,
A contract (carried boldly to the light
To challenge observation, pioneer
Good acts by a great example) 'twixt the extremes
Of martyrised society,—on the left
The well-born, on the right the merest mob,
To treat as equals!—'tis anarchical;
It means more than it says; 'tis damnable.
Why, sir, we can't have even our coffee good,
Unless we strain it."
                   "Here, Miss Leigh!"
                                    "Lord Howe,
You're Romney's friend. What's all this waiting for?"

"I cannot tell. The bride has lost her head
(And way, perhaps!) to prove her sympathy
With the bridegroom."
                    "What,—you also, disapprove!"

"Oh, *I* approve of nothing in the world,"
He answered, "not of you, still less of me,
Nor even of Romney, though he's worth us both.
We're all gone wrong. The tune in us is lost;
And whistling down back alleys to the moon
Will never catch it."
      Let me draw Lord Howe.
A born aristocrat, bred radical,
And educated socialist, who still
Goes floating, on traditions of his kind,
Across the theoretic flood from France,
Though, like a drenched Noah on a rotten deck,
Scarce safer for his place there. He, at least,
Will never land on Ararat, he knows,
To recommence the world on the new plan:
Indeed, he thinks, said world had better end,
He sympathises rather with the fish
Outside, than with the drowned paired beasts within
Who cannot couple again or multiply,—
And that's the sort of Noah he is, Lord Howe.
He never could be anything complete,
Except a loyal, upright gentleman,
A liberal landlord, graceful diner-out,
And entertainer more than hospitable,
Whom authors dine with and forget the hock.
Whatever he believes, and it is much,
But nowise certain, now here and now there,
He still has sympathies beyond his creed
Diverting him from action. In the House,
No party counts upon him, while for all
His speeches have a noticeable weight.
Men like his books too, (he has written books)
Which, safe to lie beside a bishop's chair,
At times outreach themselves with jets of fire
At which the foremost of the progressists
May warm audacious hands in passing by.
Of stature over-tall, lounging for ease;

Light hair, that seems to carry a wind in it,
And eyes that, when they look on you, will lean
Their whole weight, half in indolence and half
In wishing you unmitigated good,
Until you know not if to flinch from him
Or thank him.—'Tis Lord Howe.

       "We're all gone wrong,"
Said he, "and Romney, that dear friend of ours,
Is nowise right. There's one true thing on earth,
That's love! he takes it up, and dresses it,
And acts a play with it, as Hamlet did,
To show what cruel uncles we have been,
And how we should be uneasy in our minds
While he, Prince Hamlet, weds a pretty maid
(Who keeps us too long waiting, we'll confess)
By symbol, to instruct us formally
To fill the ditches up 'twixt class and class,
And live together in phalansteries.
What then?—he's mad, our Hamlet! clap his play,
And bind him."

    "Ah Lord Howe, this spectacle
Pulls stronger at us than the Dane's. See there!
The crammed aisles heave and strain and steam with life.
Dear Heaven, what life!"

      "Why, yes,—a poet sees;
Which makes him different from a common man.
I, too, see somewhat, though I cannot sing;
I should have been a poet, only that
My mother took fright at the ugly world,
And bore me tongue-tied. If you'll grant me now
That Romney gives us a fine actor-piece
To make us merry on his marriage-morn,
The fable's worse than Hamlet's I'll concede.
The terrible people, old and poor and blind,
Their eyes eat out with plague and poverty
From seeing beautiful and cheerful sights,
We'll liken to a brutalised King Lear,

Led out,—by no means to clear scores with wrongs —
His wrongs are so far back, he has forgot,
(All's past like youth;) but just to witness here
A simple contract,—he, upon his side,
And Regan with her sister Goneril
And all the dappled courtiers and court-fools
On their side. Not that any of these would say
They're sorry, neither. What is done, is done,
And violence is now turned privilege,
As cream turns cheese, if buried long enough.
What could such lovely ladies have to do
With the old man there, in those ill-odorous rags,
Except to keep the wind-side of him? Lear
Is flat and quiet, as a decent grave;
He does not curse his daughters in the least:
Be these his daughters? Lear is thinking of
His porridge chiefly .. is it getting cold
At Hampstead? will the ale be served in pots?
Poor Lear, poor daughters! Bravo, Romney's play."

A murmur and a movement drew around,
A naked whisper touched us. Something wrong.
What's wrong? The black crowd, as an overstrained
Cord, quivered in vibration, and I saw ..
Was that *his* face I saw? .. his .. Romney Leigh's ..
Which tossed a sudden horror like a sponge
Into all eyes,—while himself stood white upon
The topmost altar-stair and tried to speak,
And failed, and lifted higher above his head
A letter, .. as a man who drowns and gasps.

"My brothers, bear with me! I am very weak.
I meant but only good. Perhaps I meant
Too proudly, and God snatched the circumstance
And changed it therefore. There's no marriage—none.
She leaves me,—she departs,—she disappears,
I lose her. Yet I never forced her 'ay,'

To have her 'no' so cast into my teeth
In manner of an accusation, thus.
My friends, you are dismissed. Go, eat and drink
According to the programme,—and farewell!"

He ended. There was silence in the church.
We heard a baby sucking in its sleep
At the farthest end of the aisle. Then spoke a man,
"Now, look to it, coves, that all the beef and drink
Be not filched from us like the other fun,
For beer's spilt easier than a woman's lost!
This gentry is not honest with the poor;
They bring us up, to trick us."—"Go it, Jim,"
A woman screamed back,—"I'm a tender soul,
I never banged a child at two years old
And drew blood from him, but I sobbed for it
Next moment,—and I've had a plague of seven.
I'm tender; I've no stomach even for beef,
Until I know about the girl that's lost,
That's killed, mayhap. I did misdoubt, at first,
The fine lord meant no good by her or us.
He, maybe, got the upper hand of her
By holding up a wedding-ring, and then ..
A choking finger on her throat last night,
And just a clever tale to keep us still,
As she is, poor lost innocent. 'Disappear!'
Who ever disappears except a ghost?
And who believes a story of a ghost?
I ask you,—would a girl go off, instead
Of staying to be married? a fine tale!
A wicked man, I say, a wicked man!
For my part I would rather starve on gin
Than make my dinner on his beef and beer."
At which a cry rose up—"We'll have our rights.
We'll have the girl, the girl! Your ladies there
Are married safely and smoothly every day,
And *she* shall not drop through into a trap

Because she's poor and of the people: shame!
We'll have no tricks played off by gentlefolks;
We'll see her righted."
                        Through the rage and roar
I heard the broken words which Romney flung
Among the turbulent masses, from the ground
He held still with his masterful pale face,—
As huntsmen throw the ration to the pack,
Who, falling on it headlong, dog on dog
In heaps of fury, rend it, swallow it up
With yelling hound-jaws,—his indignant words,
His suppliant words, his most pathetic words,
Whereof I caught the meaning here and there
By his gesture .. torn in morsels, yelled across,
And so devoured. From end to end, the church
Rocked round us like the sea in storm, and then
Broke up like the earth in earthquake. Men cried out
'Police'—and women stood and shrieked for God,
Or dropt and swooned; or, like a herd of deer,
(For whom the black woods suddenly grow alive,
Unleashing their wild shadows down the wind
To hunt the creatures into corners, back
And forward) madly fled, or blindly fell,
Trod screeching underneath the feet of those
Who fled and screeched.
                        The last sight left to me
Was Romney's terrible calm face above
The tumult!—the last sound was "Pull him down!
Strike—kill him!" Stretching my unreasoning arms,
As men in dreams, who vainly interpose
'Twixt gods and their undoing, with a cry
I struggled to precipitate myself
Head-foremost to the rescue of my soul
In that white face, .. till some one caught me back,
And so the world went out,—I felt no more.

What followed was told after by Lord Howe,

Who bore me senseless from the strangling crowd
In church and street, and then returned alone
To see the tumult quelled. The men of law
Had fallen as thunder on a roaring fire,
And made all silent,—while the people's smoke
Passed eddying slowly from the emptied aisles.

Here's Marian's letter, which a ragged child
Brought running, just as Romney at the porch
Looked out expectant of the bride. He sent
The letter to me by his friend Lord Howe
Some two hours after, folded in a sheet
On which his well-known hand had left a word.
Here's Marian's letter.
                    "Noble friend, dear saint,
Be patient with me. Never think me vile,
Who might to-morrow morning be your wife
But that I loved you more than such a name.
Farewell, my Romney. Let me write it once,—
My Romney.
            "'Tis so pretty a coupled word,
I have no heart to pluck it with a blot.
We say 'my God' sometimes, upon our knees,
Who is not therefore vexed: so bear with it ..
And me. I know I'm foolish, weak, and vain;
Yet most of all I'm angry with myself
For losing your last footstep on the stair
That last time of your coming,—yesterday!
The very first time I lost step of yours,
(Its sweetness comes the next to what you speak)
But yesterday sobs took me by the throat
And cut me off from music.
                    "Mister Leigh,
You'll set me down as wrong in many things.
You've praised me, sir, for truth,—and now you'll learn
I had not courage to be rightly true.
I once began to tell you how she came,

The woman .. and you stared upon the floor
In one of your fixed thoughts .. which put me out
For that day. After, some one spoke of me,
So wisely, and of you, so tenderly,
Persuading me to silence for your sake ...
Well, well! it seems this moment I was wrong
In keeping back from telling you the truth:
There might be truth betwixt us two, at least,
If nothing else. And yet 'twas dangerous.
Suppose a real angel came from heaven
To live with men and women! he'd go mad,
If no considerate hand should tie a blind
Across his piercing eyes. 'Tis thus with you:
You see us too much in your heavenly light;
I always thought so, angel,—and indeed
There's danger that you beat yourself to death
Against the edges of this alien world,
In some divine and fluttering pity.

        "Yes,
It would be dreadful for a friend of yours,
To see all England thrust you out of doors
And mock you from the windows. You might say,
Or think (that's worse), 'There's some one in the house
I miss and love still.' Dreadful!

        "Very kind,
I pray you mark, was Lady Waldemar.
She came to see me nine times, rather ten —
So beautiful, she hurts one like the day
Let suddenly on sick eyes.

       "Most kind of all,
Your cousin!—ah, most like you! Ere you came
She kissed me mouth to mouth: I felt her soul
Dip through her serious lips in holy fire.
God help me, but it made me arrogant;
I almost told her that you would not lose
By taking me to wife: though ever since
I've pondered much a certain thing she asked ..

'He loves you, Marian?'.. in a sort of mild
Derisive sadness .. as a mother asks
Her babe, 'You'll touch that star, you think?'
                    "Farewell!
I know I never touched it.
                    "This is worst:
Babes grow and lose the hope of things above;
A silver threepence sets them leaping high—
But no more stars! mark that.
                    "I've writ all night
Yet told you nothing. God, if I could die,
And let this letter break off innocent
Just here! But no—for your sake ..
                    "Here's the last:
I never could be happy as your wife,
I never could be harmless as your friend,
I never will look more into your face
Till God says, 'Look!' I charge you, seek me not,
Nor vex yourself with lamentable thoughts
That peradventure I have come to grief;
Be sure I'm well, I'm merry, I'm at ease,
But such a long way, long way, long way off,
I think you'll find me sooner in my grave,
And that's my choice, observe. For what remains,
An over-generous friend will care for me
And keep me happy .. happier ..
                    "There's a blot!
This ink runs thick .. we light girls lightly weep ...
And keep me happier .. was the thing to say,
Than as your wife I could be.—O, my star,
My saint, my soul! for surely you're my soul,
Through whom God touched me! I am not so lost
I cannot thank you for the good you did,
The tears you stopped, which fell down bitterly,
Like these—the times you made me weep for joy
At hoping I should learn to write your notes
And save the tiring of your eyes, at night;

And most for that sweet thrice you kissed my lips
Saying 'Dear Marian.'
                    "'Twould be hard to read,
This letter, for a reader half as learn'd;
But you'll be sure to master it in spite
Of ups and downs. My hand shakes, I am blind;
I'm poor at writing at the best,—and yet
I tried to make my gs the way you showed.
Farewell. Christ love you.—Say 'poor Marian' now."

Poor Marian!—wanton Marian!—was it so,
Or so? For days, her touching, foolish lines
We mused on with conjectural fantasy,
As if some riddle of a summer-cloud
On which one tries unlike similitudes
Of now a spotted Hydra-skin cast off,
And now a screen of carven ivory
That shuts the heavens' conventual secrets up
From mortals over-bold. We sought the sense:
She loved him so perhaps (such words mean love,)
That, worked on by some shrewd perfidious tongue,
(And then I thought of Lady Waldemar)
She left him, not to hurt him; or perhaps
She loved one in her class,—or did not love,
But mused upon her wild bad tramping life
Until the free blood fluttered at her heart,
And black bread eaten by the road-side hedge
Seemed sweeter than being put to Romney's school
Of philanthropical self-sacrifice
Irrevocably.—Girls are girls, beside,
Thought I, and like a wedding by one rule.
You seldom catch these birds except with chaff:
They feel it almost an immoral thing
To go out and be married in broad day,
Unless some winning special flattery should
Excuse them to themselves for 't, . . "No one parts
Her hair with such a silver line as you,

One moonbeam from the forehead to the crown!"
Or else .. "You bite your lip in such a way,
It spoils me for the smiling of the rest,"
And so on. Then a worthless gaud or two
To keep for love,—a ribbon for the neck,
Or some glass pin—they have their weight with girls.

And Romney sought her many days and weeks:
He sifted all the refuse of the town,
Explored the trains, inquired among the ships,
And felt the country through from end to end;
No Marian!—Though I hinted what I knew, —
A friend of his had reasons of her own
For throwing back the match—he would not hear:
The lady had been ailing ever since,
The shock had harmed her. Something in his tone
Repressed me; something in me shamed my doubt
To a sigh repressed too. He went on to say
That, putting questions where his Marian lodged,
He found she had received for visitors,
Besides himself and Lady Waldemar
And, that once, me—a dubious woman dressed
Beyond us both: the rings upon her hands
Had dazed the children when she threw them pence;
"She wore her bonnet as the queen might hers,
To show the crown," they said,—"a scarlet crown
Of roses that had never been in bud."

When Romney told me that,—for now and then
He came to tell me how the search advanced,
His voice dropped: I bent forward for the rest:
The woman had been with her, it appeared,
At first from week to week, then day by day,
And last, 'twas sure ..
                    I looked upon the ground
To escape the anguish of his eyes, and asked
As low as when you speak to mourners new

Of those they cannot bear yet to call dead,
"If Marian had as much as named to him
A certain Rose, an early friend of hers,
A ruined creature."
                        "Never."—Starting up
He strode from side to side about the room,
Most like some prisoned lion sprung awake,
Who has felt the desert sting him through his dreams.
"What was I to her, that she should tell me aught?
A friend! was *I* a friend? I see all clear.
Such devils would pull angels out of heaven,
Provided they could reach them; 'tis their pride;
And that's the odds 'twixt soul and body-plague!
The veriest slave who drops in Cairo's street,
Cries, 'Stand off from me,' to the passengers;
While these blotched souls are eager to infect,
And blow their bad breath in a sister's face
As if they got some ease by it."
                                I broke through.
"Some natures catch no plagues. I've read of babes
Found whole and sleeping by the spotted breast
Of one a full day dead. I hold it true,
As I'm a woman and know womanhood,
That Marian Erle, however lured from place,
Deceived in way, keeps pure in aim and heart
As snow that's drifted from the garden-bank
To the open road."
                    'Twas hard to hear him laugh.
"The figure's happy. Well—a dozen carts
And trampers will secure you presently
A fine white snow-drift. Leave it there, your snow!
'Twill pass for soot ere sunset. Pure in aim?
She's pure in aim, I grant you,—like myself,
Who thought to take the world upon my back
To carry it o'er a chasm of social ill,
And end by letting slip through impotence
A single soul, a child's weight in a soul,

Straight down the pit of hell! yes, I and she
Have reason to be proud of our pure aims."
Then softly, as the last repenting drops
Of a thunder-shower, he added, "The poor child,
Poor Marian! 'twas a luckless day for her,
When first she chanced on my philanthropy."

He drew a chair beside me, and sate down;
And I, instinctively, as women use
Before a sweet friend's grief,—when, in his ear,
They hum the tune of comfort though themselves
Most ignorant of the special words of such,
And quiet so and fortify his brain
And give it time and strength for feeling out
To reach the availing sense beyond that sound,—
Went murmuring to him what, if written here,
Would seem not much, yet fetched him better help
Than peradventure if it had been more.

I've known the pregnant thinkers of our time,
And stood by breathless, hanging on their lips,
When some chromatic sequence of fine thought
In learned modulation phrased itself
To an unconjectured harmony of truth:
And yet I've been more moved, more raised, I say,
By a simple word .. a broken easy thing
A three-years infant might at need repeat,
A look, a sigh, a touch upon the palm,
Which meant less than "I love you," than by all
The full-voiced rhetoric of those master-mouths.

"Ah dear Aurora," he began at last,
His pale lips fumbling for a sort of smile,
"Your printer's devils have not spoilt your heart:
That's well. And who knows but, long years ago
When you and I talked, you were somewhat right
In being so peevish with me? You, at least,

Have ruined no one through your dreams. Instead,
You've helped the facile youth to live youth's day
With innocent distraction, still perhaps
Suggestive of things better than your rhymes.
The little shepherd-maiden, eight years old,
I've seen upon the mountains of Vaucluse,
Asleep i' the sun, her head upon her knees,
The flocks all scattered,—is more laudable
Than any sheep-dog trained imperfectly,
Who bites the kids through too much zeal."
                                                            "I look
As if I had slept, then?"
                                        He was touched at once
By something in my face. Indeed 'twas sure
That he and I, despite a year or two
Of younger life on my side, and on his
The heaping of the years' work on the days, ·
The three-hour speeches from the member's seat,
The hot committees in and out of doors,
The pamphlets, 'Arguments,' 'Collective Views,'
Tossed out as straw before sick houses, just
To show one's sick and so be trod to dirt
And no more use,—through this world's underground
The burrowing, groping effort, whence the arm
And heart come torn,—'twas sure that he and I
Were, after all, unequally fatigued;
That he, in his developed manhood, stood
A little sunburnt by the glare of life,
While I.. it seemed no sun had shone on me,
So many seasons I had missed my Springs.
My cheeks had pined and perished from their orbs,
And all the youth-blood in them had grown white
As dew on autumn cyclamens: alone
My eyes and forehead answered for my face.

He said, "Aurora, you are changed—are ill!"

"Not so, my cousin,—only not asleep,"
I answered, smiling gently. "Let it be.
You scarcely found the poet of Vaucluse
As drowsy as the shepherds. What is art
But life upon the larger scale, the higher,
When, graduating up in a spiral line
Of still expanding and ascending gyres,
It pushes toward the intense significance
Of all things, hungry for the Infinite?
Art's life,—and where we live, we suffer and toil."

He seemed to sift me with his painful eyes.
"You take it gravely, cousin; you refuse
Your dreamland's right of common, and green rest.
You break the mythic turf where danced the nymphs,
With crooked ploughs of actual life,—let in
The axes to the legendary woods,
To pay the poll-tax. You are fallen indeed
On evil days, you poets, if yourselves
Can praise that art of yours no otherwise;
And, if you cannot, .. better take a trade
And be of use: 'twere cheaper for your youth."

"Of use!" I softly echoed, "there's the point
We sweep about for ever in argument,
Like swallows which the exasperate, dying year
Sets spinning in black circles, round and round,
Preparing for far flights o'er unknown seas.
And we, where tend we?"
                                    "Where?" he said, and sighed.
"The whole creation, from the hour we are born,
Perplexes us with questions. Not a stone
But cries behind us, every weary step,
'Where, where?' I leave stones to reply to stones.
Enough for me and for my fleshly heart
To hearken the invocations of my kind,
When men catch hold upon my shuddering nerves

And shriek, 'What help? what hope? what bread i' the house,
What fire i' the frost?' There must be some response,
Though mine fail utterly. This social Sphinx
Who sits between the sepulchres and stews,
Makes mock and mow against the crystal heavens,
And bullies God,—exacts a word at least
From each man standing on the side of God,
However paying a sphinx-price for it.
We pay it also if we hold our peace,
In pangs and pity. Let me speak and die.
Alas, you'll say I speak and kill instead."

I pressed in there. "The best men, doing their best,
Know peradventure least of what they do:
Men usefullest i' the world are simply used;
The nail that holds the wood, must pierce it first,
And He alone who wields the hammer sees
The work advanced by the earliest blow. Take heart."

"Ah, if I could have taken yours!" he said,
"But that's past now." Then rising,—"I will take
At least your kindness and encouragement.
I thank you. Dear, be happy. Sing your songs,
If that's your way! but sometimes slumber too,
Nor tire too much with following, out of breath,
The rhymes upon your mountains of Delight.
Reflect, if Art be in truth the higher life,
You need the lower life to stand upon
In order to reach up unto that higher;
And none can stand a-tiptoe in the place
He cannot stand in with two stable feet.
Remember then!—for Art's sake, hold your life."

We parted so. I held him in respect.
I comprehended what he was in heart
And sacrificial greatness. Ay, but he
Supposed me a thing too small, to deign to know:

He blew me, plainly, from the crucible
As some intruding, interrupting fly,
Not worth the pains of his analysis
Absorbed on nobler subjects. Hurt a fly!
He would not for the world: he's pitiful
To flies even. "Sing," says he, "and tease me still,
If that's your way, poor insect." That's your way!

FIFTH BOOK.

Aurora Leigh, be humble. Shall I hope
To speak my poems in mysterious tune
With man and nature?—with the lava-lymph
That trickles from successive galaxies
Still drop by drop adown the finger of God
In still new worlds?—with summer-days in this
That scarce dare breathe they are so beautiful?
With spring's delicious trouble in the ground,
Tormented by the quickened blood of roots,
And softly pricked by golden crocus-sheaves
In token of the harvest-time of flowers?
With winters and with autumns,—and beyond
With the human heart's large seasons, when it hopes
And fears, joys, grieves, and loves?—with all that strain
Of sexual passion, which devours the flesh
In a sacrament of souls? with mother's breasts
Which, round the new-made creatures hanging there,
Throb luminous and harmonious like pure spheres?—
With multitudinous life, and finally
With the great escapings of ecstatic souls,
Who, in a rush of too long prisoned flame,
Their radiant faces upward, burn away
This dark of the body, issuing on a world
Beyond our mortal?—can I speak my verse
So plainly in tune to these things and the rest,
That men shall feel it catch them on the quick,
As having the same warrant over them
To hold and move them if they will or no,

Alike imperious as the primal rhythm
Of that theurgic nature?—I must fail,
Who fail at the beginning to hold and move
One man,—and he my cousin, and he my friend,
And he born tender, made intelligent,
Inclined to ponder the precipitous sides
Of difficult questions; yet, obtuse to *me*,
Of *me*, incurious! likes me very well,
And wishes me a paradise of good,
Good looks, good means, and good digestion,—ay,
But otherwise evades me, puts me off
With kindness, with a tolerant gentleness,—
Too light a book for a grave man's reading! Go,
Aurora Leigh: be humble.
      There it is,
We women are too apt to look to one,
Which proves a certain impotence in art.
We strain our natures at doing something great,
Far less because it's something great to do,
Than haply that we, so, commend ourselves
As being not small, and more appreciable
To some one friend. We must have mediators
Betwixt our highest conscience and the judge;
Some sweet saint's blood must quicken in our palms,
Or all the life in heaven seems slow and cold:
Good only being perceived as the end of good,
And God alone pleased,—that's too poor, we think.
And not enough for us by any means.
Ay—Romney, I remember, told me once
We miss the abstract when we comprehend.
We miss it most when we aspire,—and fail.

Yet, so, I will not.—This vile woman's way
Of trailing garments, shall not trip me up:
I'll have no traffic with the personal thought
In art's pure temple. Must I work in vain,
Without the approbation of a man?

It cannot be; it shall not. Fame itself,
That approbation of the general race,
Presents a poor end, (though the arrow speed,
Shot straight with vigorous finger to the white,)
And the highest fame was never reached except
By what was aimed above it. Art for art,
And good for God Himself, the essential Good!
We'll keep our aims sublime, our eyes erect,
Although our woman-hands should shake and fail;
And if we fail . . But must we?—
                      Shall I fail?
The Greeks said grandly in their tragic phrase,
"Let no one be called happy till his death."
To which I add,—Let no one till his death
Be called unhappy. Measure not the work
Until the day's out and the labour done,
Then bring your gauges. If the day's work's scant,
Why, call it scant; affect no compromise;
And, in that we have nobly striven at least,
Deal with us nobly, women though we be,
And honour us with truth if not with praise.

My ballads prospered; but the ballad's race
Is rapid for a poet who bears weights
Of thought and golden image. He can stand
Like Atlas, in the sonnet,—and support
His own heavens pregnant with dynastic stars;
But then he must stand still, nor take a step.

In that descriptive poem called "The Hills,"
The prospects were too far and indistinct.
'Tis true my critics said, "A fine view, that!"
The public scarcely cared to climb my book
For even the finest, and the public's right;
A tree's mere firewood, unless humanised,—
Which well the Greeks knew when they stirred its bark
With close-pressed bosoms of subsiding nymphs,

And made the forest-rivers garrulous
With babble of gods. For us, we are called to mark
A still more intimate humanity
In this inferior nature, or ourselves
Must fall like dead leaves trodden underfoot
By veritable artists. Earth (shut up
By Adam, like a fakir in a box
Left too long buried) remained stiff and dry,
A mere dumb corpse, till Christ the Lord came down,
Unlocked the doors, forced open the blank eyes,
And used his kingly chrism to straighten out
The leathery tongue turned back into the throat;
Since when, she lives, remembers, palpitates
In every limb, aspires in every breath,
Embraces infinite relations. Now
We want no half-gods, Panomphæan Joves,
Fauns, Naiads, Tritons, Oreads and the rest,
To take possession of a senseless world
To unnatural vampire-uses. See the earth,
The body of our body, the green earth,
Indubitably human like this flesh
And these articulated veins through which
Our heart drives blood. There's not a flower of spring
That dies ere June, but vaunts itself allied
By issue and symbol, by significance
And correspondence, to that spirit-world
Outside the limits of our space and time,
Whereto we are bound. Let poets give it voice
With human meanings,—else they miss the thought,
And henceforth step down lower, stand confessed
Instructed poorly for interpreters,
Thrown out by an easy cowslip in the text.

Even so my pastoral failed: it was a book
Of surface-pictures—pretty, cold, and false
With literal transcript,—the worse done, I think,
For being not ill-done: let me set my mark

Against such doings, and do otherwise.
This strikes me.—If the public whom we know
Could catch me at such admissions, I should pass
For being right modest. Yet how proud we are,
In daring to look down upon ourselves!

The critics say that epics have died out
With Agamemnon and the goat-nursed gods;
I'll not believe it. I could never deem
As Payne Knight did, (the mythic mountaineer
Who travelled higher than he was born to live,
And showed sometimes the goitre in his throat
Discoursing of an image seen through fog,)
That Homer's heroes measured twelve feet high.
They were but men:—his Helen's hair turned gray
Like any plain Miss Smith's who wears a front;
And Hector's infant whimpered at a plume
As yours last Friday at a turkey-cock.
All actual heroes are essential men,
And all men possible heroes: every age,
Heroic in proportions, double-faced,
Looks backward and before, expects a morn
And claims an epos.
     Ay, but every age
Appears to souls who live in 't (ask Carlyle)
Most unheroic. Ours, for instance, ours:
The thinkers scout it, and the poets abound
Who scorn to touch it with a finger-tip:
A pewter age,—mixed metal, silver-washed;
An age of scum, spooned off the richer past,
An age of patches for old gaberdines,
An age of mere transition, meaning nought
Except that what succeeds must shame it quite
If God please. That's wrong thinking, to my mind,
And wrong thoughts make poor poems.
       Every age,
Through being beheld too close, is ill-discerned

By those who have not lived past it. We'll suppose
Mount Athos carved, as Alexander schemed,
To some colossal statue of a man.
The peasants, gathering brushwood in his ear,
Had guessed as little as the browsing goats
Of form or feature of humanity
Up there,—in fact, had travelled five miles off
Or ere the giant image broke on them,
Full human profile, nose and chin distinct,
Mouth, muttering rhythms of silence up the sky
And fed at evening with the blood of suns;
Grand torso,—hand, that flung perpetually
The largesse of a silver river down
To all the country pastures. 'Tis even thus
With times we live in,—evermore too great
To be apprehended near.
     But poets should
Exert a double vision; should have eyes
To see near things as comprehensively
As if afar they took their point of sight,
And distant things as intimately deep
As if they touched them. Let us strive for this.
I do distrust the poet who discerns
No character or glory in his times,
And trundles back his soul five hundred years,
Past moat and drawbridge, into a castle-court,
To sing—oh, not of lizard or of toad
Alive i' the ditch there,—'twere excusable,
But of some black chief, half knight, half sheep-lifter
Some beauteous dame, half chattel and half queen,
As dead as must be, for the greater part,
The poems made on their chivalric bones;
And that's no wonder: death inherits death.

Nay, if there's room for poets in this world
A little overgrown, (I think there is)
Their sole work is to represent the age,

Their age, not Charlemagne's,—this live, throbbing age,
That brawls, cheats, maddens, calculates, aspires,
And spends more passion, more heroic heat,
Betwixt the mirrors of its drawing-rooms,
Than Roland with his knights at Roncesvalles.
To flinch from modern varnish, coat or flounce,
Cry out for togas and the picturesque,
Is fatal,—foolish too. King Arthur's self
Was commonplace to Lady Guenever;
And Camelot to minstrels seemed as flat
As Fleet Street to our poets.
      Never flinch,
But still, unscrupulously epic, catch
Upon the burning lava of a song
The full-veined, heaving, double-breasted Age:
That, when the next shall come, the men of that
May touch the impress with reverent hand, and say
"Behold,—behold the paps we all have sucked!
This bosom seems to beat still, or at least
It sets ours beating: this is living art,
Which thus presents and thus records true life."

What form is best for poems? Let me think
Of forms less, and the external. Trust the spirit,
As sovran nature does, to make the form;
For otherwise we only imprison spirit
And not embody. Inward evermore
To outward,—so in life, and so in art
Which still is life.
     Five acts to make a play.
And why not fifteen? why not ten? or seven?
What matter for the number of the leaves,
Supposing the tree lives and grows? exact
The literal unities of time and place,
When 'tis the essence of passion to ignore
Both time and place? Absurd. Keep up the fire,
And leave the generous flames to shape themselves.

'Tis true the stage requires obsequiousness
To this or that convention; "exit" here
And "enter" there; the points for clapping, fixed,
Like Jacob's white-peeled rods before the rams,
And all the close-curled imagery clipped
In manner of their fleece at shearing-time.
Forget to prick the galleries to the heart
Precisely at the fourth act,—culminate
Our five pyramidal acts with one act more,—
We're lost so: Shakspeare's ghost could scarcely plead
Against our just damnation. Stand aside;
We'll muse for comfort that, last century,
On this same tragic stage on which we have failed,
A wigless Hamlet would have failed the same.

And whosoever writes good poetry
Looks just to art. He does not write for you
Or me,—for London or for Edinburgh;
He will not suffer the best critic known
To step into his sunshine of free thought
And self-absorbed conception and exact
An inch-long swerving of the holy lines.
If virtue done for popularity
Defiles like vice, can art, for praise or hire,
Still keep its splendour and remain pure art?
Eschew such serfdom. What the poet writes,
He writes: mankind accepts it if it suits,
And that's success: if not, the poem's passed
From hand to hand, and yet from hand to hand,
Until the unborn snatch it, crying out
In pity on their fathers' being so dull,
And that's success too.

                I will write no plays;
Because the drama, less sublime in this,
Makes lower appeals, submits more menially,
Adopts the standard of the public taste

To chalk its height on, wears a dog-chain round
Its regal neck, and learns to carry and fetch
The fashions of the day to please the day,
Fawns close on pit and boxes, who clap hands
Commending chiefly its docility
And humour in stage-tricks,—or else indeed
Gets hissed at, howled at, stamped at like a dog,
Or worse, we'll say. For dogs, unjustly kicked,
Yell, bite at need; but if your dramatist
(Being wronged by some five hundred nobodies
Because their grosser brains most naturally
Misjudge the fineness of his subtle wit)
Shows teeth an almond's breadth, protests the length
Of a modest phrase,—"My gentle countrymen,
"There's something in it haply of your fault,"—
Why then, besides five hundred nobodies,
He'll have five thousand and five thousand more
Against him,—the whole public,—all the hoofs
Of King Saul's father's asses, in full drove,
And obviously deserve it. He appealed
To these,—and why say more if they condemn,
Than if they praise him?—Weep, my Æschylus
But low and far, upon Sicilian shores!
For since 'twas Athens (so I read the myth)
Who gave commission to that fatal weight
The tortoise, cold and hard, to drop on thee
And crush thee,—better cover thy bald head;
She'll hear the softest hum of Hyblan bee
Before thy loudest protestation!
                                        Then
The risk's still worse upon the modern stage.
I could not, for so little, accept success,
Nor would I risk so much, in case and calm,
For manifester gains: let those who prize,
Pursue them: I stand off. And yet, forbid,
That any irreverent fancy or conceit
Should litter in the Drama's throne-room where

The rulers of our art, in whose full veins
Dynastic glories mingle, sit in strength
And do their kingly work,—conceive, command,
And, from the imagination's crucial heat,
Catch up their men and women all a-flame
For action, all alive and forced to prove
Their life by living out heart, brain, and nerve,
Until mankind makes witness, "These be men
As we are," and vouchsafes the greeting due
To Imogen and Juliet—sweetest kin
On art's side.
    'Tis that, honouring to its worth
The drama, I would fear to keep it down
To the level of the footlights. Dies no more
The sacrificial goat, for Bacchus, slain,
His filmed eyes fluttered by the whirling white
Of choral vestures,—troubled in his blood,
While tragic voices that clanged keen as swords,
Leapt high together with the altar-flame
And made the blue air wink. The waxen mask,
Which set the grand still front of Themis' son
Upon the puckered visage of a player,—
The buskin, which he rose upon and moved,
As some tall ship first conscious of the wind
Sweeps slowly past the piers,—the mouthpiece, where
The mere man's voice with all its breaths and breaks
Went sheathed in brass, and clashed on even heights
Its phrasèd thunders,—these things are no more,
Which once were. And concluding, which is clear,
The growing drama has outgrown such toys
Of simulated stature, face, and speech,
It also peradventure may outgrow
The simulation of the painted scene,
Boards, actors, prompters, gaslight, and costume,
And take for a worthier stage the soul itself,
Its shifting fancies and celestial lights,

With all its grand orchestral silences
To keep the pauses of its rhythmic sounds.

Alas, I still see something to be done,
And what I do, falls short of what I see,
Though I waste myself on doing. Long green days,
Worn bare of grass and sunshine,—long calm nights,
From which the silken sleeps were fretted out,
Be witness for me, with no amateur's
Irreverent haste and busy idleness
I set myself to art! What then? what's done?
What's done, at last?
     Behold, at last, a book.
If life-blood's necessary, which it is,—
(By that blue vein athrob on Mahomet's brow,
Each prophet-poet's book must show man's blood!
If life-blood's fertilising, I wrung mine
On every leaf of this,—unless the drops
Slid heavily on one side and left it dry.
That chances often: many a fervid man
Writes books as cold and flat as grave-yard stones
From which the lichen's scraped; and if Saint Preux
Had written his own letters, as he might,
We had never wept to think of the little mole
'Neath Julie's drooping eyelid. Passion is
But something suffered, after all.
       While Art
Sets action on the top of suffering:
The artist's part is both to be and do,
Transfixing with a special, central power
The flat experience of the common man,
And turning outward, with a sudden wrench,
Half agony, half ecstasy, the thing
He feels the inmost,—never felt the less
Because he sings it. Does a torch less burn
For burning next reflectors of blue steel,

That *he* should be the colder for his place
'Twixt two incessant fires,—his personal life's
And that intense refraction which burns back
Perpetually against him from the round
Of crystal conscience he was born into
If artist-born? O sorrowful great gift
Conferred on poets, of a twofold life,
When one life has been found enough for pain!
We, staggering 'neath our burden as mere men,
Being called to stand up straight as demi-gods,
Support the intolerable strain and stress
Of the universal, and send clearly up
With voices broken by the human sob,
Our poems to find rhymes among the stars!
But soft,—a "poet" is a word soon said,
A book's a thing soon written. Nay, indeed,
The more the poet shall be questionable,
The more unquestionably comes his book.
And this of mine—well, granting to myself
Some passion in it,—furrowing up the flats,
Mere passion will not prove a volume worth
Its gall and rags even. Bubbles round a keel
Mean nought, excepting that the vessel moves.
There's more than passion goes to make a man
Or book, which is a man too.
      I am sad.
I wonder if Pygmalion had these doubts
And, feeling the hard marble first relent,
Grow supple to the straining of his arms,
And tingle through its cold to his burning lip,
Supposed his senses mocked, supposed the toil
Of stretching past the known and seen to reach
The archetypal Beauty out of sight,
Had made his heart beat fast enough for two,
And with his own life dazed and blinded him!
Not so; Pygmalion loved,—and whoso loves
Believes the impossible.

                        But I am sad:
I cannot thoroughly love a work of mine,
Since none seems worthy of my thought and hope
More highly mated. He has shot them down,
My Phœbus Apollo, soul within my soul,
Who judges, by the attempted, what's attained,
And with the silver arrow from his height
Has struck down all my works before my face
While I said nothing. Is there aught to say?
I called the artist but a greatened man.
He may be childless also, like a man.

I laboured on alone. The wind and dust
And sun of the world beat blistering in my face;
And hope, now for me, now against me, dragged
My spirits onward, as some fallen balloon,
Which, whether caught by blossoming tree or bare,
Is torn alike. I sometimes touched my aim,
Or seemed,—and generous souls cried out, "Be strong
Take courage; now you're on our level,—now!
The next step saves you!" I was flushed with praise,
But, pausing just a moment to draw breath,
I could not choose but murmur to myself
"Is this all? all that's done? and all that's gained?
If this then be success, 'tis dismaller
Than any failure."
                        O my God, my God,
O supreme Artist, who as sole return
For all the cosmic wonder of Thy work,
Demandest of us just a word .. a name,
"My Father!" thou hast knowledge, only thou,
How dreary 'tis for women to sit still
On winter nights by solitary fires
And hear the nations praising them far off,
Too far! ay, praising our quick sense of love,
Our very heart of passionate womanhood,
Which could not beat so in the verse without

Being present also in the unkissed lips
And eyes undried because there's none to ask
The reason they grew moist.
                     To sit alone
And think for comfort how, that very night,
Affianced lovers, leaning face to face
With sweet half-listenings for each other's breath,
Are reading haply from a page of ours,
To pause with a thrill (as if their cheeks had touched)
When such a stanza, level to their mood,
Seems floating their own thought out—"So I feel
For thee,"—"And I, for thee: this poet knows
What everlasting love is!"—how, that night,
Some father, issuing from the misty roads
Upon the luminous round of lamp and hearth
And happy children, having caught up first
The youngest there until it shrink and shriek
To feel the cold chin prick its dimples through
With winter from the hills, may throw i' the lap
Of the eldest, (who has learnt to drop her lids
To hide some sweetness newer than last year's)
Our book and cry, .. "Ah you, you care for rhymes;
So here be rhymes to pore on under trees,
When April comes to let you! I've been told
They are not idle as so many are,
But set hearts beating pure as well as fast.
'Tis yours, the book; I'll write your name in it,
That so you may not lose, however lost
In poet's lore and charming reverie,
The thought of how your father thought of *you*
In riding from the town."
                     To have our books
Appraised by love, associated with love,
While *we* sit loveless! is it hard, you think?
At least 'tis mournful. Fame, indeed, 'twas said,
Means simply love. It was a man said that:
And then, there's love and love: the love of all

(To risk in turn a woman's paradox,)
Is but a small thing to the love of one.
You bid a hungry child be satisfied
With a heritage of many corn-fields: nay,
He says he's hungry,—he would rather have
That little barley-cake you keep from him
While reckoning up his harvests. So with us;
(Here, Romney, too, we fail to generalise!)
We're hungry.
    Hungry! but it's pitiful
To wail like unweaned babes and suck our thumbs
Because we're hungry. Who, in all this world,
(Wherein we are haply set to pray and fast,
And learn what good is by its opposite)
Has never hungered? Woe to him who has found
The meal enough! if Ugolino's full,
His teeth have crunched some foul unnatural thing:
For here satiety proves penury
More utterly irremediable. And since
We needs must hunger,—better, for man's love,
Than God's truth! better, for companions sweet,
Than great convictions! let us bear our weights,
Preferring dreary hearths to desert souls.
Well, well! they say we're envious, we who rhyme;
But I, because I am a woman perhaps
And so rhyme ill, am ill at envying.
I never envied Graham his breadth of style,
Which gives you, with a random smutch or two,
(Near-sighted critics analyse to smutch)
Such delicate perspectives of full life:
Nor Belmore, for the unity of aim
To which he cuts his cedarn poems, fine
As sketchers do their pencils: nor Mark Gage,
For that caressing colour and trancing tone
Whereby you're swept away and melted in
The sensual element, which with a back wave
Restores you to the level of pure souls

And leaves you with Plotinus. None of these,
For native gifts or popular applause,
I've envied; but for this,—that when by chance
Says some one,—"There goes Belmore, a great man!
He leaves clean work behind him, and requires
No sweeper up of the chips,".. a girl I know,
Who answers nothing, save with her brown eyes,
Smiles unaware as if a guardian saint
Smiled in her:—for this, too,—that Gage comes home
And lays his last book's prodigal review
Upon his mother's knee, where, years ago,
He laid his childish spelling-book and learned
To chirp and peck the letters from her mouth,
As young birds must. "Well done," she murmured then;
She will not say it now more wonderingly:
And yet the last "Well done" will touch him more,
As catching up to-day and yesterday
In a perfect chord of love: and so, Mark Gage,
I envy you your mother!—and you, Graham,
Because you have a wife who loves you so,
She half forgets, at moments, to be proud
Of being Graham's wife, until a friend observes,
"The boy here, has his father's massive brow,
Done small in wax .. if we push back the curls."

Who loves me? Dearest father,—mother sweet,—
I speak the names out sometimes by myself,
And make the silence shiver. They sound strange,
As Hindostanee to an Ind-born man
Accustomed many years to English speech;
Or lovely poet-words grown obsolete,
Which will not leave off singing. Up in heaven
I have my father,—with my mother's face
Beside him in a blotch of heavenly light;
No more for earth's familiar, household use,
No more. The best verse written by this hand,
Can never reach them where they sit, to seem

Well-done to *them*. Death quite unfellows us,
Sets dreadful odds betwixt the live and dead,
And makes us part as those at Babel did
Through sudden ignorance of a common tongue.
A living Cæsar would not dare to play
At bowls with such as my dead father is.

And yet this may be less so than appears,
This change and separation. Sparrows five
For just two farthings, and God cares for each.
If God is not too great for little cares,
Is any creature, because gone to God?
I've seen some men, veracious, nowise mad,
Who have thought or dreamed, declared and testified,
They heard the Dead a-ticking like a clock
Which strikes the hours of the eternities,
Beside them, with their natural ears,—and known
That human spirits feel the human way
And hate the unreasoning awe which waves them off
From possible communion. It may be.

At least, earth separates as well as heaven,
For instance, I have not seen Romney Leigh
Full eighteen months .. add six, you get two years.
They say he's very busy with good works,—
Has parted Leigh Hall into almshouses.
He made one day an alms house of his heart,
Which ever since is loose upon the latch
For those who pull the string.—I never did.

It always makes me sad to go abroad,
And now I'm sadder that I went to-night
Among the lights and talkers at Lord Howe's.
His wife is gracious, with her glossy braids,
And even voice, and gorgeous eyeballs, calm
As her other jewels. If she's somewhat cold,
Who wonders, when her blood has stood so long

In the ducal reservoir she calls her line
By no means arrogantly! she's not proud;
Not prouder than the swan is of the lake
He has always swum in;—'tis her element;
And so she takes it with a natural grace,
Ignoring tadpoles. She just knows perhaps
There *are* who travel without outriders,
Which isn't her fault. Ah, to watch her face,
When good Lord Howe expounds his theories
Of social justice and equality!
'Tis curious, what a tender, tolerant bend
Her neck takes: for she loves him, likes his talk,
"Such clever talk—that dear, odd Algernon!"
She listens on, exactly as if he talked
Some Scandinavian myth of Lemures,
Too pretty to dispute, and too absurd.

She's gracious to me as her husband's friend,
And would be gracious, were I not a Leigh,
Being used to smile just so, without her eyes,
On Joseph Strangways, the Leeds mesmerist,
And Delia Dobbs, the lecturer from "the States"
Upon the "Woman's question.' Then, for him,
I like him; he's my friend. And all the rooms
Were full of crinkling silks that swept about
The fine dust of most subtle courtesies..
What then?—why then, we come home to be sad.

How lovely, One I love not looked to-night!
She's very pretty, Lady Waldemar.
Her maid must use both hands to twist that coil
Of tresses, then be careful lest the rich
Bronze rounds should slip:—she missed, though, a gray hair,
A single one,—I saw it; otherwise
The woman looked immortal. How they told,
Those alabaster shoulders and bare breasts,
On which the pearls, drowned out of sight in milk,

Were lost, excepting for the ruby-clasp!
They split the amaranth velvet-bodice down
To the waist or nearly, with the audacious press
Of full-breathed beauty. If the heart within
Were half as white!—but, if it were, perhaps
The breast were closer covered and the sight
Less aspectable, by half, too.
       I heard
The young man with the German student's look—
A sharp face, like a knife in a cleft stick,
Which shot up straight against the parting line
So equally dividing the long hair,—
Say softly to his neighbour, (thirty-five
And mediæval) "Look that way, Sir Blaise.
She's Lady Waldemar—to the left,—in red—
Whom Romney Leigh, our ablest man just now,
Is soon about to marry."
      Then replied
Sir Blaise Delorme, with quiet, priestlike voice,
Too used to syllable damnations round
To make a natural emphasis worth while:
"Is Leigh your ablest man? the same, I think,
Once jilted by a recreant pretty maid
Adopted from the people? Now, in change,
He seems to have plucked a flower from the other side
Of the social hedge."
     "A flower, a flower," exclaimed
My German student,—his own eyes full-blown
Bent on her. He was twenty, certainly.

Sir Blaise resumed with gentle arrogance,
As if he had dropped his alms into a hat
And gained the right to counsel,—"My young friend,
I doubt your ablest man's ability
To get the least good or help meet for him,
For pagan phalanstery or Christian home,
From such a flowery creature."

"Beautiful!"
My student murmured rapt,—"Mark how she stirs!
Just waves her head, as if a flower indeed,
Touched far off by the vain breath of our talk."

At which that bilious Grimwald, (he who writes
For the Renovator) who had seemed absorbed
Upon the table-book of autographs,
(I dare say mentally he crunched the bones
Of all those writers, wishing them alive
To feel his tooth in earnest) turned short round
With low carnivorous laugh,—"A flower, of course!
She neither sews nor spins,—and takes no thought
Of her garments .. falling off."
       The student flinched;
Sir Blaise, the same; then both, drawing back their chairs
As if they spied black-beetles on the floor,
Pursued their talk, without a word being thrown
To the critic.
    Good Sir Blaise's brow is high
And noticeably narrow: a strong wind,
You fancy, might unroof him suddenly,
And blow that great top attic off his head
So piled with feudal relics. You admire
His nose in profile, though you miss his chin;
But, though you miss his chin, you seldom miss
His ebon cross worn innermostly, (carved
For penance by a saintly Styrian monk
Whose flesh was too much with him,) slipping through
Some unaware unbuttoned casualty
Of the under-waistcoat. With an absent air
Sir Blaise sate fingering it and speaking low,
While I, upon the sofa, heard it all.

"My dear young friend, if we could bear our eyes,
Like blessedest Saint Lucy, on a plate,
They would not trick us into choosing wives,

As doublets, by the colour. Otherwise
Our fathers chose,—and therefore, when they had hung
Their household keys about a lady's waist,
The sense of duty gave her dignity;
She kept her bosom holy to her babes,
And, if a moralist reproved her dress,
'Twas, "Too much starch!"—and not, "Too little lawn!"

"Now, pshaw!" returned the other in a heat,
A little fretted by being called "young friend,"
Or so I took it,—"for Saint Lucy's sake,
If she's the saint to swear by, let us leave
Our fathers,—plagued enough about our sons!"
(He stroked his beardless chin) "yes, plagued, sir, plagued:
The future generations lie on us
As heavy as the nightmare of a seer;
Our meat and drink grow painful prophecy:
I ask you,—have we leisure, if we liked,
To hollow out our weary hands to keep
Your intermittent rushlight of the past
From draughts in lobbies? Prejudice of sex
And marriage-law .. the socket drops them through
While we two speak,—however may protest
Some over-delicate nostrils like your own,
'Gainst odours thence arising."
                          "You are young,"
Sir Blaise objected.
                "If I am," he said
With fire,—"though somewhat less so than I seem,
The young run on before, and see the thing
That's coming. Reverence for the young, I cry.
In that new church for which the world's near ripe,
You'll have the younger in the Elder's chair,
Presiding with his ivory front of hope
O'er foreheads clawed by cruel carrion-birds
Of life's experience."
                  "Pray your blessing, sir,"

Sir Blaise replied good-humouredly,—"I plucked
A silver hair this morning from my beard,
Which left me your inferior. Would I were
Eighteen and worthy to admonish you!
If young men of your order run before
To see such sights as sexual prejudice
And marriage-law dissolved,—in plainer words,
A general concubinage expressed
In a universal pruriency,—the thing
Is scarce worth running fast for, and you'd gain
By loitering with your elders."

                     "Ah," he said,
"Who, getting to the top of Pisgah-hill,
Can talk with one at bottom of the view,
To make it comprehensible? Why, Leigh
Himself, although our ablest man, I said,
Is scarce advanced to see as far as this,
Which some are: he takes up imperfectly
The social question—by one handle—leaves
The rest to trail. A Christian socialist
Is Romney Leigh, you understand."

                          "Not I.
I disbelieve in Christian-pagans, much
As you in women-fishes. If we mix
Two colours, we lose both, and make a third
Distinct from either. Mark you! to mistake
A colour is the sign of a sick brain,
And mine, I thank the saints, is clear and cool:
A neutral tint is here impossible.
The church,—and by the church, I mean of course
The catholic, apostolic, mother-church,—
Draws lines as plain and straight as her own wall
Inside of which, are Christians, obviously,
And outside .. dogs."

                     "We thank you. Well I know
The ancient mother-church would fain still bite,
For all her toothless gums,—as Leigh himself

Would fain be a Christian still, for all his wit.
Pass that; you two may settle it, for me.
You're slow in England. In a month I learnt
At Göttingen enough philosophy
To stock your English schools for fifty years;
Pass that, too. Here alone, I stop you short,
—Supposing a true man like Leigh could stand
Unequal in the stature of his life
To the height of his opinions. Choose a wife
Because of a smooth skin?—not he, not he!
He'd rail at Venus' self for creaking shoes,
Unless she walked his way of righteousness:
And if he takes a Venus Meretrix,
(No imputation on the lady there)
Be sure that, by some sleight of Christian art,
He has metamorphosed and converted her
To a Blessed Virgin."

"Soft!" Sir Blaise drew breath
As if it hurt him,—"Soft! no blasphemy,
I pray you!"

"The first Christians did the thing:
Why not the last?" asked he of Göttingen,
With just that shade of sneering on the lip,
Compensates for the lagging of the beard,—
"And so the case is. If that fairest fair
Is talked of as the future wife of Leigh,
She's talked of too, at least as certainly,
As Leigh's disciple. You may find her name
On all his missions and commissions, schools,
Asylums, hospitals,—he had her down,
With other ladies whom her starry lead
Persuaded from their spheres, to his country-place
In Shropshire, to the famed phalanstery
At Leigh Hall, christianised from Fourier's own,
(In which he has planted out his sapling stocks
Of knowledge into social nurseries)
And there, they say, she has tarried half a week,

And milked the cows, and churned, and pressed the curd,
And said 'my sister' to the lowest drab
Of all the assembled castaways; such girls!
Ay, sided with them at the washing-tub—
Conceive, Sir Blaise, those naked perfect arms,
Round glittering arms, plunged elbow-deep in suds,
Like wild swans hid in lilies all a-shake."

Lord Howe came up. "What, talking poetry
So near the image of the unfavouring Muse?
That's you, Miss Leigh: I've watched you half an hour,
Precisely as I watched the statue called
A Pallas in the Vatican;—you mind
The face, Sir Blaise!—intensely calm and sad,
As wisdom cut it off from fellowship,—
But *that* spoke louder. Not a word from *you!*
And these two gentlemen were bold, I marked,
And unabashed by even your silence."
                                    "Ah,"
Said I, "my dear Lord Howe, you shall not speak
To a printing woman who has lost her place,
(The sweet safe corner of the household fire
Behind the heads of children) compliments,
As if she were a woman. We who have clipt
The curls before our eyes, may see at least
As plain as men do. Speak out, man to man,
No compliments, beseech you."
                                    "Friend to friend,
Let that be. We are sad to-night, I saw,
(—Good night, Sir Blaise! ah, Smith—he has slipped away)
I saw you across the room, and stayed, Miss Leigh,
To keep a crowd of lion-hunters off,
With faces toward your jungle. There were three;
A spacious lady, five feet ten and fat,
Who has the devil in her (and there's room)
For walking to and fro upon the earth,
From Chipewa to China; she requires

Your autograph upon a tinted leaf
'Twixt Queen Pomare's and Emperor Soulouque's.
Pray give it; she has energies, though fat:
For me, I'd rather see a rick on fire
Than such a woman angry. Then a youth
Fresh from the backwoods, green as the underboughs,
Asks modestly, Miss Leigh, to kiss your shoe,
And adds, he has an epic in twelve parts,
Which when you've read, you'll do it for his boot:
All which I saved you, and absorb next week
Both manuscript and man,—because a lord
Is still more potent than a poetess
With any extreme republican. Ah, ah,
You smile, at last, then."
                         "Thank you."
                                     "Leave the smile.
I'll lose the thanks for 't,—ay, and throw you in
My transatlantic girl, with golden eyes,
That draw you to her splendid whiteness as
The pistil of a water-lily draws,
Adust with gold. Those girls across the sea
Are tyrannously pretty,—and I swore
(She seemed to me an innocent, frank girl)
To bring her to you for a woman's kiss,
Not now, but on some other day or week:
—We'll call it perjury; I give her up."

"No, bring her."
                "Now," said he, "you make it hard
To touch such goodness with a grimy palm.
I thought to tease you well, and fret you cross,
And steel myself, when rightly vexed with you,
For telling you a thing to tease you more."

"Of Romney?"
            "No, no; nothing worse," he cried,
"Of Romney Leigh than what is buzzed about,—

That *he* is taken in an eye-trap too,
Like many half as wise. The thing I mean
Refers to you, not him."
                        "Refers to me."

He echoed,—"Me!" You sound it like a stone
Dropped down a dry well very listlessly
By one who never thinks about the toad
Alive at the bottom. Presently perhaps
You'll sound your "me" more proudly—till I shrink.

"Lord Howe's the toad, then, in this question?"
                                        "Brief,
We'll take it graver. Give me sofa-room,
And quiet hearing. You know Eglinton,
John Eglinton, of Eglinton in Kent?"

"Is *he* the toad?—he's rather like the snail,
Known chiefly for the house upon his back:
Divide the man and house—you kill the man;
That's Eglinton of Eglinton, Lord Howe."

He answered grave. "A reputable man,
An excellent landlord of the olden stamp
If somewhat slack in new philanthropies,
Who keeps his birthdays with a tenants' dance,
Is hard upon them when they miss the church
Or hold their children back from catechism,
But not ungentle when the aged poor
Pick sticks at hedge-sides: nay, I've heard him say,
'The old dame has a twinge because she stoops;
'That's punishment enough for felony.'"

"O tender-hearted landlord! may I take
My long lease with him, when the time arrives
For gathering winter-faggots!"
                        "He likes art,

Buys books and pictures .. of a certain kind;
Neglects no patent duty; a good son" . . .

"To a most obedient mother. Born to wear
His father's shoes, he wears her husband's too:
Indeed I've heard it's touching. Dear Lord Howe,
You shall not praise *me* so against your heart,
When I'm at worst for praise and faggots."
                                    "Be
Less bitter with me, for .. in short," he said,
"I have a letter, which he urged me so
To bring you .. I could scarcely choose but yield;
Insisting that a new love, passing through
The hand of an old friendship, caught from it
Some reconciling odour."
                    "Love, you say?
My lord, I cannot love: I only find
The rhyme for love,—and that's not love, my lord.
Take back your letter."
                    "Pause: you'll read it first?"

"I will not read it: it is stereotyped;
The same he wrote to,—anybody's name,
Anne Blythe the actress, when she died so true,
A duchess fainted in a private box:
Pauline the dancer, after the great *pas*
In which her little feet winked overhead
Like other fire-flies, and amazed the pit:
Or Baldinacci, when her F in alt
Had touched the silver tops of heaven itself
With such a pungent spirit-dart, the Queen
Laid softly, each to each, her white-gloved palms,
And sighed for joy: or else (I thank your friend)
Aurora Leigh,—when some indifferent rhymes,
Like those the boys sang round the holy ox
On Memphis-highway, chance perhaps to set
Our Apis-public lowing. Oh, he wants,

Instead of any worthy wife at home,
A star upon his stage of Eglinton?
Advise him that he is not overshrewd
In being so little modest: a dropped star
Makes bitter waters, says a Book I've read,—
And there's his unread letter."
                              "My dear friend,"
Lord Howe began ..

                    In haste I tore the phrase.
"You mean your friend of Eglinton, or me?"

"I mean you, you," he answered with some fire.
"A happy life means prudent compromise;
The tare runs through the farmer's garnered sheaves,
And though the gleaner's apron holds pure wheat
We count her poorer. Tare with wheat, we cry,
And good with drawbacks. You, you love your art,
And, certain of vocation, set your soul
On utterance. Only, in this world we have made,
(They say God made it first, but if He did
'Twas so long since, and, since, we have spoiled it so,
He scarce would know it, if He looked this way,
From hells we preach of, with the flames blown out,)
—In this bad, twisted, topsy-turvy world
Where all the heaviest wrongs get uppermost,—
In this uneven, unfostering England here,
Where ledger-strokes and sword-strokes count indeed,
But soul-strokes merely tell upon the flesh
They strike from,—it is hard to stand for art,
Unless some golden tripod from the sea
Be fished up, by Apollo's divine chance,
To throne such feet as yours, my prophetess,
At Delphi. Think,—the god comes down as fierce
As twenty bloodhounds, shakes you, strangles you,
Until the oracular shriek shall ooze in froth!
At best 'tis not all ease,—at worst too hard:

A place to stand on is a 'vantage gained,
And here's your tripod. To be plain, dear friend,
You're poor, except in what you richly give;
You labour for your own bread painfully,
Or ere you pour our wine. For art's sake, pause."

I answered slow,—as some wayfaring man,
Who feels himself at night too far from home,
Makes stedfast face against the bitter wind.
"Is art so less a thing than virtue is,
That artists first must cater for their ease
Or ever they make issue past themselves
To generous use? alas, and is it so,
That we, who would be somewhat clean, must sweep
Our ways as well as walk them, and no friend
Confirm us nobly,—"Leave results to God,
But you, be clean?" What! "prudent compromise
Makes acceptable life," you say instead,
You, you, Lord Howe?—in things indifferent, well.
For instance, compromise the wheaten bread
For rye, the meat for lentils, silk for serge,
And sleep on down, if needs, for sleep on straw;
But there, end compromise. I will not bate
One artist-dream on straw or down, my lord,
Nor pinch my liberal soul, though I be poor,
Nor cease to love high, though I live thus low."

So speaking, with less anger in my voice
Than sorrow, I rose quickly to depart;
While he, thrown back upon the noble shame
Of such high-stumbling natures, murmured words,
The right words after wrong ones. Ah, the man
Is worthy, but so given to entertain
Impossible plans of superhuman life,—
He sets his virtues on so raised a shelf,
To keep them at the grand millennial height,
He has to mount a stool to get at them;

And, meantime, lives on quite the common way,
With everybody's morals.
                    As we passed,
Lord Howe insisting that his friendly arm
Should oar me across the sparkling brawling stream
Which swept from room to room,—we fell at once
On Lady Waldemar. "Miss Leigh," she said,
And gave me such a smile, so cold and bright,
As if she tried it in a 'tiring glass
And liked it; "all to-night I've strained at you
As babes at baubles held up out of reach
By spiteful nurses, ('Never snatch,' they say,)
And there you sate, most perfectly shut in
By good Sir Blaise and clever Mister Smith
And then our dear Lord Howe! at last indeed
I almost snatched. I have a world to speak
About your cousin's place in Shropshire where
I've been to see his work .. our work,—you heard
I went? .. and of a letter yesterday,
In which if I should read a page or two
You might feel interest, though you're locked of course
In literary toil.—You'll like to hear
Your last book lies at the phalanstery,
As judged innocuous for the elder girls
And younger women who still care for books.
We all must read, you see, before we live,
Till slowly the ineffable light comes up
And, as it deepens, drowns the written word,—
So said your cousin, while we stood and felt
A sunset from his favourite beech-tree seat.
He might have been a poet if he would,
But then he saw the higher thing at once
And climbed to it. I think he looks well now,
Has quite got over that unfortunate ..
Ah, ah .. I know it moved you. Tender-heart!
You took a liking to the wretched girl.
Perhaps you thought the marriage suitable,

Who knows? a poet hankers for romance,
And so on. As for Romney Leigh, 'tis sure
He never loved her,—never. By the way,
You have not heard of *her* .. ? quite out of sight,
And out of saving? lost in every sense?"

She might have gone on talking half an hour
And I stood still, and cold, and pale, I think,
As a garden-statue a child pelts with snow
For pretty pastime. Every now and then
I put in "yes" or "no," I scarce knew why;
The blind man walks wherever the dog pulls,
And so I answered. Till Lord Howe broke in;
"What penance takes the wretch who interrupts
The talk of charming women? I, at last,
Must brave it. Pardon, Lady Waldemar!
The lady on my arm is tired, unwell,
And loyally I've promised she shall say
No harder word this evening, than .. goodnight;
The rest her face speaks for her."—Then we went.

And I breathe large at home. I drop my cloak,
Unclasp my girdle, loose the band that ties
My hair .. now could I but unloose my soul!
We are sepulchred alive in this close world,
And want more room.
     The charming woman there—
This reckoning up and writing down her talk
Affects me singularly. How she talked
To pain me! woman's spite.—You wear steel-mail;
A woman takes a housewife from her breast
And plucks the delicatest needle out
As 'twere a rose, and pricks you carefully
'Neath nails, 'neath eyelids, in your nostrils,—say,
A beast would roar so tortured,—but a man,
A human creature, must not, shall not flinch,
No, not for shame.

                        What vexes, after all,
Is just that such as she, with such as I,
Knows how to vex. Sweet heaven, she takes me up
As if she had fingered me and dog-eared me
And spelled me by the fireside half a life!
She knows my turns, my feeble points.—What then?
The knowledge of a thing implies the thing;
Of course, she found *that* in me, she saw *that*,
Her pencil underscored *this* for a fault,
And I, still ignorant. Shut the book up,—close!
And crush that beetle in the leaves.
                                        O heart,
At last we shall grow hard too, like the rest,
And call it self-defence because we are soft.

And after all, now, .. why should I be pained
That Romney Leigh, my cousin, should espouse
This Lady Waldemar? And, say, she held
Her newly-blossomed gladness in my face, ..
'Twas natural surely, if not generous,
Considering how, when winter held her fast,
I helped the frost with mine, and pained her more
Than she pains me. Pains me!—but wherefore pained
'Tis clear my cousin Romney wants a wife,—
So, good!—The man's need of the woman, here,
Is greater than the woman's of the man,
And easier served; for where the man discerns
A sex, (ah, ah, the man can generalise,
Said he) we see but one, ideally
And really: where we yearn to lose ourselves
And melt like white pearls in another's wine,
He seeks to double himself by what he loves,
And make his drink more costly by our pearls.
At board, at bed, at work and holiday,
It is not good for man to be alone,
And that's his way of thinking, first and last
And thus my cousin Romney wants a wife.

But then my cousin sets his dignity
On personal virtue. If he understands
By love, like others, self-aggrandisement,
It is that he may verily be great
By doing rightly and kindly. Once he thought,
For charitable ends set duly forth
In Heaven's white judgment-book, to marry .. ah,
We'll call her name Aurora Leigh, although
She's changed since then!—and once, for social ends,
Poor Marian Erle, my sister Marian Erle,
My woodland sister, sweet maid Marian,
Whose memory moans on in me like the wind
Through ill-shut casements, making me more sad
Than ever I find reasons for. Alas,
Poor pretty plaintive face, embodied ghost!
He finds it easy then, to clap thee off
From pulling at his sleeve and book and pen,—
He locks thee out at night into the cold
Away from butting with thy horny eyes
Against his crystal dreams, that now he's strong
To love anew? that Lady Waldemar
Succeeds my Marian?
                         After all, why not?
'He loved not Marian, more than once he loved
Aurora. If he loves at last that Third,
Albeit she prove as slippery as spilt oil
On marble floors, I will not augur him
Ill-luck for that. Good love, howe'er ill-placed,
Is better for a man's soul in the end,
Than if he loved ill what deserves love well.
A pagan, kissing for a step of Pan
The wild-goat's hoof-print on the loamy down,
Exceeds our modern thinker who turns back
The strata .. granite, limestone, coal, and clay,
Concluding coldly with, "Here's law! where's God?"

And then at worse,—if Romney loves her not,—
At worst, if he's incapable of love,
Which may be—then indeed, for such a man
Incapable of love, she's good enough;
For she, at worst too, is a woman still
And loves him .. as the sort of woman can.

My loose long hair began to burn and creep,
Alive to the very ends, about my knees:
I swept it backward as the wind sweeps flame,
With the passion of my hands. Ah, Romney laughed
One day .. (how full the memories come up!)
"—Your Florence fire-flies live on in your hair,"
He said, "it gleams so." Well, I wrung them out,
My fire-flies; made a knot as hard as life
Of those loose, soft, impracticable curls,
And then sat down and thought .. "She shall not think
Her thought of me,"—and drew my desk and wrote.

"Dear Lady Waldemar, I could not speak
With people round me, nor can sleep to-night
And not speak, after the great news I heard
Of you and of my cousin. May you be
Most happy; and the good he meant the world,
Replenish his own life. Say what I say,
And let my word be sweeter for your mouth,
As you are *you* .. I only Aurora Leigh."

That's quiet, guarded: though she hold it up
Against the light, she'll not see through it more
Than lies there to be seen. So much for pride;
And now for peace, a little. Let me stop
All writing back .. "Sweet thanks, my sweetest friend,
"You've made more joyful my great joy itself."
—No, that's too simple! she would twist it thus,
"My joy would still be as sweet as thyme in drawers,
However shut up in the dark and dry;

But violets, aired and dewed by love like yours,
Out-smell all thyme: we keep that in our clothes,
But drop the other down our bosoms till
They smell like ".. ah, I see her writing back
Just so. She'll make a nosegay of her words,
And tie it with blue ribbons at the end
To suit a poet;—pshaw!
      And then we'll have
The call to church, the broken, sad, bad dream
Dreamed out at last, the marriage-vow complete
With the marriage-breakfast; praying in white gloves,
Drawn off in haste for drinking pagan toasts
In somewhat stronger wine than any sipped
By gods since Bacchus had his way with grapes.

A postscript stops all that and rescues me.
"You need not write. I have been overworked,
And think of leaving London, England even,
And hastening to get nearer to the sun
Where men sleep better. So, adieu."—I fold
And seal,——and now I'm out of all the coil;
I breathe now, I spring upward like a branch
The ten-years school-boy with a crooked stick
May pull down to his level in search of nuts,
But cannot hold a moment. How we twang
Back on the blue sky, and assert our height,
While he stares after! Now, the wonder seems
That I could wrong myself by such a doubt.
We poets always have uneasy hearts,
Because our hearts, large-rounded as the globe,
Can turn but one side to the sun at once.
We are used to dip our artist-hands in gall
And potash, trying potentialities
Of alternated colour, till at last
We get confused, and wonder for our skin
How nature tinged it first. Well—here's the true
Good flesh-colour; I recognise my hand,—

Which Romney Leigh may clasp as just a friend's,
And keep his clean.
                    And now, my Italy.
Alas, if we could ride with naked souls
And make no noise and pay no price at all,
I would have seen thee sooner, Italy,
For still I have heard thee crying through my life,
Thou piercing silence of ecstatic graves,
Men call that name!

                        But even a witch to-day
Must melt down golden pieces in the nard
Wherewith to anoint her broomstick ere she rides;
And poets evermore are scant of gold,
And if they find a piece behind the door
It turns by sunset to a withered leaf.
The Devil himself scarce trusts his patented
Gold-making art to any who make rhymes,
But culls his Faustus from philosophers
And not from poets. "Leave my job," said God;
And so the Devil leaves him without pence,
And poverty proves plainly special grace.
In these new, just, administrative times
Men clamour for an order of merit: why?
Here's black bread on the table and no wine!

At least I am a poet in being poor,
Thank God. I wonder if the manuscript
Of my long poem, if 'twere sold outright,
Would fetch enough to buy me shoes to go
A-foot, (thrown in, the necessary patch
For the other side the Alps)? It cannot be.
I fear that I must sell this residue
Of my father's books, although the Elzevirs
Have fly-leaves over-written by his hand
In faded notes as thick and fine and brown
As cobwebs on a tawny monument

Of the old Greeks—*conferenda hæc cum his—
Corruptè citat—lege potiùs,*
And so on, in the scholar's regal way
Of giving judgment on the parts of speech,
As if he sate on all twelve thrones up-piled,
Arraigning Israel. Ay, but books and notes
Must go together. And this Proclus too,
In these dear quaint contracted Grecian types,
Fantastically crumpled like his thoughts
Which would not seem too plain; you go round twice
For one step forward, then you take it back
Because you're somewhat giddy; there's the rule
For Proclus. Ah, I stained this middle leaf
With pressing in 't my Florence iris-bell,
Long stalk and all: my father chided me
For that stain of blue blood,—I recollect
The peevish turn his voice took,—"Silly girls,
Who plant their flowers in our philosophy
To make it fine, and only spoil the book!
No more of it, Aurora." Yes—no more!
Ah, blame of love, that's sweeter than all praise
Of those who love not! 'tis so lost to me,
I cannot, in such beggared life, afford
To lose my Proclus,—not for Florence even.

The kissing Judas, Wolff, shall go instead,
Who builds us such a royal book as this
To honour a chief-poet, folio-built,
And writes above, "The house of Nobody!"
Who floats in cream, as rich as any sucked
From Juno's breasts, the broad Homeric lines,
And, while with their spondaic prodigious mouths
They lap the lucent margins as babe-gods,
Proclaims them bastards. Wolff's an atheist;
And if the Iliad fell out, as he says,
By mere fortuitous concourse of old songs,
Conclude as much too for the universe.

That Wolff, those Platos: sweep the upper shelves
As clean as this, and so I am almost rich,
Which means, not forced to think of being poor
In sight of ends.   To-morrow: no delay.
I'll wait in Paris till good Carrington
Dispose of such and, having chaffered for
My book's price with the publisher, direct
All proceeds to me.   Just a line to ask
His help.
   And now I come, my Italy,
My own hills! Are you 'ware of me, my hills,
How I burn toward you? do you feel to-night
The urgency and yearning of my soul,
As sleeping mothers feel the sucking babe
And smile?—Nay, not so much as when in heat
Vain lightnings catch at your inviolate tops
And tremble while ye are stedfast.   Still ye go
Your own determined, calm, indifferent way
Toward sunrise, shade by shade, and light by light,
Of all the grand progression nought left out,
As if God verily made you for yourselves
And would not interrupt your life with ours.

SIXTH BOOK.

THE English have a scornful insular way
Of calling the French light. The levity
Is in the judgment only, which yet stands,
For say a foolish thing but oft enough
(And here's the secret of a hundred creeds,
Men get opinions as boys learn to spell,
By re-iteration chiefly,) the same thing
Shall pass at last for absolutely wise,
And not with fools exclusively. And so
We say the French are light, as if we said
The cat mews or the milch-cow gives us milk:
Say rather, cats are milked and milch-cows mew;
For what is lightness but inconsequence,
Vague fluctuation 'twixt effect and cause
Compelled by neither? Is a bullet light,
That dashes from the gun-mouth, while the eye
Winks and the heart beats one, to flatten itself
To a wafer on the white speck on a wall
A hundred paces off? Even so direct,
So sternly undivertible of aim,
Is this French people.
                    All, idealists
Too absolute and earnest, with them all
The idea of a knife cuts real flesh;
And still, devouring the safe interval
Which Nature placed between the thought and act
With those too fiery and impatient souls,
They threaten conflagration to the world,
And rush with most unscrupulous logic on

Impossible practice. Set your orators
To blow upon them with loud windy mouths
Through watchword phrases, jest or sentiment,
Which drive our burly brutal English mobs
Like so much chaff, whichever way they blow,—
This light French people will not thus be driven.
They turn indeed,—but then they turn upon
Some central pivot of their thought and choice,
And veer out by the force of holding fast.
That's hard to understand, for Englishmen
Unused to abstract questions, and untrained
To trace the involutions, valve by valve,
In each orbed bulb-root of a general truth,
And mark what subtly fine integument
Divides opposed compartments. Freedom's self
Comes concrete to us, to be understood,
Fixed in a feudal form incarnately
To suit our ways of thought and reverence,
The special form, with us, being still the thing.
With us, I say, though I'm of Italy
By mother's birth and grave, by father's grave
And memory; let it be;—a poet's heart
Can swell to a pair of nationalities,
However ill-lodged in a woman's breast.

And so I am strong to love this noble France,
This poet of the nations, who dreams on .
And wails on (while the household goes to wreck)
For ever, after some ideal good,—
Some equal poise of sex, some unvowed love
Inviolate, some spontaneous brotherhood,
Some wealth that leaves none poor and finds none tired,
Some freedom of the many that respects
The wisdom of the few. Heroic dreams!
Sublime, to dream so; natural, to wake:
And sad, to use such lofty scaffoldings,
Erected for the building of a church,

To build instead a brothel or a prison—
May God save France!
      And if at last she sighs
Her great soul up into a great man's face,
To flush his temples out so gloriously
That few dare carp at Cæsar for being bald,
What then?—this Cæsar represents, not reigns,
And is no despot, though twice absolute:
This Head has all the people for a heart;
This purple 's lined with the democracy,—
Now let him see to it! for a rent within
Would leave irreparable rags without.

A serious riddle: find such anywhere
Except in France; and when 'tis found in France,
Be sure to read it rightly. So, I mused
Up and down, up and down, the terraced streets,
The glittering boulevards, the white colonnades
Of fair fantastic Paris who wears trees
Like plumes, as if man made them, spire and tower
As if they had grown by nature, tossing up
Her fountains in the sunshine of the squares,
As if in beauty's game she tossed the dice,
Or blew the silver down-balls of her dreams
To sow futurity with seeds of thought
And count the passage of her festive hours.

The city swims in verdure, beautiful
As Venice on the waters, the sea-swan.
What bosky gardens dropped in close-walled courts
Like plums in ladies' laps who start and laugh:
What miles of streets that run on after trees,
Still carrying all the necessary shops,
Those open caskets with the jewels seen!
And trade is art, and art 's philosophy,
In Paris. There's a silk for instance, there,
As worth an artist's study for the folds,

As that bronze opposite! nay, the bronze has faults,
Art's here too artful,—conscious as a maid
Who leans to mark her shadow on the wall
Until she lose a 'vantage in her step.
Yet Art walks forward, and knows where to walk;
The artists also are idealists,
Too absolute for nature, logical
To austerity in the application of
The special theory,—not a soul content
To paint a crooked pollard and an ass,
As the English will because they find it so
And like it somehow.—There the old Tuileries
Is pulling its high cap down on its eyes,
Confounded, conscience-stricken, and amazed
By the apparition of a new fair face
In those devouring mirrors. Through the grate
Within the gardens, what a heap of babes,
Swept up like leaves beneath the chestnut-trees
From every street and alley of the town,
By ghosts perhaps that blow too bleak this way
A-looking for their heads! dear pretty babes,
I wish them luck to have their ball-play out
Before the next change. Here the air is thronged
With statues poised upon their columns fine
As if to stand a moment were a feat,
Against that blue! What squares,—what breathing-room
For a nation that runs fast,—ay, runs against
The dentist's teeth at the corner in pale rows,
Which grin at progress, in an epigram.

I walked the day out, listening to the chink
Of the first Napoleon's bones in his second grave
By victories guarded 'neath the golden dome
That caps all Paris like a bubble. "Shall
These dry bones live," thought Louis Philippe once,
And lived to know. Herein is argument
For kings and politicians, but still more

For poets, who bear buckets to the well
Of ampler draught.

                        These crowds are very good
For meditation (when we are very strong)
Though love of beauty makes us timorous,
And draws us backward from the coarse town-sights
To count the daisies upon dappled fields
And hear the streams bleat on among the hills
In innocent and indolent repose,
While still with silken elegiac thoughts
We wind out from us the distracting world
And die into the chrysalis of a man,
And leave the best that may, to come of us,
In some brown moth. I would be bold and bear
To look into the swarthiest face of things,
For God's sake who has made them.

                                  Six days' work;
The last day shutting 'twixt its dawn and eve
The whole work bettered of the previous five!
Since God collected and resumed in man
The firmaments, the strata, and the lights,
Fish, fowl, and beast, and insect,—all their trains
Of various life caught back upon His arm,
Reorganised, and constituted MAN,
The microcosm, the adding up of works,—
Within whose fluttering nostrils, then at last
Consummating Himself the Maker sighed,
As some strong winner at the foot-race sighs
Touching the goal.

                      Humanity is great;
And, if I would not rather pore upon
An ounce of common, ugly, human dust,
An artisan's palm or a peasant's brow,
Unsmooth, ignoble, save to me and God,
Than track old Nilus to his silver roots,
Or wait on all the changes of the moon

Among the mountain-peaks of Thessaly
(Until her magic crystal round itself
For many a witch to see in)—set it down
As weakness,—strength by no means. How is this
That men of science, osteologists
And surgeons, beat some poets in respect
For nature,—count nought common or unclean,
Spend raptures upon perfect specimens
Of indurated veins, distorted joints,
Or beautiful new cases of curved spine,
While we, we are shocked at nature's falling off,
We dare to shrink back from her warts and blains,
We will not, when she sneezes, look at her,
Not even to say "God bless her"! That's our wrong;
For that, she will not trust us often with
Her larger sense of beauty and desire,
But tethers us to a lily, or a rose
And bids us diet on the dew inside,
Left ignorant that the hungry beggar-boy
(Who stares unseen against our absent eyes,
And wonders at the gods that we must be,
To pass so careless for the oranges!)
Bears yet a breastful of a fellow-world
To this world, undisparaged, undespoiled,
And (while we scorn him for a flower or two,
As being, Heaven help us, less poetical)
Contains himself both flowers and firmaments
And surging seas and aspectable stars
And all that we would push him out of sight
In order to see nearer. Let us pray
God's grace to keep God's image in repute,
That so, the poet and philanthropist
(Even I and Romney) may stand side by side,
Because we both stand face to face with men,
Contemplating the people in the rough,
Yet each so follow a vocation, his
And mine.

                    I walked on, musing with myself
On life and art, and whether after all
A larger metaphysics might not help
Our physics, a completer poetry
Adjust our daily life and vulgar wants
More fully than the special outside plans,
Phalansteries, material institutes,
The civil conscriptions and lay monasteries
Preferred by modern thinkers, as they thought
The bread of man indeed made all his life,
And washing seven times in the "People's Baths"
Were sovereign for a people's leprosy,
Still leaving out the essential prophet's word
That comes in power. On which, we thunder down
We prophets, poets,—Virtue's in the *word.*
The maker burnt the darkness up with His,
To inaugurate the use of vocal life;
And, plant a poet's word even, deep enough
In any man's breast, looking presently
For offshoots, you have done more for the man
Than if you dressed him in a broad-cloth coat
And warmed his Sunday potage at your fire.
Yet Romney leaves me . . .
                              God! what face is that?
O Romney, O Marian!
                         Walking on the quays
And pulling thoughts to pieces leisurely,
As if I caught at grasses in a field
And bit them slow between my absent lips
And shred them with my hands . .
                                  What face is that?
What a face, what a look, what a likeness! Full on mine
The sudden blow of it came down, till all
My blood swam, my eyes dazzled. Then I sprang . .

It was as if a meditative man
Were dreaming out a summer afternoon

And watching gnats a-prick upon a pond,
When something floats up suddenly, out there,
Turns over .. a dead face, known once alive ..
So old, so new! it would be dreadful now
To lose the sight and keep the doubt of this:
He plunges—ha! he has lost it in the splash.

I plunged—I tore the crowd up, either side,
And rushed on, forward, forward, after her.
Her? whom?
    A woman sauntered slow in front,
Munching an apple,—she left off amazed
As if I had snatched it: that's not she, at least.
A man walked arm-linked with a lady veiled,
Both heads dropped closer than the need of talk:
They started; he forgot her with his face,
And she, herself, and clung to him as if
My look were fatal. Such a stream of folk,
And all with cares and business of their own!
I ran the whole quay down against their eyes;
No Marian; nowhere Marian. Almost, now,
I could call Marian, Marian, with the shriek
Of desperate creatures calling for the Dead.
Where is she, was she? was she anywhere?
I stood still, breathless, gazing, straining out
In every uncertain distance, till at last
A gentleman abstracted as myself
Came full against me, then resolved the clash
In voluble excuses,—obviously
Some learned member of the Institute
Upon his way there, walking, for his health,
While meditating on the last "Discourse;"
Pinching the empty air 'twixt finger and thumb
From which the snuff being ousted by that shock
Defiled his snow-white waistcoat duly pricked
At the button-hole with honourable red;
"Madame, your pardon,"—there he swerved from me

A metre, as confounded as he had heard
That Dumas would be chosen to fill up
The next chair vacant, by his "men *in us*."
Since when was genius found respectable?
It passes in its place, indeed,—which means
The seventh floor back, or else the hospital:
Revolving pistols are ingenious things,
But prudent men (Academicians are)
Scarce keep them in the cupboard next the prunes.

And so, abandoned to a bitter mirth,
I loitered to my inn.   O world, O world,
O jurists, rhymers, dreamers, what you please,
We play a weary game of hide-and-seek!
We shape a figure of our fantasy,
Call nothing something, and run after it
And lose it, lose ourselves too in the search,
Till clash against us comes a somebody
Who also has lost something and is lost,
Philosopher against philanthropist,
Academician against poet, man
Against woman, against the living the dead,—
Then home, with a bad headache and worse jest!

To change the water for my heliotropes
And yellow roses.   Paris has such flowers.
But England, also.   'Twas a yellow rose,
By that south window of the little house,
My cousin Romney gathered with his hand
On all my birthdays for me, save the last;
And then I shook the tree too rough, too rough,
For roses to stay after.
                                Now, my maps.
·I must not linger here from Italy
Till the last nightingale is tired of song,
And the last fire-fly dies off in the maize.
My soul's in haste to leap into the sun

And scorch and seethe itself to a finer mood,
Which here, in this chill north, is apt to stand
Too stiffly in former moulds.
      That face persists.
It floats up, it turns over in my mind,
As like to Marian, as one dead is like
The same alive. In very deed a face
And not a fancy, though it vanished so;
The small fair face between the darks of hair,
I used to liken, when I saw her first,
To a point of moonlit water down a well:
The low brow, the frank space between the eyes,
Which always had the brown pathetic look
Of a dumb creature who had been beaten once
And never since was easy with the world.
Ah, ah—now I remember perfectly
Those eyes, to-day,—how overlarge they seemed,
As if some patient passionate despair
(Like a coal dropt and forgot on tapestry,
Which slowly burns a widening circle out)
Had burnt them larger, larger. And those eyes
To-day, I do remember, saw me too,
As I saw them, with conscious lids astrain
In recognition. Now a fantasy,
A simple shade or image of the brain,
Is merely passive, does not retro-act,
Is seen, but sees not.
      'Twas a real face,
Perhaps a real Marian.
      Which being so,
I ought to write to Romney, "Marian's here;
Be comforted for Marian."
      My pen fell,
My hands struck sharp together, as hands do
Which hold at nothing. Can I write to *him*
A half-truth? can I keep my own soul blind
To the other half, .. the worse? What are our souls,

If still, to run on straight a sober pace
Nor start at every pebble or dead leaf,
They must wear blinkers, ignore facts, suppress
Six tenths of the road? Confront the truth, my soul!
And oh, as truly as that was Marian's face,
The arms of that same Marian clasped a thing
. . Not hid so well beneath the scanty shawl,
I cannot name it now for what it was.

A child. Small business has a cast-away
Like Marian with that crown of prosperous wives
At which the gentlest she grows arrogant
And says, "my child." Who finds an emerald ring
On a beggar's middle finger and requires
More testimony to convict a thief?
A child's too costly for so mere a wretch;
She filched it somewhere, and it means, with her,
Instead of honour, blessing, merely shame.

I cannot write to Romney, "Here she is,
Here's Marian found! I'll set you on her track
I saw her here, in Paris, . . and her child.
She put away your love two years ago,
But, plainly, not to starve. You suffered then;
And, now that you've forgot her utterly
As any last year's annual, in whose place
You've planted a thick flowering evergreen,
I choose, being kind, to write and tell you this
To make you wholly easy—she's not dead,
But only . . damned."
     Stop there: I go too fast;
I'm cruel like the rest,—in haste to take
The first stir in the arms for a rat,
And set my barking, biting thoughts upon 't.
—A child! what then? Suppose a neighbour's sick
And asked her, "Marian, carry out my child
In this Spring air,"—I punish her for that?

Or say, the child should hold her round the neck
For good child-reasons, that he liked it so
And would not leave her—she had winning ways—
I brand her therefore that she took the child?
Not so.
        I will not write to Romney Leigh.
For now he's happy,—and she may indeed
Be guilty,—and the knowledge of her fault
Would draggle his smooth time. But I, whose days
Are not so fine they cannot bear the rain,
And who moreover having seen her face
Must see it again, . . *will* see it, by my hopes
Of one day seeing heaven too. The police
Shall track her, hound her, ferret their own soil;
We'll dig this Paris to its catacombs
But certainly we'll find her, have her out,
And save her, if she will or will not—child
Or no child,—if a child, then one to save!

The long weeks passed on without consequence.
As easy find a footstep on the sand
The morning after spring-tide, as the trace
Of Marian's feet between the incessant surfs
Of this live flood. She may have moved this way,—
But so the star-fish does, and crosses out
The dent of her small shoe. The foiled police
Renounced me. "Could they find a girl and child,
No other signalment but girl and child?
No data shown but noticeable eyes
And hair in masses, low upon the brow,
As if it were an iron crown and pressed?
Friends heighten, and suppose they specify:
Why, girls with hair and eyes are everywhere
In Paris; they had turned me up in vain
No Marian Erle indeed, but certainly
Mathildes, Justines, Victoires, . . or, if I sought
The English, Betsis, Saras, by the score.

They might as well go out into the fields
To find a speckled bean, that's somehow specked,
And somewhere in the pod."—They left me so.
Shall *I* leave Marian? have I dreamed a dream?

—I thank God I have found her! I must say
"Thank God," for finding her, although 'tis true
I find the world more sad and wicked for't.
But she—
        I'll write about her, presently.
My hand's a-tremble, as I had just caught up
My heart to write with, in the place of it.
At least you'd take these letters to be writ
At sea, in storm!—wait now . .
                A simple chance
Did all. I could not sleep last night, and, tired
Of turning on my pillow and harder thoughts,
Went out at early morning, when the air
Is delicate with some last starry touch,
To wander through the Market-place of Flowers
(The prettiest haunt in Paris), and make sure
At worst that there were roses in the world.
So wandering, musing, with the artist's eye,
That keeps the shade-side of the thing it loves,
Half-absent, whole-observing, while the crowd
Of young vivacious and black-braided heads
Dipped, quick as finches in a blossomed tree,
Among the nosegays, cheapening this and that
In such a cheerful twitter of rapid speech,—
My heart leapt in me, startled by a voice
That slowly, faintly, with long breaths that marked
The interval between the wish and word,
Inquired in stranger's French, "Would *that* be much,
That branch of flowering mountain-gorse?"—"So much!
Too much for me, then!" turning the face round
So close upon me that I felt the sigh
It turned with.

"Marian, Marian!"—face to face—
"Marian! I find you. Shall I let you go?"
I held her two slight wrists with both my hands;
"Ah Marian, Marian, can I let you go?"
—She fluttered from me like a cyclamen,
As white, which taken in a sudden wind
Beats on against the palisade.—"Let pass,"
She said at last. "I will not," I replied;
"I lost my sister Marian many days,
And sought her ever in my walks and prayers,
And, now I find her . . . do we throw away
The bread we worked and prayed for,—crumble it
And drop it, . . to do even so by thee
Whom still I've hungered after more than bread,
My sister Marian?—can I hurt thee, dear?
Then why distrust me? Never tremble so.
Come with me rather where we'll talk and live
And none shall vex us. I've a home for you
And me and no one else" . . .
      She shook her head.
"A home for you and me and no one else
Ill-suits one of us: I prefer to such,
A roof of grass on which a flower might spring,
Less costly to me than the cheapest here;
And yet I could not, at this hour, afford
A like home even. That you offer yours,
I thank you. You are good as heaven itself—
As good as one I knew before . . Farewell."

I loosed her hands,—"In *his* name, no farewell!"
(She stood as if I held her.) "For his sake,
For his sake, Romney's! by the good he meant,
Ay, always! by the love he pressed for once,—
And by the grief, reproach, abandonment,
He took in change" . .
     "He Romney! who grieved *him?*
Who had the heart for 't? what reproach touched *him?*

Be merciful,—speak quickly."
                         "Therefore come,"
I answered with authority.—"I think
We dare to speak such things and name such names
In the open squares of Paris!"
                              Not a word
She said, but in a gentle humbled way
(As one who had forgot herself in grief)
Turned round and followed closely where I went,
As if I led her by a narrow plank
Across devouring waters, step by step;
And so in silence we walked on a mile.

And then she stopped: her face was white as wax.
"We go much farther?"
                     "You are ill," I asked,
"Or tired?"
           She looked the whiter for her smile.
"There's one at home," she said, "has need of me
By this time,—and I must not let him wait."

"Not even," I asked, "to hear of Romney Leigh?"

"Not even," she said, "to hear of Mister Leigh."

"In that case," I resumed, "I go with you,
And we can talk the same thing there as here.
None waits for me: I have my day to spend."

Her lips moved in a spasm without a sound,—
But then she spoke. "It shall be as you please;
And better so—'tis shorter seen than told:
And though you will not find me worth your pains,
That, even, may be worth some pains to know
For one as good as you are."
                            Then she led
The way, and I, as by a narrow plank

Across devouring waters, followed her,
Stepping by her footsteps, breathing by her breath,
And holding her with eyes that would not slip;
And so, without a word, we walked a mile,
And so, another mile, without a word.

Until the peopled streets being all dismissed,
House-rows and groups all scattered like a flock,
The market-gardens thickened, and the long
White walls beyond, like spiders' outside threads,
Stretched, feeling blindly toward the country-fields
Through half-built habitations and half-dug
Foundations,—intervals of trenchant chalk
That bit betwixt the grassy uneven turfs
Where goats (vine-tendrils trailing from their mouths)
Stood perched on edges of the cellarage
Which should be, staring as about to leap
To find their coming Bacchus. All the place
Seemed less a cultivation than a waste.
Men work here, only,—scarce begin to live:
All 's sad, the country struggling with the town,
Like an untamed hawk upon a strong man's fist,
That beats its wings and tries to get away,
And cannot choose be satisfied so soon
To hop through court-yards with its right foot tied,
The vintage plains and pastoral hills in sight.

We stopped beside a house too high and slim
To stand there by itself, but waiting till
Five others, two on this side, three on that,
Should grow up from the sullen second floor
They pause at now, to build it to a row.
The upper windows partly were unglazed
Meantime,—a meagre, unripe house: a line
Of rigid poplars elbowed it behind,
And, just in front, beyond the lime and bricks
That wronged the grass between it and the road,

A great acacia with its slender trunk
And overpoise of multitudinous leaves
(In which a hundred fields might spill their dew
And intense verdure, yet find room enough)
Stood reconciling all the place with green.
I followed up the stair upon her step.
She hurried upward, shot across a face,
A woman's, on the landing,--"How now, now!
Is no one to have holidays but you?
You said an hour, and stay three hours, I think,
And Julie waiting for your betters here?
Why if he had waked he might have waked, for me."
—Just murmuring an excusing word she passed
And shut the rest out with the chamber-door,
Myself shut in beside her.
                  'Twas a room
Scarce larger than a grave, and near as bare;
Two stools, a pallet-bed; I saw the room:
A mouse could find no sort of shelter in 't,
Much less a greater secret; curtainless,—
The window fixed you with its torturing eye,
Defying you to take a step apart
If peradventure you would hide a thing.
I saw the whole room, I and Marian there
Alone.
       Alone? She threw her bonnet off,
Then, sighing as 'twere sighing the last time,
Approached the bed, and drew a shawl away:
You could not peel a fruit you fear to bruise
More calmly and more carefully than so,—
Nor would you find within, a rosier flushed
Pomegranate—
              There he lay upon his back,
The yearling creature, warm and moist with life
To the bottom of his dimples,—to the ends
Of the lovely tumbled curls about his face;
For since he had been covered over-much

To keep him from the light-glare, both his cheeks
Were hot and scarlet as the first live rose
The shepherd's heart-blood ebbed away into
The faster for his love. And love was here
As instant; in the pretty baby-mouth,
Shut close as if for dreaming that it sucked,
The little naked feet, drawn up the way
Of nestled birdlings; everything so soft
And tender,—to the tiny holdfast hands,
Which, closing on a finger into sleep,
Had kept the mould of 't.
                          While we stood there dumb,
For oh, that it should take such innocence
To prove just guilt, I thought, and stood there dumb,—
The light upon his eyelids pricked them wide,
And, staring out at us with all their blue,
As half perplexed between the angelhood
He had been away to visit in his sleep,
And our most mortal presence, gradually
He saw his mother's face, accepting it
In change for heaven itself with such a smile
As might have well been learnt there,—never moved,
But smiled on, in a drowse of ecstasy,
So happy (half with her and half with heaven)
He could not have the trouble to be stirred,
But smiled and lay there. Like a rose, I said?
As red and still indeed as any rose,
That blows in all the silence of its leaves,
Content in blowing to fulfil its life.

She leaned above him (drinking him as wine)
In that extremity of love, 'twill pass
For agony or rapture, seeing that love
Includes the whole of nature, rounding it
To love .. no more,—since more can never be
Than just love. Self-forgot, cast out of self,
And drowning in the transport of the sight,

Her whole pale passionate face, mouth, forehead, eyes,
One gaze, she stood: then, slowly as he smiled
She smiled too, slowly, smiling unaware,
And drawing from his countenance to hers
A fainter red, as if she watched a flame
And stood in it a-glow. "How beautiful,"
Said she.
        I answered, trying to be cold.
(Must sin have compensations, was my thought,
As if it were a holy thing like grief?
And is a woman to be fooled aside
From putting vice down, with that woman's toy
A baby?)——"Ay! the child is well enough,"
I answered. "If his mother's palms are clean
They need be glad of course in clasping such;
But if not, I would rather lay my hand,
Were I she, on God's brazen altar-bars
Red-hot with burning sacrificial lambs,
Than touch the sacred curls of such a child.

She plunged her fingers in his clustering locks,
As one who would not be afraid of fire;
And then with indrawn steady utterance said,
"My lamb, my lamb! although, through such as thou,
The most unclean got courage and approach
To God, once,—now they cannot, even with men,
Find grace enough for pity and gentle words."

"My Marian," I made answer, grave and sad,
"The priest who stole a lamb to offer him,
Was still a thief. And if a woman steals
(Through God's own barrier-hedges of true love,
Which fence out licence in securing love)
A child like this, that smiles so in her face,
She is no mother but a kidnapper,
And he's a dismal orphan, not a son,
Whom all her kisses cannot feed so full

He will not miss hereafter a pure home
To live in, a pure heart to lean against,
A pure good mother's name and memory
To hope by, when the world grows thick and bad
And he feels out for virtue."
      "Oh," she smiled
With bitter patience, "the child takes his chance;
Not much worse off in being fatherless
Than I was, fathered. He will say, belike,
His mother was the saddest creature born;
He'll say his mother lived so contrary,
To joy, that even the kindest, seeing her,
Grew sometimes almost cruel: he'll not say
She flew contrarious in the face of God
With bat-wings of her vices. Stole my child,—
My flower of earth, my only flower on earth,
My sweet, my beauty!".. Up she snatched the child,
And, breaking on him in a storm of tears,
Drew out her long sobs from their shivering roots,
Until he took it for a game, and stretched
His feet and flapped his eager arms like wings
And crowed and gurgled through his infant laugh:
"Mine, mine," she said. "I have as sure a right
As any glad proud mother in the world,
Who sets her darling down to cut his teeth
Upon her church-ring. If she talks of law,
I talk of law! I claim my mother-dues
By law,—the law which now is paramount,—
The common law, by which the poor and weak
Are trodden underfoot by vicious men,
And loathed for ever after by the good.
Let pass! I did not filch,—I found the child.

"You found him, Marian?"
      "Ay, I found him where
I found my curse,—in the gutter, with my shame!
What have you, any of you, to say to that,

Who all are happy, and sit safe and high,
And never spoke before to arraign my right
To grief itself? What, what, .. being beaten down
By hoofs of maddened oxen into a ditch,
Half-dead, whole mangled, when a girl at last
Breathes, sees .. and finds there, bedded in her flesh
Because of the extremity of the shock,
Some coin of price! .. and when a good man comes
(That's God! the best men are not quite as good)
And says, 'I dropped the coin there: take it you,
And keep it,—it shall pay you for the loss,'—
You all put up your finger—'See the thief!
'Observe what precious thing she has come to filch.
'How bad those girls are!' Oh, my flower, my pet
I dare forget I have you in my arms
And fly off to be angry with the world,
And fright you, hurt you with my tempers, till
You double up your lip? Why, that indeed
Is bad: a naughty mother!"
                              "You mistake,
I interrupted; "if I loved you not,
I should not, Marian, certainly be here."

"Alas," she said, "you are so very good;
And yet I wish indeed you had never come
To make me sob until I vex the child.
It is not wholesome for these pleasure-plats
To be so early watered by our brine.
And then, who knows? he may not like me now
As well, perhaps, as ere he saw me fret,—
One's ugly fretting! he has eyes the same
As angels, but he cannot see as deep,
And so I've kept for ever in his sight
A sort of smile to please him,—as you place
A green thing from the garden in a cup,
To make believe it grows there. Look, my sweet,
My cowslip-ball! we've done with that cross face,

And here's the face come back you used to like.
Ah, ah! he laughs! he likes me. Ah, Miss Leigh,
You're great and pure; but were you purer still,—
As if you had walked, we'll say, no otherwhere
Than up and down the new Jerusalem,
And held your trailing lutestring up yourself
From brushing the twelve stones, for fear of some
Small speck as little as a needle-prick,
White stitched on white,—the child would keep to *me*,
Would choose his poor lost Marian, like me best,
And, though you stretched your arms, cry back and cling,
As we do when God says it's time to die
And bids us go up higher. Leave us, then;
We two are happy. Does *he* push me off?
He's satisfied with me, as I with him."

"So soft to one, so hard to others! Nay,"
I cried, more angry that she melted me,
"We make henceforth a cushion of our faults
To sit and practise easy virtues on?
I thought a child was given to sanctify
A woman,—set her in the sight of all
The clear-eyed Heavens, a chosen minister
To do their business and lead spirits up
The difficult blue heights. A woman lives,
Not bettered, quickened toward the truth and good
Through being a mother?.. then she's none! although
She damps her baby's cheeks by kissing them,
As we kill roses."
    "Kill! O Christ," she said,
And turned her wild sad face from side to side
With most despairing wonder in it, "What,
What have you in your souls against me then,
All of you? am I wicked, do you think?
God knows me, trusts me with the child; but you,
You think me really wicked?"

"Complaisant,"
I answered softly, "to a wrong you've done,
Because of certain profits,—which is wrong
Beyond the first wrong, Marian. When you left
The pure place and the noble heart, to take
The hand of a seducer" ..
                  "Whom? whose hand?
I took the hand of" ..
                  Springing up erect
And lifting up the child at full arm's length,
As if to bear him like an oriflamme
Unconquerable to armies of reproach,—
"By *him*," she said, "my child's head and its curls,
By these blue eyes no woman born could dare
A perjury on, I make my mother's oath,
That if I left that Heart, to lighten it,
The blood of mine was still, except for grief!
No cleaner maid than I was, took a step
To a sadder end,—no matron-mother now
Looks backward to her early maidenhood
Through chaster pulses. I speak steadily:
And if I lie so, .. if, being fouled in will
And paltered with in soul by devil's lust,
I dared to bid this angel take my part, ..
Would God sit quiet, let us think, in heaven,
Nor strike me dumb with thunder? Yet I speak:
He clears me therefore. What, 'seduced' 's your word?
Do wolves seduce a wandering fawn in France?
Do eagles, who have pinched a lamb with claws,
Seduce it into carrion? So with me.
I was not ever, as you say, seduced,
But simply, murdered."
                  There she paused, and sighed,
With such a sigh as drops from agony
To exhaustion,—sighing while she let the babe
Slide down upon her bosom from her arms,

And all her face's light fell after him
Like a torch quenched in falling. Down she sank,
And sate upon the bedside with the child.

But I, convicted, broken utterly,
With woman's passion clung about her waist
And kissed her hair and eyes,—"I have been wrong,
Sweet Marian" . . (weeping in a tender rage)
"Sweet holy Marian! And now, Marian, now,
I'll use your oath although my lips are hard,
And by the child, my Marian, by the child,
I swear his mother shall be innocent
Before my conscience, as in the open Book
Of Him who reads for judgment. Innocent,
My sister! let the night be ne'er so dark
The moon is surely somewhere in the sky;
So surely is your whiteness to be found
Through all dark facts. But pardon, pardon me,
And smile a little, Marian,—for the child,
If not for me, my sister."
                        The poor lip
Just motioned for the smile and let it go:
And then, with scarce a stirring of the mouth,
As if a statue spoke that could not breathe,
But spoke on calm between its marble lips,—
"I'm glad, I'm very glad you clear me so.
I should be sorry that you set me down
With harlots, or with even a better name
Which misbecomes his mother. For the rest,
I am not on a level with your love,
Nor ever was, you know,—but now am worse,
Because that world of yours has dealt with me
As when the hard sea bites and chews a stone
And changes the first form of it. I've marked
A shore of pebbles bitten to one shape
From all the various life of madrepores;
And so, that little stone, called Marian Erle,

Picked up and dropped by you and another friend,
Was ground and tortured by the incessant sea
And bruised from what she was,—changed! death's a
    change,
And she, I said, was murdered; Marian's dead.
What can you do with people when they are dead,
But, if you are pious, sing a hymn and go,
Or, if you are tender, heave a sigh and go,
But go by all means,—and permit the grass
To keep its green feud up 'twixt them and you?
Then leave me,—let me rest. I'm dead, I say,
And if, to save the child from death as well,
The mother in me has survived the rest,
Why, that's God's miracle you must not tax,
I'm not less dead for that: I'm nothing more
But just a mother. Only for the child
I'm warm, and cold, and hungry, and afraid,
And smell the flowers a little and see the sun,
And speak still, and am silent,—just for him!
I pray you therefore to mistake me not
And treat me haply as I were alive;
For though you ran a pin into my soul,
I think it would not hurt nor trouble me.
Here's proof, dear lady,—in the market-place
But now, you promised me to say a word
About . . a friend, who once, long years ago,
Took God's place toward me, when He leans and loves
And does not thunder, . . whom at last I left,
As all of us leave God. You thought perhaps
I seemed to care for hearing of that friend?
Now, judge me! we have sate here half an hour
And talked together of the child and me,
And I not asked as much as, 'What's the thing
'You had to tell me of the friend . . the friend?'
He's sad, I think you said,—he's sick perhaps?
'Tis nought to Marian if he's sad or sick.
Another would have crawled beside your foot

And prayed your words out. Why, a beast, a dog,
A starved cat, if he had fed it once with milk,
Would show less hardness. But I'm dead, you see,
And that explains it."

      Poor, poor thing, she spoke
And shook her head, as white and calm as frost
On days too cold for raining any more,
But still with such a face, so much alive,
I could not choose but take it on my arm
And stroke the placid patience of its cheeks,—
Then told my story out, of Romney Leigh,
How, having lost her, sought her, missed her still,
He, broken-hearted for himself and her,
Had drawn the curtains of the world awhile
As if he had done with morning. There I stopped,
For when she gasped, and pressed me with her eyes,
"And now .. how is it with him? tell me now,"
I felt the shame of compensated grief,
And chose my words with scruple—slowly stepped
Upon the slippery stones set here and there
Across the sliding water. "Certainly,
As evening empties morning into night,
Another morning takes the evening up
With healthful, providential interchange;
And, though he thought still of her,"—

        "Yes, she knew,
She understood: she had supposed indeed
That, as one stops a hole upon a flute,
At which a new note comes and shapes the tune,
Excluding her would bring a worthier in,
And, long ere this, that Lady Waldemar
He loved so" ..

     "Loved," I started,—"loved her so!
Now tell me" ..

      "I will tell you," she replied:
"But, since we're taking oaths, you'll promise first
That he in England, he, shall never learn

In what a dreadful trap his creature here,
Round whose unworthy neck he had meant to tie
The honourable ribbon of his name,
Fell unaware and came to butchery:
Because,—I know him,—as he takes to heart
The grief of every stranger, he's not like
To banish mine as far as I should choose
In wishing him most happy. Now he leaves
To think of me, perverse, who went my way,
Unkind, and left him,—but if once he knew ..
Ah, then, the sharp nail of my cruel wrong
Would fasten me for ever in his sight,
Like some poor curious bird, through each spread wing
Nailed high up over a fierce hunter's fire,
To spoil the dinner of all tenderer folk
Come in by chance. Nay, since your Marian's dead,
You shall not hang her up, but dig a hole
And bury her in silence! ring no bells."

I answered gaily, though my whole voice wept,
"We'll ring the joy-bells, not the funeral-bells,
Because we have her back, dead or alive."

She never answered that, but shook her head;
Then low and calm, as one who, safe in heaven,
Shall tell a story of his lower life,
Unmoved by shame or anger,—so she spoke.
She told me she had loved upon her knees,
As others pray, more perfectly absorbed
In the act and inspiration. She felt his
For just his uses, not her own at all,
His stool, to sit on or put up his foot,
His cup, to fill with wine or vinegar,
Whichever drink might please him at the chance
For that should please her always: let him write
His name upon her .. it seemed natural;
It was most precious, standing on his shelf,

To wait until he chose to lift his hand.
Well, well,—I saw her then, and must have seen
How bright her life went floating on her love,
Like wicks the housewives send afloat on oil
Which feeds them to a flame that lasts the night.

To do good seemed so much his business,
That, having done it, she was fain to think,
Must fill up his capacity for joy.
At first she never mooted with herself
If *he* was happy, since he made her so,
Or if he loved her, being so much beloved.
Who thinks of asking if the sun is light,
Observing that it lightens? who's so bold,
To question God of His felicity?
Still less. And thus she took for granted first
What first of all she should have put to proof,
And sinned against him so, but only so.
"What could you hope," she said, "of such as she?
You take a kid you like, and turn it out
In some fair garden: though the creature's fond
And gentle, it will leap upon the beds
And break your tulips, bite your tender trees;
The wonder would be if such innocence
Spoiled less: a garden is no place for kids."

And, by degrees, when he who had chosen her
Brought in his courteous and benignant friends
To spend their goodness on her, which she took
So very gladly, as a part of his,—
By slow degrees it broke on her slow sense
That she too in that Eden of delight
Was out of place, and, like the silly kid,
Still did most mischief where she meant most love.
A thought enough to make a woman mad,
(No beast in this but she may well go mad)
That saying "I am thine to love and use."

May blow the plague in her protesting breath
To the very man for whom she claims to die,—
That, clinging round his neck, she pulls him down
And drowns him,—and that, lavishing her soul,
She hales perdition on him. "So, being mad,"
Said Marian . .
                    "Ah—who stirred such thoughts, you ask?
Whose fault it was, that she should have such thoughts?
None's fault, none's fault. The light comes, and we see:
But if it were not truly for our eyes,
There would be nothing seen, for all the light.
And so with Marian: if she saw at last,
The sense was in her,—Lady Waldemar
Had spoken all in vain else."
                    "O my heart,
O prophet in my heart," I cried aloud,
"Then Lady Waldemar spoke!"
                    "*Did* she speak,"
Mused Marian softly, "or did she only sign?
Or did she put a word into her face
And look, and so impress you with the word?
Or leave it in the foldings of her gown,
Like rosemary smells a movement will shake out
When no one 's conscious? who shall say, or guess?
One thing alone was certain—from the day
The gracious lady paid a visit first,
She, Marian, saw things different,—felt distrust
Of all that sheltering roof of circumstance
Her hopes were building into with clay nests:
Her heart was restless, pacing up and down
And fluttering, like dumb creatures before storms,
Not knowing wherefore she was ill at ease."

"And still the lady came," said Marian Erle,
"Much oftener than *he* knew it, Mister Leigh.
She bade me never tell him she had come,
She liked to love me better than he knew,

So very kind was Lady Waldemar:
And every time she brought with her more light,
And every light made sorrow clearer .. Well,
Ah, well! we cannot give her blame for that;
'Twould be the same thing if an angel came,
Whose right should prove our wrong. And every time
The lady came, she looked more beautiful
And spoke more like a flute among green trees,
Until at last, as one, whose heart being sad
On hearing lovely music, suddenly
Dissolves in weeping, I brake out in tears
Before her, asked her counsel,—"Had I erred
'In being too happy? would she set me straight?
'For she, being wise and good and born above
'The flats I had never climbed from, could perceive
'If such as I, might grow upon the hills;
'And whether such poor herb sufficed to grow,
'For Romney Leigh to break his fast upon 't,—
'Or would he pine on such, or haply starve?'
She wrapt me in her generous arms at once,
And let me dream a moment how it feels
To have a real mother, like some girls:
But when I looked, her face was younger .. ay,
Youth's too bright not to be a little hard,
And beauty keeps itself still uppermost,
That's true!—Though Lady Waldemar was kind
She hurt me, hurt, as if the morning-sun
Should smite us on the eyelids when we sleep,
And wake us up with headache. Ay, and soon
Was light enough to make my heart ache too:
She told me truths I asked for,—'twas my fault,—
'That Romney could not love me, if he would,
'As men call loving: there are bloods that flow
'Together like some rivers and not mix,
'Through contraries of nature. He indeed
'Was set to wed me, to espouse my class,
'Act out a rash opinion,—and, once wed,

'So just a man and gentle could not choose
'But make my life as smooth as marriage-ring,
'Bespeak me mildly, keep me a cheerful house,
'With servants, brooches, all the flowers I liked,
'And pretty dresses, silk the whole year round'..
At which I stopped her,—'This for me. And now
'For *him*.'—She hesitated,—truth grew hard;
She owned, '"Twas plain a man like Romney Leigh
'Required a wife more level to himself.
'If day by day he had to bend his height
'To pick up sympathies, opinions, thoughts,
'And interchange the common talk of life
'Which helps a man to live as well as talk,
'His days were heavily taxed. Who buys a staff
'To fit the hand, that reaches but the knee?
'He'd feel it bitter to be forced to miss
'The perfect joy of married suited pairs,
'Who, bursting through the separating hedge
'Of personal dues with that sweet eglantine
'Of equal love, keep saying, "So *we* think,
' "It strikes *us*,—that's *our* fancy." '—When I asked
If earnest will, devoted love, employed
In youth like mine, would fail to raise me up
As two strong arms will always raise a child
To a fruit hung overhead, she sighed and sighed..
'That could not be,' she feared. 'You take a pink,
'You dig about its roots and water it
'And so improve it to a garden-pink,
'But will not change it to a heliotrope,
'The kind remains. And then, the harder truth—
'This Romney Leigh, so rash to leap a pale,
'So bold for conscience, quick for martyrdom,
'Would suffer steadily and never flinch,
'But suffer surely and keenly, when his class
'Turned shoulder on him for a shameful match,
'And set him up as nine-pin in their talk
'To bowl him down with jestings.'—There, she paused

And when I used the pause in doubting that
We wronged him after all in what we feared—
'Suppose such things could never touch him more
'In his high conscience (if the things should be,)
'Than, when the queen sits in an upper room,
'The horses in the street can spatter her!'—
A moment, hope came,—but the lady closed
That door and nicked the lock and shut it out,
Observing wisely that, 'the tender heart
'Which made him over-soft to a lower class,
'Would scarcely fail to make him sensitive
'To a higher,—how they thought and what they felt.'"

"Alas, alas," said Marian, rocking slow
The pretty baby who was near asleep,
The eyelids creeping over the blue balls, —
"She made it clear, too clear—I saw the whole!
And yet who knows if I had seen my way
Straight out of it by looking, though 'twas clear.
Unless the generous lady, 'ware of this,
Had set her own house all a-fire for me
To light me forwards? Leaning on my face
Her heavy agate eyes which crushed my will,
She told me tenderly, (as when men come
To a bedside to tell people they must die)
'She knew of knowledge,—ay, of knowledge knew,
'That Romney Leigh had loved *her* formerly.
'And *she* loved *him*, she might say, now the chance
'Was past,—but that, of course, he never guessed,-
'For something came between them, something thin
'As a cobweb, catching every fly of doubt,
'To hold it buzzing at the window-pane
'And help to dim the daylight. Ah, man's pride
'Or woman's—which is greatest? most averse
'To brushing cobwebs? Well, but she and he
'Remained fast friends; it seemed not more than so,
'Because he had bound his hands and could not stir.

'An honourable man, if somewhat rash;
'And she, not even for Romney, would she spill
'A blot .. as little even as a tear ..
'Upon his marriage-contract,—not to gain
'A better joy for two than came by that:
'For, though I stood between her heart and heaven,
'She loved me wholly.'"
          Did I laugh or curse?
I think I sate there silent, hearing all,
Ay, hearing double,—Marian's tale, at once,
And Romney's marriage-vow, "*I'll keep* to THEE,"
Which means that woman-serpent. Is it time
For church now?
          "Lady Waldemar spoke more,"
Continued Marian, "but, as when a soul
Will pass out through the sweetness of a song
Beyond it, voyaging the uphill road,
Even so mine wandered from the things I heard
To those I suffered. It was afterward
I shaped the resolution to the act.
For many hours we talked. What need to talk?
The fate was clear and close; it touched my eyes;
But still the generous lady tried to keep
The case afloat, and would not let it go,
And argued, struggled upon Marian's side,
Which was not Romney's! though she little knew
What ugly monster would take up the end,—
What griping death within the drowning death
Was ready to complete my sum of death."

I thought,—Perhaps he's sliding now the ring
Upon that woman's finger ..
          She went on:
"The lady, failing to prevail her way,
Up-gathered my torn wishes from the ground
And pieced them with her strong benevolence;
And, as I thought I could breathe freer air

Away from England, going without pause
Without farewell, just breaking with a jerk
The blossomed offshoot from my thorny life,—
She promised kindly to provide the means,
With instant passage to the colonies
And full protection,—'would commit me straight
'To one who once had been her waiting-maid
'And had the customs of the world, intent
'On changing England for Australia
'Herself, to carry out her fortune so.'
For which I thanked the Lady Waldemar,
As men upon their death-beds thank last friends
Who lay the pillow straight: it is not much,
And yet 'tis all of which they are capable,
This lying smoothly in a bed to die.
And so, 'twas fixed;—and so, from day to day,
The woman named came in to visit me."

Just then the girl stopped speaking,—sate erect,
And stared at me as if I had been a ghost,
(Perhaps I looked as white as any ghost)
With large-eyed horror. "Does God make," she said,
"All sorts of creatures really, do you think?
Or is it that the Devil slavers them
So excellently, that we come to doubt
Who's stronger, He who makes, or he who mars?
I never liked the woman's face or voice
Or ways: it made me blush to look at her;
It made me tremble if she touched my hand;
And when she spoke a fondling word I shrank
As if one hated me who had power to hurt;
And, every time she came, my veins ran cold
As somebody were walking on my grave.
At last I spoke to Lady Waldemar:
'Could such an one be good to trust?' I asked.
Whereat the lady stroked my cheek and laughed
Her silver-laugh, (one must be born to laugh,

To put such music in it)—"Foolish girl,
'Your scattered wits are gathering wool beyond
'The sheep-walk reaches!—leave the thing to me.'
And therefore, half in trust, and half in scorn
That I had heart still for another fear
In such a safe despair, I left the thing.

"The rest is short. I was obedient:
I wrote my letter which delivered *him*
From Marian to his own prosperities,
And followed that bad guide. The lady? - hush,
I never blame the lady. Ladies who
Sit high, however willing to look down,
Will scarce see lower than their dainty feet;
And Lady Waldemar saw less than I,
With what a Devil's daughter I went forth
Along the swine's road, down the precipice,
In such a curl of hell-foam caught and choked,
No shriek of soul in anguish could pierce through
To fetch some help. They say there's help in heaven
For all such cries. But if one cries from hell . . .
What then?—the heavens are deaf upon that side.

"A woman . . hear me, let me make it plain, . .
A woman . . not a monster . . both her breasts
Made right to suckle babes . . she took me off
A woman also, young and ignorant
And heavy with my grief, my two poor eyes
Near washed away with weeping, till the trees,
The blessed unaccustomed trees and fields
Ran either side the train like stranger dogs
Unworthy of any notice,—took me off
So dull, so blind, so only half alive,
Not seeing by what road, nor by what ship,
Nor toward what place, nor to what end of all.
Men carry a corpse thus,—past the doorway, past
The garden-gate, the children's playground, up

The green lane,—then they leave it in the pit,
To sleep and find corruption, cheek to cheek
With him who stinks since Friday.
       "But suppose;
To go down with one's soul into the grave,
To go down half dead, half alive, I say,
And wake up with corruption, .. cheek to cheek
With him who stinks since Friday! There it is,
And that's the horror of 't, Miss Leigh.
         "You feel?
You understand?—no, do not look at me,
But understand. The blank, blind, weary way,
Which led, where'er it led, away at least;
The shifted ship, to Sydney or to France,
Still bound, wherever else, to another land;
The swooning sickness on the dismal sea,
The foreign shore, the shameful house, the night,
The feeble blood, the heavy-headed grief, ...
No need to bring their damnable drugged cup,
And yet they brought it. Hell's so prodigal
Of devil's gifts, hunts liberally in packs,
Will kill no poor small creature of the wilds
But fifty red wide throats must smoke at it,
As HIS at me .. when waking up at last ..
I told you that I waked up in the grave.

"Enough so!—it is plain enough so. True,
We wretches cannot tell out all our wrong
Without offence to decent happy folk.
I know that we must scrupulously hint
With half-words, delicate reserves, the thing
Which no one scrupled we should feel in full.
Let pass the rest, then; only leave my oath
Upon this sleeping child,—man's violence,
Not man's seduction, made me what I am,
As lost as .. I told *him* I should be lost.
When mothers fail us, can we help ourselves?

That's fatal!—And you call it being lost,
That down came next day's noon and caught me there
Half gibbering and half raving on the floor,
And wondering what had happened up in heaven,
That suns should dare to shine when God himself
Was certainly abolished.
                          "I was mad,
How many weeks, I know not,—many weeks.
I think they let me go when I was mad,
They feared my eyes and loosed me, as boys might
A mad dog which they had tortured.   Up and down
I went, by road and village, over tracts
Of open foreign country, large and strange,
Crossed everywhere by long thin poplar-lines
Like fingers of some ghastly skeleton Hand
Through sunlight and through moonlight evermore
Pushed out from hell itself to pluck me back,
And resolute to get me, slow and sure;
While every roadside Christ upon his cross
Hung reddening through his gory wounds at me,
And shook his nails in anger, and came down
To follow a mile after, wading up
The low vines and green wheat, crying 'Take the girl!
'She's none of mine from henceforth.'   Then I knew
(But this is somewhat dimmer than the rest)
The charitable peasants gave me bread
And leave to sleep in straw: and twice they tied,
At parting, Mary's image round my neck—
How heavy it seemed! as heavy as a stone;
A woman has been strangled with less weight:
I threw it in a ditch to keep it clean
And ease my breath a little, when none looked;
I did not need such safeguards:—brutal men
Stopped short, Miss Leigh, in insult, when they had seen
My face,—I must have had an awful look.
And so I lived: the weeks passed on,—I lived.
'Twas living my old tramp-life o'er again,

But, this time, in a dream, and hunted round
By some prodigious Dream-fear at my back,
Which ended yet: my brain cleared presently;
And there I sate, one evening, by the road,
I, Marian Erle, myself, alone, undone,
Facing a sunset low upon the flats
As if it were the finish of all time,
The great red stone upon my sepulchre,
Which angels were too weak to roll away."

SEVENTH BOOK.

"THE woman's motive? shall we daub ourselves
With finding roots for nettles? 'tis soft clay
And easily explored. She had the means
The monies, by the lady's liberal grace,
In trust for that Australian scheme and me,
Which so, that she might clutch with both her hands
And chink to her naughty uses undisturbed,
She served me (after all it was not strange,
'Twas only what my mother would have done)
A motherly, right damnable good turn.

"Well, after. There are nettles everywhere,
But smooth green grasses are more common still;
The blue of heaven is larger than the cloud;
A miller's wife at Clichy took me in
And spent her pity on me,— made me calm
And merely very reasonably sad.
She found me a servant's place in Paris where
I tried to take the cast-off life again,
And stood as quiet as a beaten ass
Who, having fallen through overloads, stands up
To let them charge him with another pack.

"A few months, so. My mistress, young and light,
Was easy with me, less for kindness than
Because she led, herself, an easy time
Betwixt her lover and her looking-glass,
Scarce knowing which way she was praised the most.
She felt so pretty and so pleased all day

She could not take the trouble to be cross,
But sometimes, as I stooped to tie her shoe,
Would tap me softly with her slender foot
Still restless with the last night's dancing in 't,
And say, 'Fie, pale-face! are you English girls
'All grave and silent? mass-book still, and Lent?
'And first-communion pallor on your cheeks,
'Worn past the time for 't? little fool, be gay!'
At which she vanished like a fairy, through
A gap of silver laughter.
                    "Came an hour
When all went otherwise. She did not speak,
But clenched her brows, and clipped me with her eyes
As if a viper with a pair of tongs,
Too far for any touch, yet near enough
To view the writhing creature,—then at last,
'Stand still there, in the holy Virgin's name,
'Thou Marian; thou'rt no reputable girl,
'Although sufficient dull for twenty saints!
'I think thou mock'st me and my house,' she said;
'Confess thou'lt be a mother in a month.
'Thou mask of saintship.'
                    "Could I answer her?
The light broke in so. It meant *that* then, *that?*
I had not thought of that, in all my thoughts,
Through all the cold, numb aching of my brow,
Through all the heaving of impatient life
Which threw me on death at intervals,—through all
The upbreak of the fountains of my heart
The rains had swelled too large: it could mean *that?*
Did God make mothers out of victims, then,
And set such pure amens to hideous deeds?
Why not? he overblows an ugly grave
With violets which blossom in the spring.
And *I* could be a mother in a month?
I hope it was not wicked to be glad.
I lifted up my voice and wept, and laughed,

To heaven, not her, until it tore my throat.
'Confess, confess!'—what was there to confess,
Except man's cruelty, except my wrong?
Except this anguish, or this ecstasy?
This shame or glory? The light woman there
Was small to take it in: an acorn-cup
Would take the sea in sooner.
      "'Good,' she cried:
'Unmarried and a mother, and she laughs!
'These unchaste girls are always impudent.
'Get out, intriguer! leave my house and trot.
'I wonder you should look me in the face,
'With such a filthy secret.'
      "Then I rolled
My scanty bundle up and went my way,
Washed white with weeping, shuddering head and foot
With blind hysteric passion, staggering forth
Beyond those doors. 'Twas natural of course
She should not ask me where I meant to sleep;
I might sleep well beneath the heavy Seine,
Like others of my sort; the bed was laid
For us. But any woman, womanly,
Had thought of him who should be in a month,
The sinless babe that should be in a month,
And if by chance he might be warmer housed
Than underneath such dreary dripping caves."

I broke on Marian there. "Yet she herself,
A wife, I think, had scandals of her own,
A lover not her husband."
      "Ay," she said,
"But gold and meal are measured otherwise;
I learnt so much at school," said Marian Erle.

'O crooked world," I cried, "ridiculous
If not so lamentable! 'Tis the way
With these light women of a thrifty vice,

My Marian,—always hard upon the rent
In any sister's virtue! while they keep
Their own so darned and patched with perfidy,
That, though a rag itself, it looks as well
Across a street, in balcony or coach,
As any perfect stuff might. For my part,
I'd rather take the wind-side of the stews
Than touch such women with my finger-end!
They top the poor street-walker by their lie
And look the better for being so much worse:
The devil's most devilish when respectable.
But you, dear, and your story."

       "All the rest
Is here," she said, and signed upon the child.
"I found a mistress-sempstress who was kind
And let me sew in peace among her girls.
And what was better than to draw the threads
All day and half the night for him and him?
And so I lived for him, and so he lives,
And so I know, by this time, God lives too."

She smiled beyond the sun and ended so,
And all my soul rose up to take her part
Against the world's successes, virtues, fames.
"Come with me, sweetest sister," I returned,
"And sit within my house and do me good
From henceforth, thou and thine! ye are my own
From henceforth. I am lonely in the world,
And thou art lonely, and the child is half
An orphan. Come,—and henceforth thou and I
Being still together will not miss a friend,
Nor he a father, since two mothers shall
Make that up to him. I am journeying south,
And in my Tuscan home I'll find a niche
And set thee there, my saint, the child and thee,
And burn the lights of love before thy face,
And ever at thy sweet look cross myself

From mixing with the world's prosperities;
That so, in gravity and holy calm,
We two may live on toward the truer life."

She looked me in the face and answered not,
Nor signed she was unworthy, nor gave thanks,
But took the sleeping child and held it out
To meet my kiss, as if requiting me
And trusting me at once. And thus, at once,
I carried him and her to where I live;
She's there now, in the little room, asleep,
I hear the soft child-breathing through the door,
And all three of us, at to-morrow's break,
Pass onward, homeward, to our Italy.
Oh, Romney Leigh, I have your debts to pay,
And I'll be just and pay them.
      But yourself!
To pay your debts is scarcely difficult,
To buy your life is nearly impossible,
Being sold away to Lamia. My head aches,
I cannot see my road along this dark;
Nor can I creep and grope, as fits the dark,
For these foot-catching robes of womanhood:
A man might walk a little .. but I!—He loves
The Lamia-woman,—and I, write to him
What stops his marriage, and destroys his peace,—
Or what perhaps shall simply trouble him,
Until she only need to touch his sleeve
With just a finger's tremulous white flame,
Saying, "Ah,—Aurora Leigh! a pretty tale,
"A very pretty poet! I can guess
"The motive"—then, to catch his eyes in hers
And vow she does not wonder,—and they two
To break in laughter as the sea along
A melancholy coast, and float up higher,
In such a laugh, their fatal weeds of love!
Ay, fatal, ay. And who shall answer me

Fate has not hurried tides,—and if to-night
My letter would not be a night too late,
An arrow shot into a man that's dead,
To prove a vain intention? Would I show
The new wife vile, to make the husband mad?
No, Lamia! shut the shutters, bar the doors
From every glimmer on thy serpent-skin!
I will not let thy hideous secret out
To agonise the man I love—I mean
The friend I love . . as friends love.

        It is strange,
To-day while Marian told her story like
To absorb most listeners, how I listened chief
To a voice not hers, nor yet that enemy's,
Nor God's in wrath, . . but one that mixed with mine
Long years ago among the garden-trees,
And said to *me*, to *me* too, "Be my wife,
Aurora." It is strange with what a swell
Of yearning passion, as a snow of ghosts
Might beat against the impervious door of heaven,
I thought, "Now, if I had been a woman, such
As God made women, to save men by love,—
By just my love I might have saved this man,
And made a nobler poem for the world
Than all I have failed in." But I failed besides
In this; and now he's lost! through me alone!
And, by my only fault, his empty house
Sucks in, at this same hour, a wind from hell
To keep his hearth cold, make his casements creak
For ever to the tune of plague and sin—
O Romney, O my Romney, O my friend,
My cousin and friend! my helper, when I would,
My love, that might be! mine!

        Why, how one weeps
When one's too weary! Were a witness by,
He'd say some folly . . that I loved the man,
Who knows? . . and make me laugh again for scorn.

At strongest, women are as weak in flesh,
As men, at weakest, vilest, are in soul:
So, hard for women to keep pace with men!
As well give up at once, sit down at once,
And weep as I do. Tears, tears! *why* we weep?
'Tis worth inquiry?—that we've shamed a life,
Or lost a love, or missed a world, perhaps?
By no means. Simply, that we've walked too far,
Or talked too much, or felt the wind i' the east,—
And so we weep, as if both body and soul
Broke up in water—this way.
      Poor mixed rags
Forsooth we're made of, like those other dolls
That lean with pretty faces into fairs.
It seems as if I had a man in me,
Despising such a woman.
      Yet indeed,
To see a wrong or suffering moves us all
To undo it though we should undo ourselves,
Ay, all the more, that we undo ourselves;
That's womanly, past doubt, and not ill-moved.
A natural movement therefore, on my part,
To fill the chair up of my cousin's wife,
And save him from a devil's company!
We're all so,—made so—'tis our woman's trade
To suffer torment for another's ease.
The world's male chivalry has perished out,
But women are knights-errant to the last;
And if Cervantes had been Shakespeare too,
He had made his Don a Donna.
      So it clears,
And so we rain our skies blue.
      Put away
This weakness. If, as I have just now said,
A man's within me,—let him act himself,
Ignoring the poor conscious trouble of blood
That's called the woman merely. I will write

Plain words to England,—if too late, too late,
If ill-accounted, then accounted ill;
We'll trust the heavens with something.
      "Dear Lord Howe,
You'll find a story on another leaf
Of Marian Erle,—what noble friend of yours
She trusted once, through what flagitious means,
To what disastrous ends;—the story's true.
I found her wandering on the Paris quays,
A babe upon her breast,—unnatural
Unseasonable outcast on such snow
Unthawed to this time. I will tax in this
Your friendship, friend, if that convicted She
Be not his wife yet, to denounce the facts
To himself,—but, otherwise, to let them pass
On tip-toe like escaping murderers,
And tell my cousin merely—Marian lives,
Is found, and finds her home with such a friend,
Myself, Aurora. Which good news, 'She's found,'
Will help to make him merry in his love:
I send it, tell him, for my marriage-gift,
As good as orange-water for the nerves,
Or perfumed gloves for headache,—though aware
That he, except of love, is scarcely sick:
I mean the new love this time, .. since last year.
Such quick forgetting on the part of men!
Is any shrewder trick upon the cards
To enrich them? pray instruct me how 'tis done:
First, clubs,--and while you look at clubs, 'tis spades;
That's prodigy. The lightning strikes a man,
And when we think to find him dead and charred ..
Why, there he is on a sudden, playing pipes
Beneath the splintered elm-tree! Crime and shame
And all their hoggery trample your smooth world,
Nor leave more foot-marks than Apollo's kine
Whose hoofs were muffled by the thieving god
In tamarisk-leaves and myrtle. I'm so sad,

So weary and sad to-night, I'm somewhat sour,—
Forgive me. To be blue and shrew at once,
Exceeds all toleration except yours,
But yours, I know, is infinite. Farewell.
To-morrow we take train for Italy.
Speak gently of me to your gracious wife,
As one, however far, shall yet be near
In loving wishes to your house."
                              I sign.
And now I loose my heart upon a page,
This—
        "Lady Waldemar, I'm very glad
I never liked you; which you knew so well
You spared me, in your turn, to like me much:
Your liking surely had done worse for me
Than has your loathing, though the last appears
Sufficiently unscrupulous to hurt,
And not afraid of judgment. Now, there's space
Between our faces,—I stand off, as if
I judged a stranger's portrait and pronounced
Indifferently the type was good or bad.
What matter to me that the lines are false,
I ask you? did I ever ink my lips
By drawing your name through them as a friend's,
Or touch your hands as lovers do? Thank God
I never did: and since you're proved so vile,
Ay, vile, I say,—we'll show it presently,—
I'm not obliged to nurse my friend in you,
Or wash out my own blots, in counting yours,
Or even excuse myself to honest souls
Who seek to press my lip or clasp my palm,—
'Alas, but Lady Waldemar came first!'
'Tis true, by this time you may near me so
That you're my cousin's wife. You've gambled deep
As Lucifer, and won the morning-star
In that case,—and the noble house of Leigh
Must henceforth with its good roof shelter you:

I cannot speak and burn you up between
Those rafters, I who am born a Leigh,—nor speak
And pierce your breast through Romney's, I who live
His friend and cousin,—so, you're safe. You two
Must grow together like the tares and wheat
Till God's great fire.—But make the best of time.

"And hide this letter: let it speak no more
Than I shall, how you tricked poor Marian Erle,
And set her own love digging its own grave
Within her green hope's pretty garden-ground,—
Ay, sent her forth with some one of your sort
To a wicked house in France, from which she fled
With curses in her eyes and ears and throat,
Her whole soul choked with curses,—mad in short,
And madly scouring up and down for weeks
The foreign hedgeless country, lone and lost,—
So innocent, male-fiends might slink within
Remote hell-corners, seeing her so defiled.

"But you,—you are a woman and more bold.
To do you justice, you'd not shrink to face ..
We'll say, the unfledged life in the other room,
Which, treading down God's corn, you trod in sight
Of all the dogs, in reach of all the guns,—
Ay, Marian's babe, her poor unfathered child,
Her yearling babe!—you'd face him when he wakes
And opens up his wonderful blue eyes:
You'd meet them and not wink perhaps, nor fear
God's triumph in them and supreme revenge
When righting His creation's balance-scale
(You pulled as low as Tophet) to the top
Of most celestial innocence. For me
Who am not as bold, I own those infant eyes
Have set me praying.
                    "While they look at heaven,
No need of protestation in my words

Against the place you've made them! let them look.
They'll do your business with the heavens, be sure:
I spare you common curses.
                              "Ponder this;
If haply you're the wife of Romney Leigh,
(For which inheritance beyond your birth
You sold that poisonous porridge called your soul)
I charge you, be his faithful and true wife!
Keep warm his hearth and clean his board, and, when
He speaks, be quick with your obedience;
Still grind your paltry wants and low desires
To dust beneath his heel; though, even thus,
The ground must hurt him,—it was writ of old,
'Ye shall not yoke together ox and ass,'
The nobler and ignobler. Ay, but you
Shall do your part as well as such ill things
Can do aught good. You shall not vex him,—mark,
You shall not vex him, jar him when he's sad,
Or cross him when he's eager. Understand
To trick him with apparent sympathies,
Nor let him see thee in the face too near
And unlearn thy sweet seeming. Pay the price
Of lies, by being constrained to lie on still:
'Tis easy for thy sort: a million more
Will scarcely damn thee deeper.
                              "Doing which
You are very safe from Marian and myself;
We'll breathe as softly as the infant here,
And stir no dangerous embers. Fail a point,
And show our Romney wounded, ill-content,
Tormented in his home, we open mouth,
And such a noise will follow, the last trump's
Will scarcely seem more dreadful, even to you;
You'll have no pipers after: Romney will
(I know him) push you forth as none of his,
All other men declaring it well done,
While women, even the worst, your like, will draw

Their skirts back, not to brush you in the street,
And so I warn you. I'm . . . Aurora Leigh."

The letter written I felt satisfied.
The ashes, smouldering in me, were thrown out
By handfuls from me: I had writ my heart
And wept my tears, and now was cool and calm;
And, going straightway to the neighbouring room,
I lifted up the curtains of the bed
Where Marian Erle, the babe upon her arm,
Both faces leaned together like a pair
Of folded innocences self-complete,
Each smiling from the other, smiled and slept.
There seemed no sin, no shame, no wrath, no grief.
I felt she too had spoken words that night,
But softer certainly, and said to God,
Who laughs in heaven perhaps that such as I
Should make ado for such as she. "Defiled"
I wrote? "defiled" I thought her? Stoop,
Stoop lower, Aurora! get the angels' leave
To creep in somewhere, humbly, on your knees,
Within this round of sequestration white
In which they have wrapt earth's foundlings, heaven's elect.

The next day we took train to Italy
And fled on southward in the roar of steam.
The marriage-bells of Romney must be loud,
To sound so clear through all: I was not well,
And truly, though the truth is like a jest,
I could not choose but fancy, half the way,
I stood alone i' the belfry, fifty bells
Of naked iron, mad with merriment,
(As one who laughs and cannot stop himself)
All clanking at me, in me, over me,
Until I shrieked a shriek I could not hear,
And swooned with noise,—but still, along my swoon,
Was 'ware the baffled changes backward rang,

Prepared, at each emerging sense, to beat
And crash it out with clangour. I was weak;
I struggled for the posture of my soul
In upright consciousness of place and time,
But evermore, 'twixt waking and asleep,
Slipped somehow, staggered, caught at Marian's eyes
A moment, (it is very good for strength
To know that some one needs you to be strong)
And so recovered what I called myself,
For that time.
    I just knew it when we swept
Above the old roofs of Dijon: Lyons dropped
A spark into the night, half trodden out
Unseen. But presently the winding Rhone
Washed out the moonlight large along his banks
Which strained their yielding curves out clear and clean
To hold it,—shadow of town and castle blurred
Upon the hurrying river. Such an air
Blew thence upon the forehead,—half an air
And half a water,—that I leaned and looked,
Then, turning back on Marian, smiled to mark
That she looked only on her child, who slept,
His face toward the moon too.
    So we passed
The liberal open country and the close,
And shot through tunnels, like a lightning-wedge
By great Thor-hammers driven through the rock,
Which, quivering through the intestine blackness, splits,
And lets it in at once: the train swept in
Athrob with effort, trembling with resolve,
The fierce denouncing whistle wailing on
And dying off smothered in the shuddering dark,
While we, self-awed, drew troubled breath, oppressed
As other Titans underneath the pile
And nightmare of the mountains. Out, at last,
To catch the dawn afloat upon the land!
—Hills, slung forth broadly and gauntly everywhere,

Not crampt in their foundations, pushing wide
Rich outspreads of the vineyards and the corn,
(As if they entertained i' the name of France)
While, down their straining sides, streamed manifest
A soil as red as Charlemagne's knightly blood,
To consecrate the verdure. Some one said,
"Marseilles!" And lo, the city of Marseilles,
With all her ships behind her, and beyond,
The scimitar of ever-shining sea
For right-hand use, bared blue against the sky!

That night we spent between the purple heaven
And purple water: I think Marian slept;
But I, as a dog a-watch for his master's foot,
Who cannot sleep or eat before he hears,
I sate upon the deck and watched the night
And listened through the stars for Italy.
Those marriage-bells I spoke of, sounded far,
As some child's go-cart in the street beneath
To a dying man who will not pass the day,
And knows it, holding by a hand he loves.
I too sate quiet, satisfied with death,
Sate silent: I could hear my own soul speak,
And had my friend,—for Nature comes sometimes
And says, "I am ambassador for God."
I felt the wind soft from the land of souls;
The old miraculous mountains heaved in sight,
One straining past another along the shore,
The way of grand dull Odyssean ghosts,
Athirst to drink the cool blue wine of seas
And stare on voyagers. Peak pushing peak
They stood: I watched, beyond that Tyrian belt
Of intense sea betwixt them and the ship,
Down all their sides the misty olive-woods
Dissolving in the weak congenial moon
And still disclosing some brown convent-tower
That seems as if it grew from some brown rock,

Or many a little lighted village, dropt
Like a fallen star upon so high a point,
You wonder what can keep it in its place
From sliding headlong with the waterfalls
Which powder all the myrtle and orange groves
With spray of silver. Thus my Italy
Was stealing on us. Genoa broke with day,
The Doria's long pale palace striking out,
From green hills in advance of the white town,
A marble finger dominant to ships,
Seen glimmering through the uncertain gray of dawn.

And then I did not think, "my Italy,"
I thought, "my father!" O my father's house,
Without his presence!—Places are too much
Or else too little, for immortal man,—
Too little, when love's May o'ergrows the ground,
Too much, when that luxuriant robe of green
Is rustling to our ankles in dead leaves.
'Tis only good to be or here or there,
Because we had a dream on such a stone,
Or this or that,—but, once being wholly waked
And come back to the stone without the dream,
We trip upon 't,—alas, and hurt ourselves;
Or else it falls on us and grinds us flat,
The heaviest grave-stone on this burying earth.
—But while I stood and mused, a quiet touch
Fell light upon my arm, and turning round,
A pair of moistened eyes convicted mine.
"What, Marian! is the babe astir so soon?"
"He sleeps," she answered; "I have crept up thrice,
And seen you sitting, standing, still at watch.
I thought it did you good till now, but now" . . .
"But now," I said, "you leave the child alone."
"And you're alone," she answered,—and she looked
As if I too were something. Sweet the help
Of one we have helped! Thanks, Marian, for such help.

I found a house at Florence on the hill
Of Bellosguardo. 'Tis a tower which keeps
A post of double-observation o'er
That valley of Arno (holding as a hand
The outspread city,) straight toward Fiesole
And Mount Morello and the setting sun,
The Vallombrosan mountains opposite,
Which sunrise fills as full as crystal cups
Turned red to the brim because their wine is red.
No sun could die nor yet be born unseen
By dwellers at my villa: morn and eve
Were magnified before us in the pure
Illimitable space and pause of sky,
Intense as angels' garments blanched with God,
Less blue than radiant. From the outer wall
Of the garden, drops the mystic floating gray
Of olive-trees, (with interruptions green
From maize and vine) until 'tis caught and torn
Upon the abrupt black line of cypresses
Which signs the way to Florence. Beautiful
The city lies along the ample vale,
Cathedral, tower and palace, piazza and street,
The river trailing like a silver cord
Through all, and curling loosely, both before
And after, over the whole stretch of land
Sown whitely up and down its opposite slopes
With farms and villas.
                    Many weeks had passed,
No word was granted.—Last, a letter came
From Vincent Carrington:—"My dear Miss Leigh,
You've been as silent as a poet should,
When any other man is sure to speak.
If sick, if vexed, if dumb, a silver piece
Will split a man's tongue,—straight he speaks and says,
'Received that cheque.' But you! .. I send you funds
To Paris, and you make no sign at all.

Remember I'm responsible and wait
A sign of you, Miss Leigh.
                    "Meantime your book
Is eloquent as if you were not dumb;
And common critics, ordinarily deaf
To such fine meanings, and, like deaf men, loth
To seem deaf, answering chance-wise, yes or no,
'It must be' or 'it must not,' (most pronounced
When least convinced) pronounce for once aright:
You'd think they really heard,—and so they do ..
The burr of three or four who really hear
And praise your book aright: Fame's smallest trump
Is a great ear-trumpet for the deaf as posts,
No other being effective. Fear not, friend;
We think here you have written a good book,
And you, a woman! It was in you—yes,
I felt 'twas in you: yet I doubted half
If that od-force of German Reichenbach,
Which still from female finger-tips burns blue,
Could strike out as our masculine white heats
To quicken a man. Forgive me. All my heart
Is quick with yours since, just a fortnight since,
I read your book and loved it.
                    "Will you love
My wife, too? Here's my secret I might keep
A month more from you! but I yield it up
Because I know you'll write the sooner for 't,
Most women (of your height even) counting love
Life's only serious business. Who's my wife
That shall be in a month, you ask? nor guess?
Remember what a pair of topaz eyes
You once detected, turned against the wall,
That morning in my London painting-room;
The face half-sketched, and slurred; the eyes alone!
But you .. you caught them up with yours, and said
'Kate Ward's eyes, surely.'—Now I own the truth:
I had thrown them there to keep them safe from Jove,

They would so naughtily find out their way
To both the heads of both my Danaës
Where just it made me mad to look at them.
Such eyes! I could not paint or think of eyes
But those,—and so I flung them into paint
And turned them to the wall's care. Ay, but now
I've let them out, my Kate's: I've painted her,
(I change my style and leave mythologies)
The whole sweet face; it looks upon my soul
Like a face on water, to beget itself.
A half-length portrait, in a hanging cloak
Like one you wore once; 'tis a little frayed,—
I pressed too for the nude harmonious arm—
But she, she'd have her way, and have her cloak;
She said she could be like you only so,
And would not miss the fortune. Ah, my friend,
You'll write and say she shall not miss your love
Through meeting mine? in faith, she would not change.
She has your books by heart more than my words,
And quotes you up against me till I'm pushed
Where, three months since, her eyes were: nay, in fact,
Nought satisfied her but to make me paint
Your last book folded in her dimpled hands
Instead of my brown palette as I wished,
And, grant me, the presentment had been newer;
She'd grant me nothing: I compounded for
The naming of the wedding-day next month,
And gladly too. 'Tis pretty, to remark
How women can love women of your sort,
And tie their hearts with love-knots to your feet,
Grow insolent about you against men
And put us down by putting up the lip,
As if a man,—there *are* such, let us own,
Who write not ill,—remains a man, poor wretch,
While you——! Write weaker than Aurora Leigh,
And there'll be women who believe of you
(Besides my Kate) that if you walked on sand

You would not leave a foot-print.
                              "Are you put
To wonder by my marriage, like poor Leigh?
'Kate Ward!' he said. 'Kate Ward!' he said anew.
'I thought . . .' he said, and stopped,—'I did not think . .'
And then he dropped to silence.
                              "Ah, he's changed.
I had not seen him, you're aware, for long,
But went of course. I have not touched on this
Through all this letter,—conscious of your heart,
And writing lightlier for the heavy fact,
As clocks are voluble with lead.
                              "How poor,
To say I'm sorry! dear Leigh, dearest Leigh.
In those old days of Shropshire,—pardon me,—
When he and you fought many a field of gold
On what you should do, or you should not do,
Make bread or verses, (it just came to that)
I thought you'd one day draw a silken peace
Through a golden ring. I thought so: foolishly,
The event proved,—for you went more opposite
To each other, month by month, and year by year,
Until this happened. God knows best, we say,
But hoarsely. When the fever took him first,
Just after I had writ to you in France,
They tell me Lady Waldemar mixed drinks
And counted grains, like any salaried nurse,
Excepting that she wept too. Then Lord Howe,
You're right about Lord Howe, Lord Howe's a trump,
And yet, with such in his hand, a man like Leigh
May lose as *he* does. There's an end to all,
Yes, even this letter, though this second sheet
May find you doubtful. Write a word for Kate:
She reads my letters always, like a wife,
And if she sees her name I'll see her smile
And share the luck. So, bless you, friend of two!
I will not ask you what your feeling is

At Florence with my pictures; I can hear
Your heart a-flutter over the snow-hills:
And, just to pace the Pitti with you once,
I'd give a half-hour of to-morrow's walk
With Kate . . I think so.   Vincent Carrington."

The noon was hot; the air scorched like the sun
And was shut out.   The closed persiani threw
Their long-scored shadows on my villa-floor,
And interlined the golden atmosphere
Straight, still,—across the pictures on the wall,
The statuette on the console, (of young Love
And Psyche made one marble by a kiss)
The low couch where I leaned, the table near,
The vase of lilies Marian pulled last night
Each green leaf and each white leaf ruled in black
As if for writing some new text of fate)
And the open letter, rested on my knee,
But there the lines swerved, trembled, though I sate
Untroubled, plainly, reading it again
And three times.   Well, he's married; that is clear.
No wonder that he's married, nor much more
That Vincent 's therefore "sorry."   Why, of course
The lady nursed him when he was not well,
Mixed drinks,—unless nepenthe was the drink
'Twas scarce worth telling.   But a man in love
Will see the whole sex in his mistress' hood,
The prettier for its lining of fair rose,
Although he catches back and says at last,
"I'm sorry."   Sorry.   Lady Waldemar
At prettiest, under the said hood, preserved
From such a light as I could hold to her face
To flare its ugly wrinkles out to shame,
Is scarce a wife for Romney, as friends judge,
Aurora Leigh or Vincent Carrington,
That's plain.   And if he's "conscious of my heart" . .
It may be natural, though the phrase is strong;

(One 's apt to use strong phrases, being in love)
And even that stuff of "fields of gold," "gold rings,"
And what he "thought," poor Vincent, what he "thought,"
May never mean enough to ruffle me.
—Why, this room stifles. Better burn than choke;
Best have air, air, although it comes with fire,—
Throw open blinds and windows to the noon
And take a blister on my brow instead
Of this dead weight! best, perfectly be stunned
By those insufferable cicale, sick
And hoarse with rapture of the summer-heat,
That sing, like poets, till their hearts break,—sing
Till men say, "It's too tedious."
      Books succeed,
And lives fail. Do I feel it so, at last?
Kate loves a worn-out cloak for being like mine,
While I live self-despised for being myself,
And yearn toward some one else, who yearns away
From what he is, in his turn. Strain a step
For ever, yet gain no step? Are we such,
We cannot, with our admirations even,
Our tip-toe aspirations, touch a thing
That's higher than we? is all a dismal flat,
And God alone above each, as the sun
O'er level lagunes, to make them shine and stink,—
Laying stress upon us with immediate flame,
While we respond with our miasmal fog
And call it mounting higher because we grow
More highly fatal?
    Tush, Aurora Leigh!
You wear your sackcloth looped in Cæsar's way
And brag your failings as mankind's. Be still.
There *is* what's higher, in this very world,
Than you can live, or catch at. Stand aside,
And look at others—instance little Kate!
She'll make a perfect wife for Carrington.
She always has been looking round the earth

For something good and green to alight upon
And nestle into, with those soft-winged eyes,
Subsiding now beneath his manly hand
'Twixt trembling lids of inexpressive joy.
I will not scorn her, after all, too much,
That so much she should love me: a wise man
Can pluck a leaf, and find a lecture in 't;
And I, too, .. God has made me,—I've a heart
That's capable of worship, love, and loss;
We say the same of Shakespeare's. I'll be meek
And learn to reverence, even this poor myself.

The book, too—pass it. "A good book," says he,
"And you a woman." I had laughed at that,
But long since. I'm a woman,—it is true;
Alas, and woe to us, when we feel it most!
Then, least care have we for the crowns and goals
And compliments on writing our good books.

The book has some truth in it, I believe,
And truth outlives pain, as the soul does life.
I know we talk our Phædons to the end,
Through all the dismal faces that we make,
O'er-wrinkled with dishonouring agony
From decomposing drugs. I have written truth,
And I a woman,—feebly, partially,
Inaptly in presentation, Romney 'll add,
Because a woman. For the truth itself,
That's neither man's nor woman's, but just God's,
None else has reason to be proud of truth:
Himself will see it sifted, disenthralled,
And kept upon the height and in the light,
As far as and no farther than 'tis truth;
For, now He has left off calling firmaments
And strata, flowers and creatures, very good,
He says it still of truth, which is His own.

Truth, so far, in my book;—the truth which draws
Through all things upwards,—that a twofold world
Must go to a perfect cosmos. Natural things
And spiritual,—who separates those two
In art, in morals, or the social drift,
Tears up the bond of nature and brings death,
Paints futile pictures, writes unreal verse,
Leads vulgar days, deals ignorantly with men,
Is wrong, in short, at all points. We divide
This apple of life, and cut it through the pips,—
The perfect round which fitted Venus' hand
Has perished as utterly as if we ate
Both halves. Without the spiritual, observe,
The natural's impossible,—no form,
No motion: without sensuous, spiritual
Is inappreciable,—no beauty or power:
And in this twofold sphere the twofold man
(For still the artist is intensely a man)
Holds firmly by the natural, to reach
The spiritual beyond it,—fixes still
The type with mortal vision, to pierce through,
With eyes immortal, to the antetype
Some call the ideal,—better called the real,
And certain to be called so presently
When things shall have their names. Look long enough
On any peasant's face here, coarse and lined,
You'll catch Antinous somewhere in that clay,
As perfect featured as he yearns at Rome
From marble pale with beauty; then persist,
And, if your apprehension's competent,
You'll find some fairer angel at his back,
As much exceeding him as he the boor,
And pushing him with empyreal disdain
For ever out of sight. Ay, Carrington
Is glad of such a creed: an artist must,
Who paints a tree, a leaf, a common stone
With just his hand, and finds it suddenly

A-piece with and conterminous to his soul.
Why else do these things move him, leaf, or stone?
The bird's not moved, that pecks at a spring-shoot;
Nor yet the horse, before a quarry a-graze:
But man, the two-fold creature, apprehends
The two-fold manner, in and outwardly,
And nothing in the world comes single to him,
A mere itself,—cup, column, or candlestick,
All patterns of what shall be in the Mount;
The whole temporal show related royally,
And built up to eterne significance
Through the open arms of God. "There's nothing great
Nor small," has said a poet of our day,
Whose voice will ring beyond the curfew of eve
And not be thrown out by the matin's bell:
And truly, I reiterate, nothing's small!
No lily-muffled hum of a summer-bee,
But finds some coupling with the spinning stars;
No pebble at your foot, but proves a sphere;
No chaffinch, but implies the cherubim;
And, (glancing on my own thin, veinèd wrist,)
In such a little tremour of the blood
The whole strong clamour of a vehement soul
Doth utter itself distinct. Earth's crammed with heaven,
And every common bush afire with God;
But only he who sees, takes off his shoes,
The rest sit round it and pluck blackberries,
And daub their natural faces unaware
More and more from the first similitude.

Truth, so far, in my book! a truth which draws
From all things upward. I, Aurora, still
Have felt it hound me through the wastes of life
As Jove did Io; and, until that Hand
Shall overtake me wholly and on my head
Lay down its large unfluctuating peace,
The feverish gad-fly pricks me up and down.

It must be.   Art's the witness of what Is
Behind this show.   If this world's show were all,
Then imitation would be all in Art;
There, Jove's hand gripes us!—For we stand here, we,
If genuine artists, witnessing for God's
Complete, consummate, undivided work;
—That every natural flower which grows on earth
Implies a flower upon the spiritual side,
Substantial, archetypal, all a-glow
With blossoming causes,—not so far away,
But we, whose spirit-sense is somewhat cleared,
May catch at something of the bloom and breath,—
Too vaguely apprehended, though indeed
Still apprehended, consciously or not,
And still transferred to picture, music, verse,
For thrilling audient and beholding souls
By signs and touches which are known to souls.
How known, they know not,—why, they cannot find,
So straight call out on genius, say, "A man
Produced this," when much rather they should say,
"'Tis insight and he saw this."
                                Thus is Art
Self-magnified in magnifying a truth
Which, fully recognised, would change the world
And shift its morals.   If a man could feel,
Not one day, in the artist's ecstasy,
But every day, feast, fast, or working-day,
The spiritual significance burn through
The hieroglyphic of material shows,
Henceforward he would paint the globe with wings,
And reverence fish and fowl, the bull, the tree,
And even his very body as a man,—
Which now he counts so vile, that all the towns
Make offal of their daughters for its use,
On summer-nights, when God is sad in heaven
To think what goes on in his recreant world
He made quite other; while that moon He made

To shine there, at the first love's covenant,
Shines still, convictive as a marriage-ring
Before adulterous eyes.
     How sure it is,
That, if we say a true word, instantly
We feel 'tis God's, not ours, and pass it on
Like bread at sacrament we taste and pass
Nor handle for a moment, as indeed
We dared to set up any claim to such!
And I—my poem,—let my readers talk.
I'm closer to it—I can speak as well:
I'll say with Romney, that the book is weak,
The range uneven, the points of sight obscure,
The music interrupted.
     Let us go.
The end of woman (or of man, I think)
Is not a book. Alas, the best of books
Is but a word in Art, which soon grows cramped,
Stiff, dubious-statured with the weight of years,
And drops an accent or digamma down
Some cranny of unfathomable time,
Beyond the critic's reaching. Art itself,
We've called the larger life, must feel the soul
Live past it. For more's felt than is perceived,
And more's perceived than can be interpreted,
And Love strikes higher with his lambent flame
Than Art can pile the faggots.
     Is it so?
When Jove's hand meets us with composing touch,
And when at last we are hushed and satisfied,
Then Io does not call it truth, but love?
Well, well! my father was an Englishman:
My mother's blood in me is not so strong
That I should bear this stress of Tuscan noon
And keep my wits. The town, there, seems to seethe
In this Medæan boil-pot of the sun,
And all the patient hills are bubbling round

As if a prick would leave them flat. Does heaven
Keep far off, not to set us in a blaze?
Not so,—let drag your fiery fringes, heaven,
And burn us up to quiet. Ah, we know
Too much here, not to know what's best for peace;
We have too much light here, not to want more fire
To purify and end us. We talk, talk,
Conclude upon divine philosophies,
And get the thanks of men for hopeful books,
Whereat we take our own life up, and .. pshaw!
Unless we piece it with another's life
(A yard of silk to carry out our lawn)
As well suppose my little handkerchief
Would cover Samminiato, church and all,
If out I threw it past the cypresses,
As, in this ragged, narrow life of mine,
Contain my own conclusions.
       But at least
We'll shut up the persiani and sit down,
And when my head 's done aching, in the cool,
Write just a word to Kate and Carrington.
May joy be with them! she has chosen well,
And he not ill.
     I should be glad, I think,
Except for Romney. Had *he* married Kate,
I surely, surely, should be very glad.
This Florence sits upon me easily,
With native air and tongue. My graves are calm,
And do not too much hurt me. Marian 's good
Gentle and loving,—lets me hold the child,
Or drags him up the hills to find me flowers
And fill these vases ere I 'm quite awake,—
My grandiose red tulips, which grow wild,
Or Dante's purple lilies, which he blew
To a larger bubble with his prophet breath,
Or one of those tall flowering reeds that stand
In Arno, like a sheaf of sceptres left

By some remote dynasty of dead gods
To suck the stream for ages and get green,
And blossom wheresoe'er a hand divine
Had warmed the place with ichor. Such I find
At early morning laid across my bed,
And wake up pelted with a childish laugh
Which even Marian's low precipitous "hush"
Has vainly interposed to put away,—
While I, with shut eyes, smile and motion for
The dewy kiss that's very sure to come
From mouth and cheeks, the whole child's face at once
Dissolved on mine,—as if a nosegay burst
Its string with the weight of roses overblown,
And dropt upon me. Surely I should be glad.
The little creature almost loves me now,
And calls my name, "Alola," stripping off
The *rs* like thorns, to make it smooth enough
To take between his dainty, milk-fed lips,
God love him! I should certainly be glad,
Except, God help me, that I'm sorrowful
Because of Romney.
    Romney, Romney! Well,
This grows absurd!—too like a tune that runs
I' the head, and forces all things in the world,
Wind, rain, the creaking gnat, or stuttering fly,
To sing itself and vex you,—yet perhaps
A paltry tune you never fairly liked,
Some "I'd be a butterfly," or "C'est l'amour:"
We're made so,—not such tyrants to ourselves
But still we are slaves to nature. Some of us
Are turned, too, overmuch like some poor verse
With a trick of ritournelle: the same thing goes
And comes back ever.
    Vincent Carrington
Is "sorry," and I'm sorry; but *he's* strong
To mount from sorrow to his heaven of love,
And when he says at moments, "Poor, poor Leigh,

Who'll never call his own so true a heart,
So fair a face even,"—he must quickly lose
The pain of pity, in the blush he makes
By his very pitying eyes. The snow, for him,
Has fallen in May and finds the whole earth warm,
And melts at the first touch of the green grass.

But Romney,—he has chosen, after all.
I think he had as excellent a sun
To see by, as most others, and perhaps
Has scarce seen really worse than some of us
When all's said. Let him pass. I'm not too much
A woman, not to be a man for once
And bury all my Dead like Alaric,
Depositing the treasures of my soul
In this drained water-course, then letting flow
The river of life again with commerce-ships
And pleasure-barges full of silks and songs.
Blow, winds, and help us.
                    Ah, we mock ourselves
With talking of the winds; perhaps as much
With other resolutions. How it weighs,
This hot, sick air! and how I covet here
The Dead's provision on the river-couch,
With silver curtains drawn on tinkling rings!
Or else their rest in quiet crypts,—laid by
From heat and noise;—from those cicale, say,
And this more vexing heart-beat.
                            So it is:
We covet for the soul, the body's part,
To die and rot. Even so, Aurora, ends
Our aspiration who bespoke our place
So far in the east. The occidental flats
Had fed us fatter, therefore? we have climbed
Where herbage ends? we want the beast's part now,
And tire of the angel's?—Men define a man,
The creature who stands front-ward to the stars,

The creature who looks inward to himself,
The tool-wright, laughing creature. 'Tis enough:
We'll say instead, the inconsequent creature, man,
For that's his specialty. What creature else
Conceives the circle, and then walks the square?
Loves things proved bad, and leaves a thing proved good?
You think the bee makes honey half a year,
To loathe the comb in winter and desire
The little ant's food rather? But a man—
Note men!—they are but women after all,
As women are but Auroras!—there are men
Born tender, apt to pale at a trodden worm,
Who paint for pastime, in their favourite dream,
Spruce auto-vestments flowered with crocus-flames.
There are, too, who believe in hell, and lie;
There are, too, who believe in heaven, and fear:
There are, who waste their souls in working out
Life's problem on these sands betwixt two tides,
Concluding,—"Give us the oyster's part, in death."

Alas, long-suffering and most patient God,
Thou needst be surelier God to bear with us
Than even to have made us! thou aspire, aspire
From henceforth for me! thou who hast thyself
Endured this fleshhood, knowing how as a soaked
And sucking vesture it can drag us down
And choke us in the melancholy Deep,
Sustain me, that with thee I walk these waves,
Resisting!—breathe me upward, thou in me
Aspiring who art the way, the truth, the life,—
That no truth henceforth seem indifferent,
No way to truth laborious, and no life,
Not even this life I live, intolerable!

The days went by. I took up the old days,
With all their Tuscan pleasures worn and spoiled,
Like some lost book we dropt in the long grass

On such a happy summer-afternoon
When last we read it with a loving friend,
And find in autumn when the friend is gone,
The grass cut short, the weather changed, too late,
And stare at, as at something wonderful
For sorrow,—thinking how two hands before
Had held up what is left to only one,
And how we smiled when such a vehement nail
Impressed the tiny dint here which presents
This verse in fire for ever.   Tenderly
And mournfully I lived.   I knew the birds
And insects,—which looked fathered by the flowers
And emulous of their hues: I recognised
The moths, with that great overpoise of wings
Which make a mystery of them how at all
They can stop flying: butterflies, that bear
Upon their blue wings such red embers round,
They seem to scorch the blue air into holes
Each flight they take: and fire-flies, that suspire
In short soft lapses of transported flame
Across the tingling Dark, while overhead
The constant and inviolable stars
Outburn those light-of-love: melodious owls,
(If music had but one note and was sad,
'Twould sound just so); and all the silent swirl
Of bats that seem to follow in the air
Some grand circumference of a shadowy dome
To which we are blind: and then the nightingales,
Which pluck our heart across a garden-wall
(When walking in the town) and carry it
So high into the bowery almond-trees
We tremble and are afraid, and feel as if
The golden flood of moonlight unaware
Dissolved the pillars of the steady earth
And made it less substantial.   And I knew
The harmless opal snakes, the large-mouthed frogs
(Those noisy vaunters of their shallow streams);

And lizards, the green lightnings of the wall,
Which, if you sit down quiet, nor sigh loud,
Will flatter you and take you for a stone,
And flash familiarly about your feet
With such prodigious eyes in such small heads!—
I knew them, (though they had somewhat dwindled from
My childish imagery,) and kept in mind
How last I sate among them equally,
In fellowship and mateship, as a child
Feels equal still toward insect, beast, and bird,
Before the Adam in him has foregone
All privilege of Eden,—making friends
And talk with such a bird or such a goat,
And buying many a two-inch-wide rush-cage
To let out the caged cricket on a tree,
Saying, "Oh, my dear grillino, were you cramped?
And are you happy with the ilex-leaves?
And do you love me who have let you go?
Say *yes* in singing, and I'll understand."

But now the creatures all seemed farther off,
No longer mine, nor like me, only *there*,
A gulph between us. I could yearn indeed,
Like other rich men, for a drop of dew
To cool this heat,—a drop of the early dew,
The irrecoverable child-innocence
(Before the heart took fire and withered life)
When childhood might pair equally with birds;
But now . . the birds were grown too proud for us,
Alas, the very sun forbids the dew.

And I, I had come back to an empty nest,
Which every bird's too wise for. How I heard
My father's step on that deserted ground,
His voice along that silence, as he told
The names of bird and insect, tree and flower,
And all the presentations of the stars

Across Valdarno, interposing still
"My child," "my child." When fathers say "my child,"
'Tis easier to conceive the universe,
And life's transitions down the steps of law.

I rode once to the little mountain-house
As fast as if to find my father there,
But, when in sight of 't, within fifty yards,
I dropped my horse's bridle on his neck
And paused upon his flank. The house's front
Was cased with lingots of ripe Indian corn
In tesselated order and device
Of golden patterns, not a stone of wall
Uncovered,—not an inch of room to grow
A vine-leaf. The old porch had disappeared;
And right in the open doorway sate a girl
At plaiting straws, her black hair strained away
To a scarlet kerchief caught beneath her chin
In Tuscan fashion,—her full ebon eyes,
Which looked too heavy to be lifted so,
Still dropt and lifted toward the mulberry-tree
On which the lads were busy with their staves
In shout and laughter, stripping every bough
As bare as winter, of those summer leaves
My father had not changed for all the silk
In which the ugly silkworms hide themselves.
Enough. My horse recoiled before my heart
I turned the rein abruptly. Back we went
As fast, to Florence.
     That was trial enough
Of graves. I would not visit, if I could,
My father's, or my mother's any more,
To see if stone-cutter or lichen beat
So early in the race, or throw my flowers,
Which could not out-smell heaven or sweeten earth.
They live too far above, that I should look
So far below to find them: let me think

That rather they are visiting my grave,
Called life here, (undeveloped yet to life)
And that they drop upon me, now and then,
For token or for solace, some small weed
Least odorous of the growths of paradise,
To spare such pungent scents as kill with joy.

My old Assunta, too, was dead, was dead—
O land of all men's past! for me alone,
It would not mix its tenses. I was past,
It seemed, like others,—only not in heaven.
And many a Tuscan eve I wandered down
The cypress alley like a restless ghost
That tries its feeble ineffectual breath
Upon its own charred funeral-brands put out
Too soon, where black and stiff stood up the trees
Against the broad vermilion of the skies.
Such skies!—all clouds abolished in a sweep
Of God's skirt, with a dazzle to ghosts and men,
As down I went, saluting on the bridge
The hem of such before 'twas caught away
Beyond the peaks of Lucca. Underneath,
The river, just escaping from the weight
Of that intolerable glory, ran
In acquiescent shadow murmurously;
While, up beside it, streamed the festa-folk
With fellow-murmurs from their feet and fans,
And *issimo* and *ino* and sweet poise
Of vowels in their pleasant scandalous talk;
Returning from the grand-duke's dairy-farm
Before the trees grew dangerous at eight,
(For, "trust no tree by moonlight," Tuscans say)
To eat their ice at Donay's tenderly,—
Each lovely lady close to a cavalier
Who holds her dear fan while she feeds her smile
On meditative spoonfuls of vanille

And listens to his hot-breathed vows of love
Enough to thaw her cream and scorch his beard.

'Twas little matter. I could pass them by
Indifferently, not fearing to be known.
No danger of being wrecked upon a friend,
And forced to take an iceberg for an isle!
The very English, here, must wait and learn
To hang the cobweb of their gossip out
To catch a fly. I'm happy. It's sublime,
This perfect solitude of foreign lands!
To be, as if you had not been till then,
And were then, simply that you chose to be:
To spring up, not be brought forth from the ground,
Like grasshoppers at Athens, and skip thrice
Before a woman makes a pounce on you
And plants you in her hair!—possess, yourself,
A new world all alive with creatures new,
New sun, new moon, new flowers, new people—ah,
And be possessed by none of them! no right
In one, to call your name, inquire your where,
Or what you think of Mister Some-one's book,
Or Mister Other's marriage or decease,
Or how's the headache which you had last week,
Or why you look so pale still, since it's gone?
—Such most surprising riddance of one's life
Comes next one's death; 'tis disembodiment
Without the pang. I marvel, people choose
To stand stock-still like fakirs, till the moss
Grows on them and they cry out, self-admired,
"How verdant and how virtuous!" Well, I'm glad:
Or should be, if grown foreign to myself
As surely as to others.
     Musing so,
I walked the narrow unrecognising streets,
Where many a palace-front peers gloomily

Through stony vizors iron-barred, (prepared
Alike, should foe or lover pass that way,
For guest or victim) and came wandering out
Upon the churches with mild open doors
And plaintive wail of vespers, where a few,
Those chiefly women, sprinkled round in blots
Upon the dusky pavement, knelt and prayed
Toward the altar's silver glory. Oft a ray
(I liked to sit and watch) would tremble out,
Just touch some face more lifted, more in need,
(Of course a woman's)—while I dreamed a tale
To fit its fortunes. There was one who looked
As if the earth had suddenly grown too large
For such a little humpbacked thing as she;
The pitiful black kerchief round her neck
Sole proof she had had a mother. One, again,
Looked sick for love,—seemed praying some soft saint
To put more virtue in the new fine scarf
She spent a fortnight's meals on, yesterday,
That cruel Gigi might return his eyes
From Giuliana. There was one, so old,
So old, to kneel grew easier than to stand,—
So solitary, she accepts at last
Our Lady for her gossip, and frets on
Against the sinful world which goes its rounds
In marrying and being married, just the same
As when 'twas almost good and had the right,
(Her Gian alive, and she herself eighteen).
"And yet, now even, if Madonna willed,
She'd win a tern in Thursday's lottery
And better all things. Did she dream for nought,
That, boiling cabbage for the fast-day's soup,
It smelt like blessed entrails! such a dream
For nought! would sweetest Mary cheat her so,
And lose that certain candle, straight and white
As any fair grand-duchess in her teens,

Which otherwise should flare here in a week?
Benigna sis, thou beauteous Queen of heaven!"

I sate there musing, and imagining
Such utterance from such faces: poor blind souls
That writhe toward heaven along the devil's trail,—
Who knows, I thought, but He may stretch his hand
And pick them up? 'tis written in the Book
He heareth the young ravens when they cry,
And yet they cry for carrion.—O my God,
And we, who make excuses for the rest,
We do it in our measure. Then I knelt,
And dropped my head upon the pavement too,
And prayed, since I was foolish in desire
Like other creatures, craving offal-food,
That He would stop his ears to what I said,
And only listen to the run and beat
Of this poor, passionate, helpless blood—
                                      And then
I lay, and spoke not: but He heard in heaven.

So many Tuscan evenings passed the same.
I could not lose a sunset on the bridge,
And would not miss a vigil in the church,
And liked to mingle with the out-door crowd
So strange and gay and ignorant of my face,
For men you know not, are as good as trees.
And only once, at the Santissima,
I almost chanced upon a man I knew,
Sir Blaise Delorme. He saw me certainly,
And somewhat hurried, as he crossed himself,
The smoothness of the action,—then half bowed,
But only half, and merely to my shade,
I slipped so quick behind the porphyry plinth
And left him dubious if 'twas really I
Or peradventure Satan's usual trick

To keep a mounting saint uncanonised.
But he was safe for that time, and I too;
The argent angels in the altar-flare
Absorbed his soul next moment.   The good man!
In England we were scarce acquaintances,
That here in Florence he should keep my thought
Beyond the image on his eye, which came
And went: and yet his thought disturbed my life
For, after that, I oftener sat at home
On evenings, watching how they fined themselves
With gradual conscience to a perfect night,
Until the moon, diminished to a curve,
Lay out there like a sickle for His hand
Who cometh down at last to reap the earth.
At such times, ended seemed my trade of verse;
I feared to jingle bells upon my robe
Before the four-faced silent cherubim:
With God so near me, could I sing of God?
I did not write, nor read, nor even think,
But sate absorbed amid the quickening glooms,
Most like some passive broken lump of salt
Dropt in by chance to a bowl of œnomel,
To spoil the drink a little and lose itself,
Dissolving slowly, slowly, until lost.

EIGHTH BOOK.

ONE eve it happened, when I sate alone,
Alone, upon the terrace of my tower,
A book upon my knees to counterfeit
The reading that I never read at all,
While Marian, in the garden down below,
Knelt by the fountain I could just hear thrill
The drowsy silence of the exhausted day,
And peeled a new fig from that purple heap
In the grass beside her, turning out the red
To feed her eager child (who sucked at it
With vehement lips across a gap of air
As he stood opposite, face and curls a-flame
With that last sun-ray, crying, "give me, give,"
And stamping with imperious baby-feet,
We're all born princes)—something startled me,—
The laugh of sad and innocent souls, that breaks
Abruptly, as if frightened at itself.
'Twas Marian laughed. I saw her glance above
In sudden shame that I should hear her laugh,
And straightway dropped my eyes upon my book,
And knew, the first time, 'twas Boccaccio's tale,
The Falcon's, of the lover who for love
Destroyed the best that loved him. Some of us
Do it still, and then we sit and laugh no more.
Laugh *you*, sweet Marian,—you've the right to laugh,
Since God himself is for you, and a child!
For me there's somewhat less,—and so I sigh.

The heavens were making room to hold the night,

The sevenfold heavens unfolding all their gates
To let the stars out slowly (prophesied
In close-approaching advent, not discerned),
While still the cue-owls from the cypresses
Of the Poggio called and counted every pulse
Of the skyey palpitation. Gradually
The purple and transparent shadows slow
Had filled up the whole valley to the brim,
And flooded all the city, which you saw
As some drowned city in some enchanted sea,
Cut off from nature,—drawing you who gaze,
With passionate desire, to leap and plunge
And find a sea-king with a voice of waves,
And treacherous soft eyes, and slippery locks
You cannot kiss but you shall bring away
Their salt upon your lips. The duomo-bell
Strikes ten, as if it struck ten fathoms down,
So deep; and twenty churches answer it
The same, with twenty various instances.
Some gaslights tremble along squares and streets;
The Pitti's palace-front is drawn in fire;
And, past the quays, Maria Novella Place,
In which the mystic obelisks stand up
Triangular, pyramidal, each based
Upon its four-square brazen tortoises,
To guard that fair church, Buonarroti's Bride,
That stares out from her large blind dial-eyes,
(Her quadrant and armillary dials, black
With rhythms of many suns and moons) in vain
Inquiry for so rich a soul as his.
Methinks I have plunged, I see it all so clear . . .
And, O my heart, . . . the sea-king!

                              In my ears
The sound of waters. There he stood, my king!

I felt him, rather than beheld him. Up

I rose, as if he were my king indeed,
And then sate down, in trouble at myself,
And struggling for my woman's empery.
'Tis pitiful; but women are so made:
We'll die for you perhaps,—'tis probable;
But we'll not spare you an inch of our full height:
We'll have our whole just stature,—five feet four,
Though laid out in our coffins: pitiful.
—"You, Romney!——Lady Waldemar is here?"

He answered in a voice which was not his.
"I have her letter; you shall read it soon.
But first, I must be heard a little, I,
Who have waited long and travelled far for that,
Although you thought to have shut a tedious book
And farewell. Ah, you dog-eared such a page,
And here you find me."
      Did he touch my hand,
Or but my sleeve? I trembled, hand and foot,—
He must have touched me.—"Will you sit?" I asked,
And motioned to a chair; but down he sate,
A little slowly, as a man in doubt,
Upon the couch beside me,—couch and chair
Being wheeled upon the terrace.
       "You are come,
My cousin Romney?—this is wonderful.
But all is wonder on such summer-nights;
And nothing should surprise us any more,
Who see that miracle of stars. Behold."

I signed above, where all the stars were out,
As if an urgent heat had started there
A secret writing from a sombre page,
A blank, last moment, crowded suddenly
With hurrying splendours.
      "Then you do not know"
He murmured.

"Yes, I know," I said, "I know.
I had the news from Vincent Carrington.
And yet I did not think you'd leave the work
In England, for so much even,—though of course
You'll make a work-day of your holiday,
And turn it to our Tuscan people's use,—
Who much need helping since the Austrian boar
(So bold to cross the Alp to Lombardy
And dash his brute front unabashed against
The steep snow-bosses of that shield of God
Who soon shall rise in wrath and shake it clear,)
Came hither also, raking up our grape
And olive-gardens with his tyrannous tusk,
And rolling on our maize with all his swine."

"You had the news from Vincent Carrington,"
He echoed,—picking up the phrase beyond,
As if he knew the rest was merely talk
To fill a gap and keep out a strong wind;
"You had, then, Vincent's personal news?"
                                    "His own,"
I answered. "All that ruined world of yours
Seems crumbling into marriage. Carrington
Has chosen wisely."
                    "Do you take it so?"
He cried, "and is it possible at last" . .
He paused there,—and then, inward to himself,
"Too much at last, too late!—yet certainly" . .
(And there his voice swayed as an Alpine plank
That feels a passionate torrent underneath)
"The knowledge, had I known it first or last,
Could scarce have changed the actual case for *me*.
And best for *her* at this time."
                                Nay, I thought,
He loves Kate Ward, it seems, now, like a man,
Because he has married Lady Waldemar!
Ah, Vincent's letter said how Leigh was moved

To hear that Vincent was betrothed to Kate.
With what cracked pitchers go we to deep wells
In this world! Then I spoke,—"I did not think,
My cousin, you had ever known Kate Ward."

"In fact I never knew her. 'Tis enough
That Vincent did, and therefore chose his wife
For other reasons than those topaz eyes
We've heard of. Not to undervalue them,
For all that. One takes up the world with eyes."

—Including Romney Leigh, I thought again,
Albeit he knows them only by repute.
How vile must all men be, since *he's* a man.

His deep pathetic voice, as if he guessed
I did not surely love him, took the word;
"You never got a letter from Lord Howe
A month back, dear Aurora?"

        "None," I said.

"I felt it was so," he replied: "yet, strange!
Sir Blaise Delorme has passed through Florence?"
              "Ay,
By chance I saw him in Our Lady's church,
(I saw him, mark you, but he saw not me)
Clean-washed in holy water from the count
Of things terrestrial,—letters, and the rest;
He had crossed us out together with his sins.
Ay, strange; but only strange that good Lord Howe
Preferred him to the post because of pauls.
For me I'm sworn to never trust a man—
At least with letters."

      "There were facts to tell,
To smooth with eye and accent. Howe supposed ..

Well, well, no matter! there was dubious need;
You heard the news from Vincent Carrington.
And yet perhaps you had been startled less
To see me, dear Aurora, if you had read
That letter."
                —Now he sets me down as vexed.
I think I've draped myself in woman's pride
To a perfect purpose.   Oh, I'm vexed, it seems!
My friend Lord Howe deputes his friend Sir Blaise
To break as softly as a sparrow's egg
That lets a bird out tenderly, the news
Of Romney's marriage to a certain saint;
To *smooth with eye and accent*,—indicate
His possible presence.   Excellently well
You've played your part, my Lady Waldemar,—
As I've played mine.
                "Dear Romney." I began,
"You did not use, of old, to be so like
A Greek king coming from a taken Troy
'Twas needful that precursors spread your path
With three-piled carpets, to receive your foot
And dull the sound of 't.   For myself, be sure,
Although it frankly grinds the gravel here,
I still can bear it.   Yet I'm sorry too
To lose this famous letter, which Sir Blaise
Has twisted to a lighter absently
To fire some holy taper: dear Lord Howe
Writes letters good for all things but to lose;
And many a flower of London gossipry
Has dropt wherever such a stem broke off.
Of course I feel that, lonely among my vines,
Where nothing's talked of, save the blight again,
And no more Chianti!   Still the letter's use
As preparation . . . . . Did I start indeed?
Last night I started at a cockchafer,
And shook a half-hour after.   Have you learnt
No more of women, 'spite of privilege,

Than still to take account too seriously
Of such weak flutterings? Why, we like it, sir,
We get our powers and our effects that way:
The trees stand stiff and still at time of frost,
If no wind tears them; but, let summer come,
When trees are happy,— and a breath avails
To set them trembling through a million leaves
In luxury of emotion. Something less
It takes to move a woman: let her start
And shake at pleasure,—nor conclude at yours,
The winter's bitter,—but the summer's green."

He answered, "Be the summer ever green
With you, Aurora!—though you sweep your sex
With somewhat bitter gusts from where you live
Above them,—whirling downward from your heights
Your very own pine-cones, in a grand disdain
Of the lowland burrs with which you scatter them.
So high and cold to others and yourself,
A little less to Romney were unjust,
And thus, I would not have you. Let it pass:
I feel content so. You can bear indeed
My sudden step beside you: but for me,
'Twould move me sore to hear your softened voice,—
Aurora's voice,—if softened unaware
In pity of what I am."
                              Ah friend, I thought,
As husband of the Lady Waldemar
You're granted very sorely pitiable!
And yet Aurora Leigh must guard her voice
From softening in the pity of your case,
As if from lie or licence. Certainly
We'll soak up all the slush and soil of life
With softened voices, ere we come to *you*.

At which I interrupted my own thought
And spoke out calmly. "Let us ponder, friend,

Whate'er our state we must have made it first;
And though the thing displease us, ay, perhaps
Displease us warrantably, never doubt
That other states, thought possible once, and then
Rejected by the instinct of our lives,
If then adopted had displeased us more
Than this in which the choice, the will, the love,
Has stamped the honour of a patent act
From henceforth. What we choose may not be good,
But, that we choose it, proves it good for *us*
Potentially, fantastically, now
Or last year, rather than a thing we saw,
And saw no need for choosing. Moths will burn
Their wings,—which proves that light is good for moths,
Who else had flown not where they agonise."

"Ay, light is good," he echoed, and there paused;
And then abruptly, .. "Marian. Marian's well?"

I bowed my head but found no word. 'Twas hard
To speak of *her* to Lady Waldemar's
New husband. How much did he know, at last?
How much? how little?——He would take no sign,
But straight repeated,—"Marian. Is she well?"

"She's well," I answered.

      She was there in sight
An hour back, but the night had drawn her home,
Where still I heard her in an upper room,
Her low voice singing to the child in bed,
Who restless with the summer-heat and play
And slumber snatched at noon, was long sometimes
In falling off, and took a score of songs
And mother-hushes ere she saw him sound.

"She's well," I answered.

"Here?" he asked.
"Yes, here."

He stopped and sighed. "That shall be presently,
But now this must be. I have words to say,
And would be alone to say them, I with you,
And no third troubling."

"Speak then," I returned,
"She will not vex you."

At which, suddenly
He turned his face upon me with its smile
As if to crush me. "I have read your book,
Aurora."

"You have read it," I replied,
"And I have writ it,—we have done with it,
And now the rest?"

"The rest is like the first,"
He answered,—"for the book is in my heart,
Lives in me, wakes in me, and dreams in me:
My daily bread tastes of it,—and my wine
Which has no smack of it, I pour it out,
It seems unnatural drinking."

Bitterly
I took the word up; "Never waste your wine.
The book lived in me ere it lived in you;
I know it closer than another does,
And how it's foolish, feeble, and afraid,
And all unworthy so much compliment.
Beseech you, keep your wine,—and, when you drink,
Still wish some happier fortune to a friend,
Than even to have written a far better book."

He answered gently, "That is consequent:
The poet looks beyond the book he has made,

Or else he had not made it. If a man
Could make a man, he'd henceforth be a god
In feeling what a little thing is man:
It is not my case. And this special book,
I did not make it, to make light of it:
It stands above my knowledge, draws me up;
'Tis high to me. It may be that the book
Is not so high, but I so low, instead;
Still high to me. I mean no compliment:
I will not say there are not, young or old,
Male writers, ay, or female, let it pass,
Who'll write us richer and completer books.
A man may love a woman perfectly,
And yet by no means ignorantly maintain
A thousand women have not larger eyes:
Enough that she alone has looked at him
With eyes that, large or small, have won his soul.
And so, this book, Aurora,—so, your book."

"Alas," I answered, "is it so, indeed?"
And then was silent.

      "Is it so, indeed,
He echoed, "that *alas* is all your word?"
I said,—"I'm thinking of a far-off June,
When you and I, upon my birthday once,
Discoursed of life and art, with both untried.
I'm thinking, Romney, how 'twas morning then,
And now 'tis night."

      "And now," he said, "'tis night.

"I'm thinking," I resumed, "'tis somewhat sad,
That if I had known, that morning in the dew,
My cousin Romney would have said such words
On such a night at close of many years,
In speaking of a future book of mine,

It would have pleased me better as a hope,
Than as an actual grace it can at all:
That's sad, I'm thinking."
                          "Ay," he said, "'tis night."

"And there," I added lightly, "are the stars!
And here, we'll talk of stars and not of books."

"You have the stars," he murmured,—"it is well.
Be like them! shine, Aurora, on my dark,
Though high and cold and only like a star,
And for this short night only,—you, who keep
The same Aurora of the bright June day
That withered up the flowers before my face,
And turned me from the garden evermore
Because I was not worthy. Oh, deserved,
Deserved! that I, who verily had not learnt
God's lesson half, attaining as a dunce
To obliterate good words with fractious thumbs
And cheat myself of the context,—*I* should push
Aside, with male ferocious impudence,
The world's Aurora who had conned her part
On the other side the leaf! ignore her so,
Because she was a woman and a queen,
And had no beard to bristle through her song,
My teacher, who has taught me with a book,
My Miriam, whose sweet mouth, when nearly drowned
I still heard singing on the shore! Deserved,
That here I should look up unto the stars
And miss the glory" ..
                     "Can I understand?"
I broke in. "You speak wildly, Romney Leigh,
Or I hear wildly. In that morning-time
We recollect, the roses were too red,
The trees too green, reproach too natural
If one should see not what the other saw:
And now, it's night, remember; we have shades

In place of colours; we are now grown cold,
And old, my cousin Romney. Pardon me,—
I'm very happy that you like my book,
And very sorry that I quoted back
A ten years' birthday. 'Twas so mad a thing
In any woman, I scarce marvel much
You took it for a venturous piece of spite,
Provoking such excuses as indeed
I cannot call you slack in."
      "Understand,"
He answered sadly, "something, if but so.
This night is softer than an English day,
And men may well come hither when they're sick,
To draw in easier breath from larger air.
'Tis thus with me; I come to you,—to you,
My Italy of women, just to breathe
My soul out once before you, ere I go,
As humble as God makes me at the last
(I thank Him), quite out of the way of men
And yours, Aurora,—like a punished child,
His cheeks all blurred with tears and naughtiness,
To silence in a corner. I am come
To speak, beloved" ..
     "Wisely, cousin Leigh,
And worthily of us both!"
      "Yes, worthily;
For this time I must speak out and confess
That I, so truculent in assumption once,
So absolute in dogma, proud in aim,
And fierce in expectation,—I, who felt
The whole world tugging at my skirts for help,
As if no other man than I, could pull,
Nor woman, but I led her by the hand,
Nor cloth hold, but I had it in my coat,
Do know myself to-night for what I was
On that June-day, Aurora. Poor bright day,
Which meant the best .. a woman and a rose,

And which I smote upon the cheek with words
Until it turned and rent me! Young you were,
That birthday, poet, but you talked the right:
While I, .. I built up follies like a wall
To intercept the sunshine and your face.
Your face! that's worse."
      "Speak wisely, cousin Leigh."

"Yes, wisely, dear Aurora, though too late:
But then, not wisely. I was heavy then,
And stupid, and distracted with the cries
Of tortured prisoners in the polished brass
Of that Phalarian bull, society,
Which seems to bellow bravely like ten bulls
But, if you listen, moans and cries instead
Despairingly, like victims tossed and gored
And trampled by their hoofs. I heard the cries
Too close: I could not hear the angels lift
A fold of rustling air, nor what they said
To help my pity. I beheld the world
As one great famishing carnivorous mouth,—
A huge, deserted, callow, blind bird Thing,
With piteous open beak that hurt my heart,
Till down upon the filthy ground I dropped,
And tore the violets up to get the worms.
Worms, worms, was all my cry: an open mouth,
A gross want, bread to fill it to the lips,
No more. That poor men narrowed their demands
To such an end, was virtue, I supposed,
Adjudicating that to see it so
Was reason. Oh, I did not push the case
Up higher, and ponder how it answers when
The rich take up the same cry for themselves,
Professing equally,—'An open mouth
A gross need, food to fill us, and no more.'
Why that's so far from virtue, only vice
Can find excuse for 't! that makes libertines,

And slurs our cruel streets from end to end
With eighty thousand women in one smile,
Who only smile at night beneath the gas.
The body's satisfaction and no more,
Is used for argument against the soul's,
Here too; the want, here too, implies the right.
—How dark I stood that morning in the sun,
My best Aurora (though I saw your eyes)
When first you told me .. oh, I recollect
The sound, and how you lifted your small hand,
And how your white dress and your burnished curls
Went greatening round you in the still blue air,
As if an inspiration from within
Had blown them all out when you spoke the words,
Even these,—'You will not compass your poor ends
'Of barley-feeding and material ease,
'Without the poet's individualism
'To work your universal. It takes a soul,
'To move a body,—it takes a high-souled man,
'To move the masses, even to a cleaner stye:
'It takes the ideal, to blow an inch inside
'The dust of the actual: and your Fouriers failed,
'Because not poets enough to understand
'That life develops from within.' I say
Your words,—I could say other words of yours,
For none of all your words will let me go;
Like sweet verbena which, being brushed against,
Will hold us three hours after by the smell
In spite of long walks upon windy hills.
But these words dealt in sharper perfume,—these
Were ever on me, stinging through my dreams,
And saying themselves for ever o'er my acts
Like some unhappy verdict. That I failed,
Is certain. Stye or no stye, to contrive
The swine's propulsion toward the precipice,
Proved easy and plain. I subtly organised
And ordered, built the cards up high and higher,

Till, some one breathing, all fell flat again;
In setting right society's wide wrong,
Mere life 's so fatal. So I failed indeed
Once, twice, and oftener,—hearing through the rents
Of obstinate purpose, still those words of yours,
'*You will not compass your poor ends, not you!*'
But harder than you said them; every time
Still farther from your voice, until they came
To overcrow me with triumphant scorn
Which vexed me to resistance. Set down this
For condemnation,—I was guilty here;
I stood upon my deed and fought my doubt,
As men will,—for I doubted,—till at last
My deed gave way beneath me suddenly
And left me what I am:—the curtain dropped,
My part quite ended, all the footlights quenched,
My own soul hissing at me through the dark,
I ready for confession,—I was wrong,
I've sorely failed, I've slipped the ends of life,
I yield, you have conquered."
                              "Stay," I answered him;
"I've something for your hearing, also. I
Have failed too."
                  "You!" he said, "you're very great;
The sadness of your greatness fits you well:
As if the plume upon a hero's casque
Should nod a shadow upon his victor face."

I took him up austerely,—"You have read
My book, but not my heart; for recollect,
'Tis writ in Sanscrit which you bungle at.
I've surely failed, I know, if failure means
To look back sadly on work gladly done,—
To wander on my mountains of Delight,
So called, (I can remember a friend's words
As well as you, sir), weary and in want
Of even a sheep-path, thinking bitterly . .

Well, well! no matter. I but say so much,
To keep you, Romney Leigh, from saying more,
And let you feel I am not so high indeed,
That I can bear to have you at my foot,—
Or safe, that I can help you. That June-day,
Too deeply sunk in craterous sunsets now
For you or me to dig it up alive,—
To pluck it out all bleeding with spent flame
At the roots, before those moralising stars
We have got instead,—that poor lost day, you said
Some words as truthful as the thing of mine
You cared to keep in memory; and I hold
If I, that day, and, being the girl I was,
Had shown a gentler spirit, less arrogance,
It had not hurt me. You will scarce mistake
The point here: I but only think, you see,
More justly, that's more humbly, of myself,
Than when I tried a crown on and supposed . . .
Nay, laugh, sir,—I'll laugh with you!—pray you, laugh.
I've had so many birthdays since that day
I've learnt to prize mirth's opportunities,
Which come too seldom. Was it you who said
I was not changed? the same Aurora? Ah,
We could laugh there, too! Why, Ulysses' dog
Knew *him*, and wagged his tail and died: but if
I had owned a dog, I too, before my Troy,
And if you brought him here, . . I warrant you
He'd look into my face, bark lustily,
And live on stoutly, as the creatures will
Whose spirits are not troubled by long loves.
A dog would never know me, I'm so changed,
Much less a friend . . except that you're misled
By the colour of the hair, the trick of the voice,
Like that Aurora Leigh's."

                      "Sweet trick of voice!
I would be a dog for this, to know it at last,
And die upon the falls of it. O love,

O best Aurora! are you then so sad
You scarcely had been sadder as my wife?"

"Your wife, sir! I must certainly be changed,
If I, Aurora, can have said a thing
So light, it catches at the knightly spurs
Of a noble gentleman like Romney Leigh
And trips him from his honourable sense
Of what befits" . .
                "You wholly misconceive,"
He answered.
                I returned,—"I'm glad of it.
But keep from misconception, too, yourself:
I am not humbled to so low a point,
Nor so far saddened. If I am sad at all,
Ten layers of birthdays on a woman's head
Are apt to fossilise her girlish mirth,
Though ne'er so merry: I'm perforce more wise,
And that, in truth, means sadder. For the rest,
Look here, sir: I was right upon the whole
That birthday morning. 'Tis impossible
To get at men excepting through their souls,
However open their carnivorous jaws;
And poets get directlier at the soul,
Than any of your œconomists:—for which
You must not overlook the poet's work
When scheming for the world's necessities.
The soul 's the way. Not even Christ Himself
Can save man else than as He holds man's soul;
And therefore did He come into our flesh,
As some wise hunter creeping on his knees
With a torch, into the blackness of a cave,
To face and quell the beast there,—take the soul,
And so possess the whole man, body and soul.
I said, so far, right, yes: not farther, though:
We both were wrong that June-day,—both as wrong
As an east wind had been. I who talked of art,

And you who grieved for all men's griefs .. what then?
We surely made too small a part for God
In these things. What we are, imports us more
Than what we eat; and life, you've granted me,
Develops from within. But innermost
Of the inmost, most interior of the interne,
God claims his own, Divine humanity
Renewing nature,—or the piercingest verse,
Prest in by subtlest poet, still must keep
As much upon the outside of a man
As the very bowl in which he dips his beard.
—And then, .. the rest; I cannot surely speak:
Perhaps I doubt more than you doubted then,
If I, the poet's veritable charge,
Have borne upon my forehead. If I have,
It might feel somewhat liker to a crown,
The foolish green one even.—Ah, I think,
And chiefly when the sun shines, that I've failed.
But what then, Romney? Though we fail indeed,
You .. I .. a score of such weak workers, .. He
Fails never. If He cannot work by us,
He will work over us. Does He want a man,
Much less a woman, think you? Every time
The star winks there, so many souls are born,
Who all shall work too. Let our own be calm.
We should be ashamed to sit beneath those stars,
Impatient that we're nothing."

                         "Could we sit
Just so for ever, sweetest friend," he said,
"My failure would seem better than success.
And yet indeed your book has dealt with me
More gently, cousin, than you ever will!
Your book brought down entire the bright June-day,
And set me wandering in the garden-walks,
And let me watch the garland in a place
You blushed so .. nay, forgive me, do not stir,—
I only thank the book for what it taught,

And what, permitted. Poet, doubt yourself,
But never doubt that you're a poet to me
From henceforth. You have written poems, sweet,
Which moved me in secret, as the sap is moved
In still March-branches, signless as a stone:
But this last book o'ercame me like soft rain
Which falls at midnight, when the tightened bark
Breaks out into unhesitating buds
And sudden protestations of the spring.
In all your other books, I saw but *you:*
A man may see the moon so, in a pond,
And not be nearer therefore to the moon,
Nor use the sight .. except to drown himself:
And so I forced my heart back from the sight,
For what had *I*, I thought, to do with *her*,
Aurora .. Romney? But, in this last book,
You showed me something separate from yourself,
Beyond you, and I bore to take it in
And let it draw me. You have shown me truth,
O June-day friend, that help me now at night
When June is over! truths not yours, indeed,
But set within my reach by means of you,
Presented by your voice and verse the way
To take them clearest. Verily I was wrong;
And verily many thinkers of this age,
Ay, many Christian teachers, half in heaven,
Are wrong in just my sense who understood
Our natural world too insularly, as if
No spiritual counterpart completed it
Consummating its meaning, rounding all
To justice and perfection, line by line,
Form by form, nothing single nor alone,
The great below clenched by the great above,
Shade here authenticating substance there,
The body proving spirit, as the effect
The cause: we meantime being too grossly apt
To hold the natural, as dogs a bone,

(Though reason and nature beat us in the face)
So obstinately, that we'll break our teeth
Or ever we let go. For everywhere
We're too materialistic,—eating clay
(Like men of the west) instead of Adam's corn
And Noah's wine, clay by handfuls, clay by lumps,
Until we're filled up to the throat with clay,
And grow the grimy colour of the ground
On which we are feeding. Ay, materialist
The age's name is. God himself, with some,
Is apprehended as the bare result
Of what his hand materially has made,
Expressed in such an algebraic sign
Called God;—that is, to put it otherwise,
They add up nature to a nought of God
And cross the quotient. There are many even,
Whose names are written in the Christian church
To no dishonour, diet still on mud
And splash the altars with it. You might think
The clay, Christ laid upon their eyelids when,
Still blind, he called them to the use of sight,
Remained there to retard its exercise
With clogging incrustations. Close to heaven,
They see for mysteries, through the open doors,
Vague puffs of smoke from pots of earthenware;
And fain would enter, when their time shall come,
With quite another body than Saint Paul
Has promised,—husk and chaff, the whole barley-corn,
Or where's the resurrection?"

      "Thus it is,"
I sighed. And he resumed with mournful face.
"Beginning so, and filling up with clay
The wards of this great key, the natural world,
And fumbling vainly therefore at the lock.
Of the spiritual, we feel ourselves shut in
With all the wild-beast roar of struggling life,
The terrors and compunctions of our souls,

As saints with lions,—we who are not saints,
And have no heavenly lordship in our stare
To awe them backward. Ay, we are forced, so pent,
To judge the whole too partially, . . confound
Conclusions. Is there any common phrase
Significant, with the adverb heard alone,
The verb being absent, and the pronoun out?
But we, distracted in the roar of life,
Still insolently at God's adverb snatch,
And bruit against Him that his thought is void,
His meaning hopeless,—cry, that everywhere
The government is slipping from his hand,
Unless some other Christ (say Romney Leigh)
Come up and toil and moil and change the world,
Because the First has proved inadequate,
However we talk bigly of His work
And piously of His person. We blaspheme
At last, to finish our doxology,
Despairing on the earth for which He died."

"So now," I asked, "you have more hope of men?"

"I hope," he answered. "I am come to think
That God will have his work done, as you said,
And that we need not be disturbed too much
For Romney Leigh or others having failed
With this or that quack nostrum,—recipes
For keeping summits by annulling depths,
For wrestling with luxurious lounging sleeves,
And acting heroism without a scratch.
We fail,—what then? Aurora, if I smiled
To see you, in your lovely morning-pride,
Try on the poet's wreath which suits the noon,
(Sweet cousin, walls must get the weather stain
Before they grow the ivy!) certainly
I stood myself there worthier of contempt,
Self-rated, in disastrous arrogance,

As competent to sorrow for mankind
And even their odds. A man may well despair,
Who counts himself so needful to success.
I failed: I throw the remedy back on God,
And sit down here beside you, in good hope."

"And yet take heed," I answered, "lest we lean
Too dangerously on the other side,
And so fail twice. Be sure, no earnest work
Of any honest creature, howbeit weak,
Imperfect, ill-adapted, fails so much,
It is not gathered as a grain of sand
To enlarge the sum of human action used
For carrying out God's end. No creature works
So ill, observe, that therefore he's cashiered.
The honest earnest man must stand and work,
The woman also,—otherwise she drops
At once below the dignity of man,
Accepting serfdom. Free men freely work.
Whoever fears God, fears to sit at ease."

He cried, "True. After Adam, work was curse;
The natural creature labours, sweats, and frets.
But, after Christ, work turns to privilege,
And henceforth, one with our humanity,
The Six-day Worker working still in us
Has called us freely to work on with Him
In high companionship. So, happiest!
I count that Heaven itself is only work
To a surer issue. Let us work, indeed.
But no more work as Adam,—nor as Leigh
Erewhile, as if the only man on earth
Responsible for all the thistles blown
And tigers couchant, struggling in amaze
Against disease and winter, snarling on
For ever, that the world's not paradise.
Oh cousin, let us be content, in work,

To do the thing we can, and not presume
To fret because it's little. 'Twill employ
Seven men, they say, to make a perfect pin;
Who makes the head, content to miss the point,
Who makes the point, agreed to leave the join:
And if a man should cry, 'I want a pin,
'And I must make it straightway, head and point,'
His wisdom is not worth the pin he wants.
Seven men to a pin,—and not a man too much!
Seven generations, haply, to this world,
To right it visibly a finger's breadth,
And mend its rents a little. Oh, to storm
And say, 'This world here is intolerable;
'I will not eat this corn, nor drink this wine,
'Nor love this woman, flinging her my soul
'Without a bond for 't as a lover should,
'Nor use the generous leave of happiness
'As not too good for using generously'—
(Since virtue kindles at the touch of joy
Like a man's cheek laid on a woman's hand,
And God, who knows it, looks for quick returns
From joys)—to stand and claim to have a life
Beyond the bounds of the individual man,
And raze all personal cloisters of the soul
To build up public stores and magazines,
As if God's creatures otherwise were lost,
The builder surely saved by any means!
To think,—I have a pattern on my nail,
And I will carve the world new after it
And solve so these hard social questions,—nay,
Impossible social questions, since their roots
Strike deep in Evil's own existence here
Which God permits because the question's hard
To abolish evil nor attaint free-will.
Ay, hard to God, but not to Romney Leigh!
For Romney has a pattern on his nail,
(Whatever may be lacking on the Mount)

And, not being overnice to separate
What's element from what's convention, hastes
By line on line to draw you out a world,
Without your help indeed, unless you take
His yoke upon you and will learn of him,
So much he has to teach! so good a world!
The same, the whole creation's groaning for!
No rich nor poor, no gain nor loss nor stint;
No potage in it able to exclude
A brother's birthright, and no right of birth,
The potage,—both secured to every man,
And perfect virtue dealt out like the rest
Gratuitously, with the soup at six,
To whoso does not seek it."
       "Softly, sir,"
I interrupted, —"I had a cousin once
I held in reverence. If he strained too wide,
It was not to take honour but give help;
The gesture was heroic. If his hand
Accomplished nothing . . (well, it is not proved)
That empty hand thrown impotently out
Were sooner caught, I think, by One in heaven,
Than many a hand that reaped a harvest in
And keeps the scythe's glow on it. Pray you, then,
For my sake merely, use less bitterness
In speaking of my cousin."
       "Ah," he said,
"Aurora! when the prophet beats the ass,
The angel intercedes." He shook his head—
"And yet to mean so well and fail so foul,
Expresses ne'er another beast than man;
The antithesis is human. Harken, dear;
There's too much abstract willing, purposing,
In this poor world. We talk by aggregates,
And think by systems, and, being used to face
Our evils in statistics, are inclined

To cap them with unreal remedies
Drawn out in haste on the other side the slate."

"That's true," I answered, fain to thrown up though
And make a game of 't,—"Yes, we generalise
Enough to please you. If we pray at all,
We pray no longer for our daily bread
But next centenary's harvests. If we give,
Our cup of water is not tendered till
We lay down pipes and found a Company
With Branches. Ass or angel, 'tis the same:
A woman cannot do the thing she ought,
Which means whatever perfect thing she can,
In life, in art, in science, but she fears
To let the perfect action take her part,
And rest there: she must prove what she can do
Before she does it, prate of woman's rights,
Of woman's mission, woman's function, till
The men (who are prating too on their side) cry,
'A woman's function plainly is .. to talk.'
Poor souls, they are very reasonably vexed;
They cannot hear each other talk."
        "And you,
An artist, judge so?"
       "I, an artist,—yes:
Because, precisely, I'm an artist, sir,
And woman, if another sate in sight,
I'd whisper,—Soft, my sister! not a word!
By speaking we prove only we can speak,
Which he, the man here, never doubted. What
He doubts is, whether we can *do* the thing
With decent grace we've not yet done at all.
Now, do it; bring your statue,—you have room!
He'll see it even by the starlight here;
And if 'tis e'er so little like the god
Who looks out from the marble silently

Along the track of his own shining dart
Through the dusk of ages, there's no need to speak;
The universe shall henceforth speak for you,
And witness, 'She who did this thing, was born
To do it,—claims her license in her work.'
And so with more works. Whoso cures the plague,
Though twice a woman, shall be called a leech:
Who rights a land's finances, is excused
For touching coppers, though her hands be white,—
But we, we talk!"
    "It is the age's mood,"
He said; "we boast, and do not. We put up
Hostelry signs where'er we lodge a day,
Some red colossal cow with mighty paps
A Cyclops' fingers could not strain to milk,—
Then bring out presently our saucerful
Of curds. We want more quiet in our works,
More knowledge of the bounds in which we work;
More knowledge that each individual man
Remains an Adam to the general race,
Constrained to see, like Adam, that he keep
His personal state's condition honestly,
Or vain all thoughts of his to help the world,
Which still must be developed from its *one*
If bettered in its many. We indeed,
Who think to lay it out new like a park,
We take a work on us which is not man's,
For God alone sits far enough above
To speculate so largely. None of us
(Not Romney Leigh) is mad enough to say,
We'll have a grove of oaks upon that slope
And sink the need of acorns. Government,
If veritable and lawful, is not given
By imposition of the foreign hand,
Nor chosen from a pretty pattern-book
Of some domestic idealogue who sits
And coldly chooses empire, where as well

He might republic. Genuine government
Is but the expression of a nation, good
Or less good,—even as all society,
Howe'er unequal, monstrous, crazed and cursed,
Is but the expression of men's single lives,
The loud sum of the silent units. What,
We'd change the aggregate and yet retain
Each separate figure? whom do we cheat by that?
Now, not even Romney."
          "Cousin, you are sad.
Did all your social labour at Leigh Hall
And elsewhere, come to nought then?"
              "It *was* nought,"
He answered mildly. "There is room indeed
For statues still, in this large world of God's.
But not for vacuums,—so I am not sad;
Not sadder than is good for what I am.
My vain phalanstery dissolved itself;
My men and women of disordered lives,
I brought in orderly to dine and sleep,
Broke up those waxen masks I made them wear,
With fierce contortions of the natural face,—
And cursed me for my tyrannous constraint
In forcing crooked creatures to live straight;
And set the country hounds upon my back
To bite and tear me for my wicked deed
Of trying to do good without the church
Or even the squires, Aurora. Do you mind
Your ancient neighbours? The great book-club teems
With 'sketches,' 'summaries,' and 'last tracts' but twelve,
On socialistic troublers of close bonds
Betwixt the generous rich and grateful poor.
The vicar preached from 'Revelations' (till
The doctor woke), and found me with 'the frogs'
On three successive Sundays; ay, and stopped
To weep a little (for he's getting old)
That such perdition should o'ertake a man

Of such fair acres,—in the parish, too!
He printed his discourses 'by request,'
And if your book shall sell as his did, then
Your verses are less good than I suppose.
The women of the neighbourhood subscribed,
And sent me a copy bound in scarlet silk,
Tooled edges, blazoned with the arms of Leigh:
I own that touched me."
                        "What, the pretty ones?
Poor Romney!"
                "Otherwise the effect was small:
I had my windows broken once or twice
By liberal peasants naturally incensed
At such a vexer of Arcadian peace,
Who would not let men call their wives their own
To kick like Britons, and made obstacles
When things went smoothly as a baby drugged,
Toward freedom and starvation,—bringing down
The wicked London tavern-thieves and drabs
To affront the blessed hillside drabs and thieves
With mended morals, quotha,—fine new lives!—
My windows paid for 't. I was shot at, once,
By an active poacher who had hit a hare
From the other barrel, (tired of springeing game
So long upon my acres, undisturbed,
And restless for the country's virtue,—yet
He missed me) ay, and pelted very oft
In riding through the village. 'There he goes
'Who'd drive away our Christian gentlefolks,
'To catch us undefended in the trap
'He baits with poisonous cheese, and lock us up
'In that pernicious prison of Leigh Hall
'With all his murderers! Give another name
'And say Leigh Hell, and burn it up with fire.'
And so they did, at last, Aurora."
                                    "Did?"

"You never heard it, cousin? Vincent's news
Came stinted, then."
                    "They did; they burnt Leigh Hall!

"You're sorry, dear Aurora? Yes indeed,
They did it perfectly: a thorough work,
And not a failure, this time. Let us grant
'Tis somewhat easier, though, to burn a house
Than build a system;—yet that's easy, too,
In a dream. Books, pictures,—ay, the pictures! what,
You think your dear Vandykes would give them pause?
Our proud ancestral Leighs, with those peaked beards,
Or bosoms white as foam thrown up on rocks
From the old-spent wave. Such calm defiant looks
They flared up with! now nevermore to twit
The bones in the family-vault with ugly death.
Not one was rescued, save the Lady Maud,
Who threw you down, that morning you were born,
The undeniable lineal mouth and chin
To wear for ever for her gracious sake,
For which good deed I saved her; the rest went:
And you, you're sorry, cousin. Well, for me,
With all my phalansterians safely out,
(Poor hearts, they helped the burners, it was said,
And certainly a few clapped hands and yelled)
The ruin did not hurt me as it might,—
As when for instance I was hurt one day
A certain letter being destroyed. In fact,
To see the great house flare so .. oaken floors,
Our fathers made so fine with rushes once
Before our mothers furbished them with trains,
Carved wainscoats, panelled walls, the favourite slide
For draining off a martyr, (or a rogue)
The echoing galleries, half a half-mile long,
And all the various stairs that took you up
And took you down, and took you round about
Upon their slippery darkness, recollect,

All helping to keep up one blazing jest!
The flames through all the casements pushing forth
Like red-hot devils crinkled into snakes,
All signifying,—'Look you, Romney Leigh,
'We save the people from your saving, here,
'Yet so as by fire! we make a pretty show
'Besides,—and that's the best you've ever done.'
—To see this, almost moved myself to clap!
The 'vale et plaude' came too with effect
When, in the roof fell, and the fire that paused,
Stunned momently beneath the stroke of slates
And tumbling rafters, rose at once and roared,
And wrapping the whole house (which disappeared
In a mounting whirlwind of dilated flame,)
Blew upward, straight, its drift of fiery chaff
In the face of Heaven, which blenched, and ran up higher."

"Poor Romney!"
     "Sometimes when I dream," he said,
"I hear the silence after, 'twas so still.
For all those wild beasts, yelling, cursing round,
Were suddenly silent, while you counted five,
So silent, that you heard a young bird fall
From the top-nest in the neighbouring rookery,
Through edging over-rashly toward the light.
The old rooks had already fled too far,
To hear the screech they fled with, though you saw
Some flying still, like scatterings of dead leaves
In autumn-gusts, seen dark against the sky,—
All flying,—ousted, like the House of Leigh."

"Dear Romney!"
    "Evidently 'twould have been
A fine sight for a poet, sweet, like you,
To make the verse blaze after. I myself,
Even I, felt something in the grand old trees,
Which stood that moment like brute Druid gods

Amazed upon the rim of ruin, where,
As into a blackened socket, the great fire
Had dropped,—still throwing up splinters now and then
To show them gray with all their centuries,
Left there to witness that on such a day
The House went out."
    "Ah!"
        "While you counted five,
I seemed to feel a little like a Leigh,—
But then it passed, Aurora. A child cried,
And I had enough to think of what to do
With all those houseless wretches in the dark,
And ponder where they'd dance the next time, they
Who had burnt the viol."
      "Did you think of that?
Who burns his viol will not dance, I know,
To cymbals, Romney."
      "O my sweet sad voice,"
He cried,—"O voice that speaks and overcomes!
The sun is silent, but Aurora speaks."

"Alas," I said, "I speak I know not what:
I'm back in childhood, thinking as a child,
A foolish fancy—will it make you smile?
I shall not from the window of my room
Catch sight of those old chimneys any more."

"No more," he answered. "If you pushed one day
Through all the green hills to our fathers' house,
You'd come upon a great charred circle, where
The patient earth was singed an acre round,
With one stone-stair, symbolic of my life,
Ascending, winding, leading up to nought!
'Tis worth a poet's seeing. Will you go?"

I made no answer. Had I any right
To weep with this man, that I dared to speak?

A woman stood between his soul and mine,
And waved us off from touching evermore,
With those unclean white hands of hers. Enough.
We had burnt our viols and were silent.
                                          So,
The silence lengthened till it'pressed. I spoke,
To breathe: "I think you were ill afterward."

"More ill," he answered, "had been scarcely ill.
I hoped this feeble fumbling at life's knot
Might end concisely,—but I failed to die,
As formerly I failed to live,—and thus
Grew willing, having tried all other ways,
To try just God's. Humility's so good,
When pride's impossible. Mark us, how we make
Our virtues, cousin, from our worn-out sins,
Which smack of them from henceforth. Is it right,
For instance, to wed here while you love there?
And yet because a man sins once, the sin
Cleaves to him, in necessity to sin,
That if he sin not *so*, to damn himself,
He sins *so*, to damn others with himself:
And thus, to wed here, loving there, becomes
A duty. Virtue buds a dubious leaf
Round mortal brows; your ivy's better, dear.
—Yet she, 'tis certain, is my very wife,
The very lamb left mangled by the wolves
Through my own bad shepherding: and could I choose
But take her on my shoulder past this stretch
Of rough, uneasy wilderness, poor lamb,
Poor child, poor child?—Aurora, my beloved
I will not vex you any more to-night,
But, having spoken what I came to say,
The rest shall please you. What she can, in me,—
Protection, tender liking, freedom, ease,
She shall have surely, liberally, for her
And hers, Aurora. Small amends they'll make

For hideous evils which she had not known
Except by me, and for this imminent loss,
This forfeit presence of a gracious friend,
Which also she must forfeit for my sake,
Since, ... drop your hand in mine a moment, sweet,
We're parting!——ah, my snowdrop, what a touch,
As if the wind had swept it off! you grudge
Your gelid sweetness on my palm but so,
A moment? angry, that I could not bear
You .. speaking, breathing, living, side by side
With some one called my wife .. and live, myself?
Nay, be not cruel—you must understand!
Your lightest footfall on a floor of mine
Would shake the house, my lintel being uncrossed
'Gainst angels: henceforth it is night with me,
And so, henceforth, I put the shutters up:
Auroras must not come to spoil my dark."

He smiled so feebly, with an empty hand
Stretched sideway from me,—as indeed he looked
To any one but me to give him help;
And, while the moon came suddenly out full,
The double-rose of our Italian moons,
Sufficient plainly for the heaven and earth,
(The stars struck dumb and washed away in dews
Of golden glory, and the mountains steeped
In divine languor) he, the man, appeared
So pale and patient, like the marble man
A sculptor puts his personal sadness in
To join his grandeur of ideal thought,—
As if his mallet struck me from my height
Of passionate indignation, I who had risen
Pale, doubting paused, ... Was Romney mad indeed?
Had all this wrong of heart made sick the brain!

Then quiet, with a sort of tremulous pride,
"Go, cousin," I said coldly; "a farewell

Was sooner spoken 'twixt a pair of friends
In those old days, than seems to suit you now.
Howbeit, since then, I've writ a book or two,
I'm somewhat dull still in the manly art
Of phrase and metaphrase. Why, any man
Can carve a score of white Loves out of snow,
As Buonarroti in my Florence there,
And set them on the wall in some safe shade,
As safe, sir, as your marriage! very good;
Though if a woman took one from the ledge
To put it on the table by her flowers
And let it mind her of a certain friend,
'Twould drop at once (so better), would not bear
Her nail-mark even, where she took it up
A little tenderly,—so best, I say:
For me, I would not touch the fragile thing
And risk to spoil it half an hour before
The sun shall shine to melt it: leave it there.
I'm plain at speech, direct in purpose: when
I speak, you'll take the meaning as it is,
And not allow for puckerings in the silk
By clever stitches:—I'm a woman, sir,
I use the woman's figures naturally,
As you the male license. So, I wish you well.
I'm simply sorry for the griefs you've had,
And not for your sake only, but mankind's.
This race is never grateful: from the first,
One fills their cup at supper with pure wine,
Which back they give at cross-time on a sponge,
In vinegar and gall."
     "If gratefuller,"
He murmured, "by so much less pitiable!
God's self would never have come down to die,
Could man have thanked him for it."
       "Happily
'Tis patent that, whatever," I resumed,
"You suffered from this thanklessness of men,

You sink no more than Moses' bulrush-boat
When once relieved of Moses,—for you're light,
You're light, my cousin! which is well for you,
And manly. For myself,—now mark me, sir,
They burnt Leigh Hall; but if, consummated
To devils, heightened beyond Lucifers,
They had burnt instead, a star or two of those
We saw above there just a moment back,
Before the moon abolished them,—destroyed
And riddled them in ashes through a sieve
On the head of the foundering universe,—what then?
If you and I remained still you and I,
It could not shift our places as mere friends,
Nor render decent you should toss a phrase
Beyond the point of actual feeling!—nay,
You shall not interrupt me: as you said,
We're parting. Certainly, not once nor twice
To-night you've mocked me somewhat, or yourself,
And I, at least, have not deserved it so
That I should meet it unsurprised. But now,
Enough: we're parting .. parting. Cousin Leigh,
I wish you well through all the acts of life
And life's relations, wedlock not the least,
And it shall 'please me,' in your words, to know
You yield your wife, protection, freedom, ease,
And very tender liking. May you live
So happy with her, Romney, that your friends
Shall praise her for it. Meantime some of us
Are wholly dull in keeping ignorant
Of what she has suffered by you, and what debt
Of sorrow your rich love sits down to pay:
But if 'tis sweet for love to pay its debt,
'Tis sweeter still for love to give its gift,
And you, be liberal in the sweeter way,
You can, I think. At least, as touches me,
You owe her, cousin Romney, no amends.
She is not used to hold my gown so fast,

You need entreat her now to let it go;
The lady never was a friend of mine,
Nor capable,—I thought you knew as much,—
Of losing for your sake so poor a prize
As such a worthless friendship. Be content,
Good cousin, therefore, both for her and you!
I'll never spoil your dark, nor dull your noon,
Nor vex you when you're merry, or at rest:
You shall not need to put a shutter up
To keep out this Aurora,—though your north
Can make Auroras which vex nobody,
Scarce known from night, I fancied! let me add,
My larks fly higher than some windows. Well,
You've read your Leighs. Indeed 'twould shake a house,
If such as I came in with outstretched hand
Still warm and thrilling from the clasp of one ..
Of one we know, .. to acknowledge, palm to palm,
As mistress there, the Lady Waldemar.

"Now God be with us" .. with a sudden clash
Of voice he interrupted—"what name's that?
You spoke a name, Aurora."
                        "Pardon me;
I would that, Romney, I could name your wife
Nor wound you, yet be worthy."
                        "Are we mad?"
He echoed—"wife! mine! Lady Waldemar!
I think you said my wife." He sprang to his feet,
And threw his noble head back toward the moon
As one who swims against a stormy sea,
Then laughed with such a helpless, hopeless scorn,
I stood and trembled.
                        "May God judge me so,"
He said at last,—"I came convicted here,
And humbled sorely if not enough. I came,
Because this woman from her crystal soul
Had shown me something which a man calls light;

Because too, formerly, I sinned by her
As then and ever since I have, by God,
Through arrogance of nature,—though I loved . .
Whom best, I need not say, since that is writ
Too plainly in the book of my misdeeds:
And thus I came here to abase myself,
And fasten, kneeling, on her regent brows
A garland which I startled thence one day
Of her beautiful June-youth. But here again
I'm baffled,—fail in my abasement as
My aggrandisement: there's no room left for me
At any woman's foot who misconceives
My nature, purpose, possible actions. What!
Are you the Aurora who made large my dreams
To frame your greatness? you conceive so small?
You stand so less than woman through being more,
And lose your natural instinct (like a beast)
Through intellectual culture? since indeed
I do not think that any common she
Would dare adopt such monstrous forgeries
For the legible life-signature of such
As I, with all my blots,—with all my blots!
At last then, peerless cousin, we are peers,
At last we're even. Ah, you've left your height,
And here upon my level we take hands,
And here I reach you to forgive you, sweet,
And that's a fall, Aurora. Long ago
You seldom understood me,—but before,
I could not blame you. Then, you only seemed
So high above, you could not see below;
But now I breathe,—but now I pardon!—nay,
We're parting. Dearest, men have burnt my house,
Maligned my motives,—but not one, I swear,
Has wronged my soul as this Aurora has,
Who called the Lady Waldemar my wife."

"Not married to her! yet you said" . .

                                        "Again?
"Nay, read the lines" (he held a letter out)
"She sent you through me."
                        By the moonlight there,
I tore the meaning out with passionate haste
Much rather than I read it. Thus it ran.

NINTH BOOK.

Even thus. I pause to write it out at length.
The letter of the Lady Waldemar.

"I prayed your cousin Leigh to take you this,
He says he'll do it. After years of love,
Or what is called so, when a woman frets
And fools upon one string of a man's name,
And fingers it for ever till it breaks,—
He may perhaps do for her such a thing,
And she accept it without detriment
Although she should not love him any more.
And I, who do not love him, nor love you,
Nor you, Aurora,—choose you shall repent
Your most ungracious letter and confess,
Constrained by his convictions, (he's convinced,)
You've wronged me foully. Are you made so ill,
You woman—to impute such ill to *me?*
We both had mothers,—lay in their bosom once.
And after all, I thank you, Aurora Leigh,
For proving to myself that there are things
I would not do,—not for my life, nor him,
Though something I have somewhat overdone,—
For instance, when I went to see the gods
One morning on Olympus, with a step
That shook the thunder from a certain cloud,
Committing myself vilely. Could I think,
The Muse I pulled my heart out from my breast

To soften, had herself a sort of heart,
And loved my mortal? He at least loved her,
I heard him say so,—'twas my recompense,
When, watching at his bedside fourteen days,
He broke out ever like a flame at whiles
Between the heats of fever,—'Is it thou?
'Breathe closer, sweetest mouth!' and when at last
The fever gone, the wasted face extinct,
As if it irked him much to know me there,
He said, ''Twas kind, 'twas good, 'twas womanly,
(And fifty praises to excuse no love)
'But was the picture safe he had ventured for?'
And then, half wandering,—'I have loved her well,
'Although she could not love me,'—'Say instead,'
I answered, 'she does love you.'—'Twas my turn
To rave: I would have married him so changed,
Although the world had jeered me properly
For taking up with Cupid at his worst,
The silver quiver worn off on his hair.
'No, no,' he murmured, 'no, she loves me not;
'Aurora Leigh does better: bring her book
'And read it softly, Lady Waldemar,
'Until I thank your friendship more for that
'Than even for harder service.' So I read
Your book, Aurora, for an hour that day:
I kept its pauses, marked its emphasis;
My voice, empaled upon its hooks of rhyme,
Not once would writhe, nor quiver, nor revolt;
I read on calmly,—calmly shut it up,
Observing, 'There's some merit in the book;
'And yet the merit in 't is thrown away,
'As chances still with women if we write
'Or write not: we want string to tie our flowers,
'So drop them as we walk, which serves to show
'The way we went. Good morning, Mister Leigh;
'You'll find another reader the next time.

'A woman who does better than to love,
'I hate; she will do nothing very well:
'Male poets are preferable, straining less
'And teaching more.' I triumphed o'er you both,
And left him.
        "When I saw him afterward
I had read your shameful letter, and my heart.
He came with health recovered, strong though pale,
Lord Howe and he, a courteous pair of friends,
To say what men dare say to women, when
Their debtors. But I stopped them with a word,
And proved I had never trodden such a road
To carry so much dirt upon my shoe.
Then, putting into it something of disdain,
I asked forsooth his pardon, and my own,
For having done no better than to love,
And that not wisely,—though 'twas long ago,
And had been mended radically since.
I told him, as I tell you now, Miss Leigh,
And proved, I took some trouble for his sake
(Because I knew he did not love the girl)
To spoil my hands with working in the stream
Of that poor bubbling nature,—till she went,
Consigned to one I trusted, my own maid
Who once had lived full five months in my house,
(Dressed hair superbly) with a lavish purse
To carry to Australia where she had left
A husband, said she. If the creature lied,
The mission failed, we all do fail and lie
More or less—and I'm sorry—which is all
Expected from us when we fail the most
And go to church to own it. What I meant,
Was just the best for him, and me, and her . .
Best even for Marian!—I am sorry for't,
And very sorry. Yet my creature said
She saw her stop to speak in Oxford Street

To one .. no matter! I had sooner cut
My hand off (though 'twere kissed the hour before,
And promised a duke's troth-ring for the next)
Than crush her silly head with so much wrong.
Poor child! I would have mended it with gold,
Until it gleamed like St. Sophia's dome
When all the faithful troop to morning prayer:
But he, he nipped the bud of such a thought
With that cold Leigh look which I fancied once,
And broke in, 'Henceforth she was called his wife:
'His wife required no succour: he was bound
'To Florence, to resume this broken bond;
'Enough so. Both were happy, he and Howe,
'To acquit me of the heaviest charge of all—'
—At which I shot my tongue against my fly
And struck him; 'Would he carry,—he was just,
'A letter from me to Aurora Leigh,
'And ratify from his authentic mouth
'My answer to her accusation?'—'Yes,
'If such a letter were prepared in time.'
—He's just, your cousin,—ay, abhorrently:
He'd wash his hands in blood, to keep them clean.
And so, cold, courteous, a mere gentleman,
He bowed, we parted.
                    "Parted. Face no more,
Voice no more, love no more! wiped wholly out
Like some ill scholar's scrawl from heart and slate,—
Ay, spit on and so wiped out utterly
By some coarse scholar! I have been too coarse,
Too human. Have we business, in our rank,
With blood i' the veins? I will have henceforth none,
Not even to keep the colour at my lip:
A rose is pink and pretty without blood,
Why not a woman? When we've played in vain
The game, to adore,—we have resources still,
And can play on at leisure, being adored:

Here's Smith already swearing at my feet
That I'm the typic She.   Away with Smith!—
Smith smacks of Leigh,—and henceforth I'll admit
No socialist within three crinolines,
To live and have his being.   But for you,
Though insolent your letter and absurd,
And though I hate you frankly,—take my Smith!
For when you have seen this famous marriage tied,
A most unspotted Erle to a noble Leigh
(His love astray on one he should not love),
Howbeit you may not want his love, beware,
You'll want some comfort.   So I leave you Smith,
Take Smith!—he talks Leigh's subjects, somewhat worse;
Adopts a thought of Leigh's, and dwindles it;
Goes leagues beyond, to be no inch behind;
Will mind you of him, as a shoe-string may
Of a man: and women, when they are made like you,
Grow tender to a shoe-string, footprint even,
Adore averted shoulders in a glass,
And memories of what, present once, was loathed.
And yet, you loathed not Romney,—though you played
At 'fox and goose' about him with your soul;
Pass over fox, you rub out fox,—ignore
A feeling, you eradicate it,—the act 's
Identical.
                     "I wish you joy, Miss Leigh,
You've made a happy marriage for your friend,
And all the honour, well-assorted love,
Derives from you who love him, whom he loves!
You need not wish *me* joy to think of it;
I have so much.   Observe, Aurora Leigh,
Your droop of eyelid is the same as his,
And, but for you, I might have won his love,
And, to you, I have shown my naked heart;
For which three things, I hate, hate, hate you.   Hush
Suppose a fourth!—I cannot choose but think

That, with him, I were virtuouser than you
Without him: so I hate you from this gulf
And hollow of my soul, which opens out
To what, except for you, had been my heaven,
And is, instead, a place to curse by! LOVE."

An active kind of curse. I stood there cursed,
Confounded. I had seized and caught the sense
Of the letter, with its twenty stinging snakes,
In a moment's sweep of eyesight, and I stood
Dazed.—"Ah! not married."
       "You mistake," he said,
"I'm married. Is not Marian Erle my wife?
As God sees things, I have a wife and child;
And I, as I'm a man who honours God,
Am here to claim them as my child and wife."

I felt it hard to breathe, much less to speak.
Nor word of mine was needed. Some one else
Was there for answering. "Romney," she began,
"My great good angel, Romney."
       Then at first,
I knew that Marian Erle was beautiful.
She stood there, still and pallid as a saint,
Dilated, like a saint in ecstasy,
As if the floating moonshine interposed
Betwixt her foot and the earth, and raised her up
To float upon it. "I had left my child,
Who sleeps," she said, "and having drawn this way
I heard you speaking, .. friend!—Confirm me now.
You take this Marian, such as wicked men
Have made her, for your honourable wife?"

The thrilling, solemn, proud, pathetic voice.
He stretched his arms out toward that thrilling voice,
As if to draw it on to his embrace.

—"I take her as God made her, and as men
Must fail to unmake her, for my honoured wife."

She never raised her eyes, nor took a step,
But stood there in her place, and spoke again.
—"You take this Marian's child, which is her shame
In sight of men and women, for your child,
Of whom you will not ever feel ashamed?"

The thrilling, tender, proud, pathetic voice.
He stepped on toward it, still with outstretched arms,
As if to quench upon his breast that voice.
—"May God so father me, as I do him,
And so forsake me, as I let him feel
He's orphaned haply. Here I take the child
To share my cup, to slumber on my knee,
To play his loudest gambol at my foot,
To hold my finger in the public ways,
Till none shall need inquire, 'Whose child is this,'
The gesture saying so tenderly, 'My own.'"

She stood a moment silent in her place;
Then turning towards me very slow and cold,
—"And you,—what say you?—will you blame me much,
If, careful for that outcast child of mine,
I catch this hand that's stretched to me and him,
Nor dare to leave him friendless in the world
Where men have stoned me? Have I not the right
To take so mere an aftermath from life,
Else found so wholly bare? Or is it wrong
To let your cousin, for a generous bent,
Put out his ungloved fingers among briars
To set a tumbling bird's nest somewhat straight?
You will not tell him, though we're innocent,
We are not harmless, .. and that both our harms
Will stick to his good smooth noble life like burrs,

Never to drop off though he shakes the cloak?
You've been my friend: you will not now be his?
You've known him that he's worthy of a friend,
And you're his cousin, lady, after all,
And therefore more than free to take his part,
Explaining, since the nest is surely spoilt
And Marian what you know her,—though a wife,
The world would hardly understand her case
Of being just hurt and honest; while, for him,
'Twould ever twit him with his bastard child
And married harlot. Speak, while yet there's time.
You would not stand and let a good man's dog
Turn round and rend him, because his, and reared
Of a generous breed,—and will you let his act,
Because it's generous? Speak. I'm bound to you,
And I'll be bound by only you, in this."
The thrilling, solemn voice, so passionless,
Sustained, yet low, without a rise or fall,
As one who had authority to speak,
And not as Marian.
     I looked up to feel
If God stood near me, and beheld his heaven
As blue as Aaron's priestly robe appeared
To Aaron when he took it off to die.
And then I spoke—"Accept the gift, I say,
My sister Marian, and be satisfied.
The hand that gives, has still a soul behind
Which will not let it quail for having given,
Though foolish worldlings talk they know not what
Of what they know not. Romney's strong enough
For this: do you be strong to know he's strong:
He stands on Right's side; never flinch for him,
As if he stood on the other. You'll be bound
By me? I am a woman of repute;
No fly-blow gossip ever specked my life;
My name is clean and open as this hand,

Whose glove there's not a man dares blab about
As if he had touched it freely. Here's my hand
To clasp your hand, my Marian, owned as pure!
As pure,—as I'm a woman and a Leigh!—
And, as I'm both, I'll witness to the world
That Romney Leigh is honoured in his choice
Who chooses Marian for his honoured wife."

Her broad wild woodland eyes shot out a light,
Her smile was wonderful for rapture. "Thanks,
My great Aurora." Forward then she sprang,
And dropping her impassioned spaniel head
With all its brown abandonment of curls
On Romney's feet, we heard the kisses drawn
Through sobs upon the foot, upon the ground—
"O Romney! O my angel! O unchanged,
Though since we've parted I have past the grave!
But Death itself could only better *thee*,
Not change thee!—*Thee* I do not thank at all:
I but thank God who made thee what thou art,
So wholly godlike."
                When he tried in vain
To raise her to his embrace, escaping thence
As any leaping fawn from a huntsman's grasp,
She bounded off and 'lighted beyond reach,
Before him, with a staglike majesty
Of soft, serene defiance,—as she knew
He could not touch her, so was tolerant
He had cared to try. She stood there with her great
Drowned eyes, and dripping cheeks, and strange sweet
        smile
That lived through all, as if one held a light
Across a waste of waters,—shook her head
To keep some thoughts down deeper in her soul,—
Then, white and tranquil like a summer-cloud
Which, having rained itself to a tardy peace,

Stands still in heaven as if it ruled the day,
Spoke out again—"Although, my generous friend,
Since last we met and parted you're unchanged,
And, having promised faith to Marian Erle,
Maintain it, as she were not changed at all;
And though that's worthy, though that's full of balm
To any conscious spirit of a girl
Who once has loved you as I loved you once,—
Yet still it will not make her .. if she's dead,
And gone away where none can give or take
In marriage,—able to revive, return
And wed you,—will it, Romney? Here's the point
My friend, we'll see it plainer: you and I
Must never, never, never join hands so.
Nay, let me say it,—for I said it first
To God, and placed it, rounded to an oath,
Far, far above the moon there, at His feet,
As surely as I wept just now at yours,—
We never, never, never join hands so.
And now, be patient with me; do not think
I'm speaking from a false humility.
The truth is, I am grown so proud with grief,
And He has said so often through his nights
And through his mornings, 'Weep a little still,
'Thou foolish Marian, because women must,
'But do not blush at all except for sin,'—
That I, who felt myself unworthy once
Of virtuous Romney and his high-born race,
Have come to learn,—a woman, poor or rich,
Despised or honoured, is a human soul,
And what her soul is, that, she is herself,
Although she should be spit upon of men,
As is the pavement of the churches here,
Still good enough to pray in. And being chaste
And honest, and inclined to do the right,
And love the truth, and live my life out green

And smooth beneath his steps, I should not fear
To make him thus a less uneasy time
Than many a happier woman.   Very proud
You see me.   Pardon, that I set a trap
To hear a confirmation in your voice,
Both yours and yours.   It is so good to know
'Twas really God who said the same before;
And thus it is in heaven, that first God speaks,
And then his angels.   Oh, it does me good,
It wipes me clean and sweet from devil's dirt,
That Romney Leigh should think me worthy still
Of being his true and honourable wife!
Henceforth I need not say, on leaving earth,
I had no glory in it.   For the rest,
The reason 's ready (master, angel, friend,
Be patient with me) wherefore you and I
Can never, never, never join hands so.
I know you'll not be angry like a man
(For *you* are none) when I shall tell the truth,
Which is, I do not love you, Romney Leigh,
I do not love you.   Ah well! catch my hands,
Miss Leigh, and burn into my eyes with yours, —
I swear I do not love him.   Did I once?
'Tis said that women have been bruised to death
And yet, if once they loved, that love of theirs
Could never be drained out with all their blood:
I've heard such things and pondered.   Did I indeed
Love once; or did I only worship?   Yes,
Perhaps, O friend, I set you up so high
Above all actual good or hope of good
Or fear of evil, all that could be mine,
I haply set you above love itself,
And out of reach of these poor woman's arms,
Angelic Romney.   What was in my thought?
To be your slave, your help, your toy, your tool.
To be your love .. I never thought of that:

To give you love .. still less. I gave you love?
I think I did not give you anything;
I was but only yours,—upon my knees,
All yours, in soul and body, in head and heart,
A creature you had taken from the ground
Still crumbling through your fingers to your feet
To join the dust she came from. Did I love,
Or did I worship? judge, Aurora Leigh!
But, if indeed I loved, 'twas long ago,—
So long! before the sun and moon were made,
Before the hells were open,—ah, before
I heard my child cry in the desert night,
And knew he had no father. It may be
I 'm not as strong as other woman are,
Who, torn and crushed, are not undone from love:
It may be I am colder than the dead,
Who, being dead, love always. But for me,
Once killed, this ghost of Marian loves no more,
No more .. except the child! .. no more at all.
I told your cousin, sir, that I was dead;
And now, she thinks I'll get up from my grave,
And wear my chin-cloth for a wedding-veil,
And glide along the churchyard like a bride
While all the dead keep whispering through the withes,
'You would be better in your place with us,
'You pitiful corruption!' At the thought,
The damps break out on me like leprosy
Although I'm clean. Ay, clean as Marian Erle!
As Marian Leigh, I know, I were not clean:
Nor have I so much life that I should love,
Except the child. Ah God! I could not bear
To see my darling on a good man's knees,
And know, by such a look, or such a sigh,
Or such a silence, that he thought sometimes,
'This child was fathered by some cursed wretch' ..
For, Romney,—angels are less tender-wise

Than God and mothers: even *you* would think
What *we* think never. He is ours, the child;
And we would sooner vex a soul in heaven
By coupling with it the dead body's thought,
It left behind it in a last month's grave,
Than, in my child, see other than . . my child.
We only, never call him fatherless
Who has God and his mother. O my babe,
My pretty, pretty blossom, an ill-wind
Once blew upon my breast! can any think
I'd have another,—one called happier,
A fathered child, with father's love and race
That's worn as bold and open as a smile,
To vex my darling when he's asked his name
And has no answer? What! a happier child
Than mine, my best,—who laughed so loud to-night
He could not sleep for pastime? Nay, I swear
By life and love, that, if I lived like some,
And loved like . . *some*, ay, loved you, Romney Leigh,
As some love, (eyes that have wept so much, see clear,)
I've room for no more children in my arms,
My kisses are all melted on one mouth,
I would not push my darling to a stool
To dandle babies. Here's a hand shall keep
For ever clean without a marriage-ring,
To tend my boy until he cease to need
One steadying finger of it, and desert
(Not miss) his mother's lap, to sit with men.
And when I miss him (not he me) I'll come
And say, 'Now give me some of Romney's work,
To help your outcast orphans of the world
And comfort grief with grief.' For you, meantime,
Most noble Romney, wed a noble wife,
And open on each other your great souls,—
I need not farther bless you. If I dared
But strain and touch her in her upper sphere

And say, 'Come down to Romney—pay my debt!
I should be joyful with the stream of joy
Sent through me. But the moon is in my face ..
I dare not,—though I guess the name he loves;
I'm learned with my studies of old days,
Remembering how he crushed his under-lip
When some one came and spoke, or did not come:
Aurora, I could touch her with my hand,
And fly because I dare not."
      She was gone.
He smiled so sternly that I spoke in haste.
"Forgive her—she sees clearly for herself:
Her instinct 's holy."
     "*I* forgive!" he said,
"I only marvel how she sees so sure,
While others" .. there he paused,—then hoarse, abrupt,—
"Aurora! you forgive us, her and me?
For her, the thing she sees, poor loyal child,
If once corrected by the thing I know,
Had been unspoken, since she loves you well,
Has leave to love you:—while for me, alas,
If once or twice I let my heart escape
This night, .. remember, where hearts slip and fall
They break beside: we're parting,—parting,—ah,
You do not love, that you should surely know
What that word means. Forgive, be tolerant;
It had not been, but that I felt myself
So safe in impuissance and despair,
I could not hurt you though I tossed my arms
And sighed my soul out. The most utter wretch
Will choose his postures when he comes to die,
However in the presence of a queen;
And you'll forgive me some unseemly spasms
Which meant no more than dying. Do you think
I had ever come here in my perfect mind,
Unless I had come here in my settled mind

Bound Marian's, bound to keep the bond and give
My name, my house, my hand, the things I could,
To Marian? For even *I* could give as much:
Even I, affronting her exalted soul
By a supposition that she wanted these,
Could act the husband's coat and hat set up
To creak i' the wind and drive the world-crows off
From pecking in her garden. Straw can fill
A hole to keep out vermin. Now, at last,
I own heaven's angels round her life suffice
To fight the rats of our society,
Without this Romney: I can see it at last;
And here is ended my pretension which
The most pretended. Over-proud of course,
Even so!—but not so stupid .. blind .. that I,
Whom thus the great Taskmaster of the world
Has set to meditate mistaken work,
My dreary face against a dim blank wall
Throughout man's natural lifetime,—could pretend
Or wish .. O love, I have loved you! O my soul,
I have lost you!—but I swear by all yourself,
And all you might have been to me these years
If that June-morning had not failed my hope,—
I'm not so bestial, to regret that day
This night,—this night, which still to you is fair!
Nay, not so blind, Aurora. I attest
Those stars above us which I cannot see . . ."

"You cannot" ..
                "That if Heaven itself should stoop,
Remix the lots, and give me another chance,
I'd say, 'No other!'—I'd record my blank.
Aurora never should be wife of mine."

"Not see the stars?"
               " 'Tis worse still, not to see

To find your hand, although we're parting, dear.
A moment let me hold it ere we part;
And understand my last words—these, at last!
I would not have you thinking when I'm gone
That Romney dared to hanker for your love
In thought or vision, if attainable,
(Which certainly for me it never was)
And wished to use it for a dog to-day
To help the blind man stumbling. God forbid!
And now I know He held you in his palm,
And kept you open-eyed to all my faults,
To save you at last from such a dreary end.
Believe me, dear, that, if I had known like Him
What loss was coming on me, I had done
As well in this as He has.—Farewell you
Who are still my light,—farewell! How late it is:
I know that, now. You've been too patient, sweet.
I will but blow my whistle toward the lane,
And some one comes,—the same who brought me here.
Get in—Good-night."
     "A moment. Heavenly Christ!
A moment. Speak once, Romney. 'Tis not true.
I hold your hands, I look into your face—
You see me?"
    "No more than the blessed stars.
Be blessed too, Aurora. Nay, my sweet,
You tremble. Tender-hearted! Do you mind
Of yore, dear, how you used to cheat old John,
And let the mice out slily from his traps,
Until he marvelled at the soul in mice
Which took the cheese and left the snare? The same
Dear soft heart always! 'Twas for this I grieved
Howe's letter never reached you. Ah, you had heard
Of illness,—not the issue, not the extent:
My life long sick with tossings up and down,
The sudden revulsion in the blazing house,

The strain and struggle both of body and soul,
Which left fire running in my veins for blood:
Scarce lacked that thunderbolt of the falling beam
Which nicked me on the forehead as I passed
The gallery-door with a burden. Say heaven's bolt,
Not William Erle's, not Marian's father's,— tramp
And poacher, whom I found for what he was,
And, eager for her sake to rescue him,
Forth swept from the open highway of the world,
Road-dust and all,—till, like a woodland boar
Most naturally unwilling to be tamed,
He notched me with his tooth. But not a word
To Marian! and I do not think, besides,
He turned the tilting of the beam my way,—
And if he laughed, as many swear, poor wretch,
Nor he nor I supposed the hurt so deep.
We'll hope his next laugh may be merrier,
In a better cause."
    "Blind, Romney?"
           "Ah, my friend,
You'll learn to say it in a cheerful voice.
I, too, at first desponded. To be blind,
Turned out of nature, mulcted as a man,
Refused the daily largesse of the sun
To humble creatures! When the fever's heat
Dropped from me, as the flame did from my house,
And left me ruined like it, stripped of all
The hues and shapes of aspectable life,
A mere bare blind stone in the blaze of day,
A man, upon the outside of the earth,
As dark as ten feet under, in the grave,—
Why that seemed hard."
    "No hope?"
        "A tear! you weep,
Divine Aurora? tears upon my hand!
I've seen you weeping for a mouse, a bird,—

But, weep for me, Aurora? Yes, there's hope.
Not hope of sight,—I could be learned, dear,
And tell you in what Greek and Latin name
The visual nerve is withered to the root,
Though the outer eyes appear indifferent,
Unspotted in their crystals. But there's hope.
The spirit, from behind this dethroned sense,
Sees, waits in patience till the walls break up
From which the bas-relief and fresco have dropt:
There's hope. The man here, once so arrogant
And restless, so ambitious, for his part,
Of dealing with statistically packed
Disorders (from a pattern on his nail),
And packing such things quite another way,—
Is now contented. From his personal loss
He has come to hope for others when they lose,
And wear a gladder faith in what we gain ..
Through bitter experience, compensation sweet,
Like that tear, sweetest. I am quiet now,
As tender surely for the suffering world,
But quiet,—sitting at the wall to learn,
Content henceforth to do the thing I can:
For, though as powerless, said I, as a stone,
A stone can still give shelter to a worm,
And it is worth while being a stone for that:
There's hope, Aurora."
                      "Is there hope for me?
For me?—and is there room beneath the stone
For such a worm?—And if I came and said ..
What all this weeping scarce will let me say,
And yet what women cannot say at all
But weeping bitterly .. (the pride keeps up,
Until the heart breaks under it) .. I love,—
I love you, Romney" ...
                      "Silence!" he exclaimed.
"A woman's pity sometimes makes her mad.

A man's distraction must not cheat his soul
To take advantage of it. Yet, 'tis hard—
Farewell, Aurora."
                    "But I love you, sir;
And when a woman says she loves a man,
The man must hear her, though he love her not,
Which .. hush! .. he has leave to answer in his turn;
She will not surely blame him. As for me,
You call it pity,—think I'm generous?
'Twere somewhat easier, for a woman proud
As I am, and I'm very vilely proud,
To let it pass as such, and press on you
Love born of pity,—seeing that excellent loves
Are born so, often, nor the quicklier die,—
And this would set me higher by the head
Than now I stand. No matter: let the truth
Stand high; Aurora must be humble: no,
My love's not pity merely. Obviously
I'm not a generous woman, never was,
Or else, of old, I had not looked so near
To weights and measures, grudging you the power
To give, as first I scorned your power to judge
For me, Aurora. I would have no gifts
Forsooth, but God's,—and I would use *them* too
According to my pleasure and my choice,
As He and I were equals, you below,
Excluded from that level of interchange
Admitting benefaction. You were wrong
In much? you said so. I was wrong in most.
Oh, most! You only thought to rescue men
By half-means, half-way, seeing half their wants,
While thinking nothing of your personal gain.
But I who saw the human nature broad
At both sides, comprehending too the soul's,
And all the high necessities of Art,
Betrayed the thing I saw, and wronged my own life

For which I pleaded. Passioned to exalt
The artist's instinct in me at the cost
Of putting down the woman's, I forgot
No perfect artist is developed here
From any imperfect woman. Flower from root,
And spiritual from natural, grade by grade
In all our life. A handful of the earth
To make God's image! the despised poor earth,
The healthy odorous earth,—I missed with it
The divine Breath that blows the nostrils out
To ineffable inflatus,—ay, the breath
Which love is. Art is much, but love is more.
O Art, my Art, thou'rt much, but Love is more!
Art symbolises heaven, but Love is God
And makes heaven. I, Aurora, fell from mine.
I would not be a woman like the rest,
A simple woman who believes in love
And owns the right of love because she loves,
And, hearing she's beloved, is satisfied
With what contents God: I must analyse,
Confront, and question; just as if a fly
Refused to warm itself in any sun
Till such was *in leone:* I must fret
Forsooth because the month was only May,
Be faithless of the kind of proffered love,
And captious, lest it miss my dignity,
And scornful, that my lover sought a wife
To use .. to use! O Romney, O my love,
I am changed since then, changed wholly,—for indeed
If now you'd stoop so low to take my love
And use it roughly, without stint or spare,
As men use common things with more behind,
(And, in this, ever would be more behind)
To any mean and ordinary end,—
The joy would set me like a star, in heaven,
So high up, I should shine because of height

And not of virtue. Yet in one respect,
Just one, beloved, I am in no wise changed:
I love you, loved you .. loved you first and last,
And love you on for ever. Now I know
I loved you always, Romney. She who died
Knew that, and said so; Lady Waldemar
Knows that; .. and Marian. I had known the same,
Except that I was prouder than I knew,
And not so honest. Ay, and, as I live,
I should have died so, crushing in my hand
This rose of love, the wasp inside and all,
Ignoring ever to my soul and you
Both rose and pain,—except for this great loss,
This great despair,—to stand before your face
And know you do not see me where I stand.
You think, perhaps, I am not changed from pride,
And that I chiefly bear to say such words,
Because you cannot shame me with your eyes?
O calm, grand eyes, extinguished in a storm,
Blown out like lights o'er melancholy seas,
Though shrieked for by the shipwrecked,—O my Dark,
My Cloud,—to go before me every day
While I go ever toward the wilderness,—
I would that you could see me bare to the soul!
If this be pity, 'tis so for myself,
And not for Romney! *he* can stand alone;
A man like *him* is never overcome:
No woman like me, counts him pitiable
While saints applaud him. He mistook the world;
But I mistook my own heart, and that slip
Was fatal. Romney,—will you leave me here?
So wrong, so proud, so weak, so unconsoled,
So mere a woman!—and I love you so,
I love you, Romney—"
     Could I see his face
I wept so? Did I drop against his breast,

Or did his arms constrain me? were my cheeks
Hot, overflooded, with my tears, or his?
And which of our two large explosive hearts
So shook me? That, I know not. There were words
That broke in utterance .. melted, in the fire,—
Embrace, that was convulsion, .. then a kiss
As long and silent as the ecstatic night,
And deep, deep, shuddering breaths, which meant beyond
Whatever could be told by word or kiss.

But what he said .. I have written day by day,
With somewhat even writing. Did I think
That such a passionate rain would intercept
And dash this last page? What he said, indeed,
I fain would write it down here like the rest,
To keep it in my eyes, as in my ears,
The heart's sweet scripture, to be read at night
When weary, or at morning when afraid,
And lean my heaviest oath on when I swear
That, when all's done, all tried, all counted here,
All great arts, and all good philosophies,
This love just puts its hand out in a dream
And straight outstretches all things.
       What he said,
I fain would write. But if an angel spoke
In thunder, should we haply know much more
Than that it thundered? If a cloud came down
And wrapt us wholly, could we draw its shape,
As if on the outside and not overcome?
And so he spake. His breath against my face
Confused his words, yet made them more intense,
(As when the sudden finger of the wind
Will wipe a row of single city-lamps
To a pure white line of flame, more luminous
Because of obliteration) more intense,
The intimate presence carrying in itself

Complete communication, as with souls
Who, having put the body off, perceive
Through simply being. Thus, 'twas granted me
To know he loved me to the depth and height
Of such large natures, ever competent,
With grand horizons by the sea or land,
To love's grand sunrise. Small spheres hold small fires
But he loved largely, as a man can love
Who, baffled in his love, dares live his life,
Accept the ends which God loves, for his own,
And lift a constant aspect.
                          From the day
I brought to England my poor searching face,
(An orphan even of my father's grave)
He had loved me, watched me, watched his soul in mine,
Which in me grew and heightened into love.
For he, a boy still, had been told the tale
Of how a fairy bride from Italy
With smells of oleanders in her hair,
Was coming through the vines to touch his hand;
Whereat the blood of boyhood on the palm
Made sudden heats. And when at last I came,
And lived before him, lived, and rarely smiled,
He smiled and loved me for the thing I was,
As every child will love the year's first flower
(Not certainly the fairest of the year,
But, in which, the complete year seems to blow)
The poor sad snowdrop,—growing between drifts,
Mysterious medium 'twixt the plant and frost,
So faint with winter while so quick with spring,
And doubtful if to thaw itself away
With that snow near it. Not that Romney Leigh
Had loved me coldly. If I thought so once,
It was as if I had held my hand in fire
And shook for cold. But now I understood
For ever, that the very fire and heat

Of troubling passion in him burned him clear,
And shaped, to dubious order, word and act:
That, just because he loved me over all,
All wealth, all lands, all social privilege,
To which chance made him unexpected heir,
And, just because on all these lesser gifts,
Constrained by conscience and the sense of wrong
He had stamped with steady hand God's arrow-mark
Of dedication to the human need,
He thought it should be so too, with his love.
He, passionately loving, would bring down
His love, his life, his best, (because the best)
His bride of dreams, who walked so still and high
Through flowery poems as through meadow-grass,
The dust of golden lilies on her feet,
That *she* should walk beside him on the rocks
In all that clang and hewing out of men,
And help the work of help which was his life,
And prove he kept back nothing,—not his soul.
And when I failed him,—for I failed him, I,
And when it seemed he had missed my love, he thought
"Aurora makes room for a working-noon,"
And so, self-girded with torn strips of hope,
Took up his life as if it were for death,
(Just capable of one heroic aim,)
And threw it in the thickest of the world,—
At which men laughed as if he had drowned a dog.
No wonder,—since Aurora failed him first!
The morning and the evening made his day.

But oh, the night! oh, bitter-sweet! oh, sweet!
O dark, O moon and stars, O ecstasy
Of darkness! O great mystery of love,
In which absorbed, loss, anguish, treason's self
Enlarges rapture,—as a pebble dropt
In some full wine-cup over-brims the wine!

While we two sate together, leaned that night
So close my very garments crept and thrilled
With strange electric life, and both my cheeks
Grew red, then pale, with touches from my hair
In which his breath was,—while the golden moon
Was hung before our faces as the badge
Of some sublime inherited despair,
Since ever to be seen by only one,—
A voice said, low and rapid as a sigh,
Yet breaking, I felt conscious, from a smile,
"Thank God, who made me blind, to make me see!
Shine on, Aurora, dearest light of souls,
Which rul'st for evermore both day and night!
I am happy."
         I flung closer to his breast,
As sword that, after battle, flings to sheath;
And, in that hurtle of united souls,
The mystic motions which in common moods
Are shut beyond our sense, broke in on us,
And, as we sate, we felt the old earth spin,
And all the starry turbulence of worlds
Swing round us in their audient circles, till,
If that same golden moon were overhead
Or if beneath our feet, we did not know.

And then calm, equal, smooth with weights of joy,
His voice rose, as some chief musician's song
Amid the old Jewish temple's Selah-pause,
And bade me mark how we two met at last
Upon this moon-bathed promontory of earth,
To give up much on each side, then take all.
"Beloved," it sang, "we must be here to work;
And men who work can only work for men,
And, not to work in vain, must comprehend
Humanity and so work humanly,
And raise men's bodies still by raising souls,

As God did first."
                    "But stand upon the earth,"
I said, "to raise them, (this is human too,
There's nothing high which has not first been low,
My humbleness, said One, has made me great!)
As God did last."
                    "And work all silently
And simply," he returned, "as God does all;
Distort our nature never for our work,
Nor count our right hands stronger for being hoofs.
The man most man, with tenderest human hands,
Works best for men,—as God in Nazareth."

He paused upon the word, and then resumed;
"Fewer programmes, we who have no prescience.
Fewer systems, we who are held and do not hold.
Less mapping out of masses to be saved,
By nations or by sexes. Fourier's void,
And Comte absurd,—and Cabet, puerile.
Subsist no rules of life outside of life,
No perfect manners, without Christian souls:
The Christ himself had been no Lawgiver
Unless He had given the life, too, with the law."

I echoed thoughtfully—"The man, most man,
Works best for men, and, if most man indeed,
He gets his manhood plainest from his soul:
While obviously this stringent soul itself
Obeys the old law of development,
The Spirit ever witnessing in ours,
And Love, the soul of soul, within the soul,
Evolving it sublimely. First, God's love."

"And next," he smiled, "the love of wedded souls,
Which still presents that mystery's counterpart.
Sweet shadow-rose, upon the water of life,

Of such a mystic substance, Sharon gave
A name to! human, vital, fructuous rose,
Whose calyx holds the multitude of leaves,
Loves filial, loves fraternal, neighbour-loves
And civic—all fair petals, all good scents,
All reddened, sweetened from one central Heart!"

"Alas," I cried, "it was not long ago,
You swore this very social rose smelt ill."

"Alas," he answered, "is it a rose at all?
The filial's thankless, the fraternal's hard,
The rest is lost. I do but stand and think,
Across the waters of a troubled life
This Flower of Heaven so vainly overhangs,
What perfect counterpart would be in sight
If tanks were clearer. Let us clean the tubes,
And wait for rains. O poet, O my love,
Since *I* was too ambitious in my deed
And thought to distance all men in success,
(Till God came on me, marked the place and said,
"Ill-doer, henceforth keep within this line,
Attempting less than others,"—and I stand
And work among Christ's little ones, content,)
Come thou, my compensation, my dear sight,
My morning-star, my morning,—rise and shine,
And touch my hills with radiance not their own.
Shine out for two, Aurora, and fulfil
My falling-short that must be! work for two,
As I, though thus restrained, for two, shall love!
Gaze on, with inscient vision toward the sun,
And, from his visceral heat, pluck out the roots
Of light beyond him. Art's a service,—mark:
A silver key is given to thy clasp,
And thou shalt stand unwearied, night and day,
And fix it in the hard, slow-turning wards,

To open, so, that intermediate door
Betwixt the different planes of sensuous form
And form insensuous, that inferior men
May learn to feel on still through these to those,
And bless thy ministration. The world waits
For help. Beloved, let us love so well,
Our work shall still be better for our love,
And still our love be sweeter for our work,
And both commended, for the sake of each,
By all true workers and true lovers born.
Now press the clarion on thy woman's lip
(Love's holy kiss shall still keep consecrate)
And breathe thy fine keen breath along the brass,
And blow all class-walls level as Jericho's
Past Jordan,—crying from the top of souls,
To souls, that, here assembled on earth's flats,
They get them to some purer eminence
Than any hitherto beheld for clouds!
What height we know not,—but the way we know,
And how by mounting ever, we attain,
And so climb on. It is the hour for souls,
That bodies, leavened by the will and love,
Be lightened to redemption. The world's old,
But the old world waits the time to be renewed.
Toward which, new hearts in individual growth
Must quicken, and increase to multitude
In new dynasties of the race of men;
Developed whence, shall grow spontaneously
New churches, new œconomies, new laws
Admitting freedom, new societies
Excluding falsehood: HE shall make all new.

My Romney!—Lifting up my hand in his,
As wheeled by Seeing spirits toward the east,
He turned instinctively, where, faint and far,
Along the tingling desert of the sky,

Beyond the circle of the conscious hills,
Were laid in jasper-stone as clear as glass
The first foundations of that new, near Day
Which should be builded out of heaven to God.
He stood a moment with erected brows
In silence, as a creature might who gazed,—
Stood calm, and fed his blind, majestic eyes
Upon the thought of perfect noon: and when
I saw his soul saw,—"Jasper first," I said,
"And second, sapphire; third, chalcedony;
The rest in order,—last, an amethyst."

THE END.

www.ingramcontent.com/pod-product-compliance
Lightning Source LLC
Chambersburg PA
CBHW021204230426
43667CB00006B/543